AUTOCAD® 2013 AND AUTOCAD LT® 2013

ESSENTIALS

Scott Onstott

WILEY

John Wiley & Sons, Inc.

Senior Acquisitions Editor: Willem Knibbe
Development Editor: Gary Scwartz
Technical Editor: Ian le Cheminant
Production Editor: Rebecca Anderson
Copy Editor: Elizabeth Welch
Editorial Manager: Pete Gaughan
Production Manager: Tim Tate
Vice President and Executive Group Publisher: Richard Swadley
Vice President and Publisher: Neil Edde
Book Designer: Happenstance Type-O-Rama
Compositor: Craig W. Johnson, Happenstance Type-O-Rama
Proofreader: James Saturnio, Word One New York
Indexer: Robert Swanson
Project Coordinator, Cover: Katherine Crocker
Cover Designer: Ryan Sneed
Cover Image: © Maciej Noskowski / iStockPhoto

Dear Reader,

Thank you for choosing *AutoCAD® 2013 and AutoCAD LT® 2013 Essentials*. This book is part of a family of premium-quality Sybex books, all of which are written by outstanding authors who combine practical experience with a gift for teaching.

Sybex was founded in 1976. More than 30 years later, we're still committed to producing consistently exceptional books. With each of our titles, we're working hard to set a new standard for the industry. From the paper we print on, to the authors we work with, our goal is to bring you the best books available.

I hope you see all that reflected in these pages. I'd be very interested to hear your comments and get your feedback on how we're doing. Feel free to let me know what you think about this or any other Sybex book by sending me an email at nedde@wiley.com. If you think you've found a technical error in this book, please visit http://sybex.custhelp.com. Customer feedback is critical to our efforts at Sybex.

Best regards,

NEIL EDDE
Vice President and Publisher
Sybex, an Imprint of Wiley

to Jenn and Merlin

Acknowledgments

A team of people has been instrumental in making this book you are holding in your hands or reading on screen a reality. I would like to express my sincere gratitude to the professional team at Sybex (an imprint of Wiley) for all their hard work.

It has been a pleasure working with my acquisitions editor, Willem Knibbe; developmental editor, Gary Schwartz; technical editor, Ian le Cheminant; and members of the editorial staff, including Pete Gaughan, Connor O'Brien, and Jenni Housh.

ABOUT THE AUTHOR

 *Scott Onstott* has published seven books with Sybex prior to the present title: *AutoCAD® 2012 and AutoCAD LT® 2012 Essentials, Adobe® Photoshop® CS6 Essentials, Enhancing Architectural Drawings and Models with Photoshop, AutoCAD®: Professional Tips and Techniques* (with Lynn Allen), *Enhancing CAD Drawings with Photoshop, Mastering Autodesk® Architectural Desktop 2006*, and *Autodesk® VIZ 2005* (with George Omura). Scott has worked on some 20 other technical books as contributing author, reviser, compilation editor, and/or technical editor.

Scott has a bachelor's degree in architecture from University of California, Berkeley, and is a former university instructor who now serves as a consultant, independent video producer, and contributor to popular industry websites. You can contact the author through his website at www.scottonstott.com.

Contents at a Glance

Introduction   *xiii*

CHAPTER 1   Getting Started   1

CHAPTER 2   Basic Drawing Skills   15

CHAPTER 3   Using Drawing Aids   39

CHAPTER 4   Editing Entities   53

CHAPTER 5   Shaping Curves   79

CHAPTER 6   Controlling Object Visibility and Appearance   97

CHAPTER 7   Organizing Objects   121

CHAPTER 8   Hatching and Gradients   145

CHAPTER 9   Working with Blocks and Xrefs   163

CHAPTER 10   Creating and Editing Text   183

CHAPTER 11   Dimensioning   197

CHAPTER 12   Keeping In Control with Constraints   217

CHAPTER 13   Working with Layouts and Annotative Objects   231

CHAPTER 14   Printing and Plotting   253

CHAPTER 15   Storing, Presenting, and Extracting Data   277

CHAPTER 16   Navigating 3D Models   299

CHAPTER 17   Modeling in 3D   317

CHAPTER 18   Presenting and Documenting 3D Design   345

APPENDIX   Autodesk AutoCAD 2013 Certification   369

Index   *375*

CONTENTS

Introduction   *xiii*

CHAPTER 1   **Getting Started**   **1**

Exploring the AutoCAD 2013 for Windows User Interface 1
    Exploring the Graphical User Interface 1
    Exploring Workspaces 7
    The AutoCAD Ribbon. 8
Setting Drawing Units 12
The Essentials and Beyond. 14

CHAPTER 2   **Basic Drawing Skills**   **15**

Navigating 2D Drawings. 15
Drawing Lines and Rectangles. 19
    Drawing Lines 19
    Drawing Rectangles 22
Canceling, Erasing, and Undoing. 23
Using Coordinate Systems 24
    Using Absolute Coordinates. 25
    Using Relative Coordinates 26
    Using Polar Coordinates. 27
Drawing Circles, Arcs, and Polygons 30
    Creating Circles 30
    Creating Arcs 33
    Drawing Polygons 34
Filleting and Chamfering Lines 36
    Joining Nonparallel Lines 36
    Joining Crossed Lines 37
The Essentials and Beyond. 38

CHAPTER 3   **Using Drawing Aids**   **39**

Grid and Snap 39
Ortho and Polar Tracking. 42
PolarSnap 44
Running Object Snaps 46

From Snap. 49

Object Snap Tracking 50

The Essentials and Beyond. 52

CHAPTER 4　Editing Entities　53

Creating Selection Sets. 53

Creating a Selection Set at the *Select Objects:* Prompt 53

Creating a Selection Set Before Deciding on a Command. 56

Move and Copy 60

Rotate and Scale 63

Working with Arrays. 67

Rectangular Arrays 67

Polar Arrays 68

Trim and Extend 71

Lengthen and Stretch. 72

Offset and Mirror. 73

Grip Editing. 76

The Essentials and Beyond. 78

CHAPTER 5　Shaping Curves　79

Drawing and Editing Curved Polylines 79

Drawing Ellipses 85

Drawing and Editing Splines 88

Working with Control Vertices 88

Working with Fit Points. 92

Blending Between Objects with Splines 95

The Essentials and Beyond. 96

CHAPTER 6　Controlling Object Visibility and Appearance　97

Changing Object Properties. 97

Setting the Current Layer 101

Altering the Layer Assignments of Objects 104

Controlling Layer Visibility. 106

Toggling Layer Status 106

Isolating Layers 109

Saving Layer States 111

Applying Linetype. 112

Assigning Properties by Object or by Layer. 115
Managing Layer Properties 117
The Essentials and Beyond. 120

CHAPTER 7   **Organizing Objects**   **121**

Defining Blocks. 121
    Drawing a Chair and Defining It as a Block 122
    Drawing a Door and Defining It as a Block. 125
Inserting Blocks 126
Editing Blocks. 131
    Editing Block Definition Geometry. 131
    Assigning Floating Properties. 133
    Nesting Blocks 135
    Exploding Blocks 137
Redefining Blocks 138
Working with Groups 141
The Essentials and Beyond. 144

CHAPTER 8   **Hatching and Gradients**   **145**

Specifying Hatch Areas. 145
    Picking Points to Determine Boundaries 145
    Selecting Objects to Define Boundaries 150
Associating Hatches with Boundaries 151
Hatching with Patterns 154
    Specifying Properties. 154
    Separating Hatch Areas 156
Hatching with Gradients 159
The Essentials and Beyond. 162

CHAPTER 9   **Working with Blocks and Xrefs**   **163**

Working with Global Blocks. 163
    Writing a Local Block Definition to a File 163
    Inserting a Drawing as a Local Block 166
    Redefining Local Blocks with Global Blocks 169
Accessing Content Globally 171
Storing Content on Tool Palettes. 175
Referencing External Drawings and Images 177
The Essentials and Beyond. 182

CHAPTER 10 **Creating and Editing Text** **183**

Creating Text Styles 183
Writing Lines of Text 185
  Creating Text to Fit 185
  Justifying Text 187
  Transforming and Creating Text 188
Writing and Formatting Paragraphs of Text Using MTEXT 189
Editing Text 192
  Editing Content and Properties 193
  Working with Columns 194
The Essentials and Beyond 195

CHAPTER 11 **Dimensioning** **197**

Styling Dimensions 197
Adding Dimensions 203
  Using Inquiry Commands 204
  Adding Dimension Objects 206
  Adding and Styling Multileaders 211
Editing Dimensions 212
The Essentials and Beyond 216

CHAPTER 12 **Keeping In Control with Constraints** **217**

Working with Geometric Constraints 217
Applying Dimensional Constraints and Creating User Parameters 220
Constraining Objects Simultaneously with Geometry and Dimensions 224
Making Parametric Changes to Constrained Objects 227
The Essentials and Beyond 229

CHAPTER 13 **Working with Layouts and Annotative Objects** **231**

Creating Annotative Styles and Objects 231
  Working with Annotative Text 232
  Working with Annotative Dimensions 235
Creating Layouts 237
Adjusting Floating Viewports 241
  Working on Layout1 241
  Working on Layout2 244
Overriding Layer Properties in Layout Viewports 247
Drawing on Layouts 248
The Essentials and Beyond 251

CHAPTER 14   **Printing and Plotting**   **253**

Configuring Output Devices. 253
    Setting Up a System Printer 254
    Setting Up an AutoCAD Plotter. 254
Creating Plot Style Tables. 258
Using Plot Style Tables 261
    Configuring New Drawings for Named Plot Style Tables. 262
    Assigning Plot Styles by Layer or by Object 265
Plotting in Modelspace 268
Plotting Layouts in Paperspace 271
Exporting to an Electronic Format 275
The Essentials and Beyond. 276

CHAPTER 15   **Storing, Presenting, and Extracting Data**   **277**

Defining Attributes and Blocks 277
Inserting Attributed Blocks 282
Editing Table Styles and Creating Tables. 285
Using Fields in Table Cells 289
Editing Table Data. 292
The Essentials and Beyond. 298

CHAPTER 16   **Navigating 3D Models**   **299**

Using Visual Styles 299
Working with Tiled Viewports 303
Navigating with the ViewCube. 305
Orbiting in 3D. 307
Using Cameras 309
Navigating with SteeringWheels 311
Saving Views 313
The Essentials and Beyond. 316

CHAPTER 17   **Modeling in 3D**   **317**

Creating Surface Models. 317
    Making Planar Surfaces. 317
    Revolving 2D Profile into a 3D Model 319
    Sweeping Out 3D Geometry 320
    Extruding 2D Geometry into 3D. 322

Editing Surface Models. 324

    Trimming Surfaces with Other Surfaces 324

    Projecting Edges on Surfaces 325

    Trimming Surfaces with Edges. 328

Creating Solid Models. 330

    Extruding Solid Objects. 330

    Lofting Solid Objects 334

Editing Solid Models. 336

    Performing Boolean Operations 336

    Editing Solids. 339

Smoothing Meshes 342

The Essentials and Beyond. 344

CHAPTER 18   **Presenting and Documenting 3D Design**   **345**

Assigning Materials. 345

Placing and Adjusting Lights 351

    Adding Artificial Lights 351

    Simulating Natural Light 357

Creating Renderings. 359

Documenting Models with Drawings. 363

The Essentials and Beyond. 368

APPENDIX   **Autodesk AutoCAD 2013 Certification**   **369**

Index   *375*

INTRODUCTION

The staying power of AutoCAD® is legendary in the ever-changing software industry, having been around for 31 years by 2013. You can rest assured that spending your time learning AutoCAD will be a wise investment, and the skills you obtain in this book will be useful for years to come.

I wish to welcome you in beginning the process of learning AutoCAD. It will give you great satisfaction to learn such a complex program and use it to design and document whatever you dream up. You'll find step-by-step tutorials that reveal a wide variety of techniques built on many years of real-world experience.

The first 14 chapters apply to both AutoCAD® 2013 and AutoCAD LT® 2013. AutoCAD LT is Autodesk's lower-cost version of AutoCAD, and it has reduced capabilities. Chapters 15 through 18 are for full AutoCAD users only as they cover advanced tools not available in AutoCAD LT, including attributes, 3D navigation, 3D modeling, and rendering.

Who Should Read This Book

This book is for students, hobbyists, and professional architects, industrial designers, engineers, builders, landscape architects, or anyone who communicates through technical drawings as part of their work.

If you're interested in certification for AutoCAD 2013, this book can be a great resource to help you prepare. See www.autodesk.com/certification for more certification information and resources.

What You Will Learn

You'll gain a solid understanding of the features of AutoCAD in this book. Each chapter features multiple exercises that take you step by step through the many complex procedures of AutoCAD. The goal of performing these steps on your own is to aim for an understanding that you can abstract into skills, which you can apply to many different real-world situations.

While each project presents different obstacles and opportunities, I urge you to focus on the concepts and techniques presented rather than memorizing the specific steps used to achieve the desired result. The actual steps performed may vary in each geometric situation.

The best way to build skills is to perform the steps on your computer exactly as they are presented in the book during your first reading. After you achieve the desired result, start over and experiment using the same techniques on your own project (whether invented or real). After you have practiced, think about how you have achieved the desired result, and try to abstract the steps performed into concepts that you'll remember. Only then will you begin to own the knowledge and get the most out of this book.

Reader Requirements

You don't need any previous experience with AutoCAD to use this book. However, you'll need familiarity with either the Windows or Mac operating system and have the basic skills necessary to use a graphical user interface successfully and to operate a computer confidently.

AutoCAD 2013 or AutoCAD LT 2013 System Requirements

The book is written for both AutoCAD 2013 and AutoCAD LT 2013. The following are system requirements for running either version on the different operating systems in which they are offered. See www.autodesk.com for the most up-to-date requirements.

General Windows System Requirements

- ► Microsoft Windows 7 Enterprise, Ultimate, Professional, or Home Premium
- ► Microsoft Windows Vista Enterprise, Business, or Ultimate (SP1 or later)
- ► Microsoft Windows XP Professional (SP2 or later)
- ► 2 GB of RAM
- ► 2 GB of free space for installation
- ► 1,280 × 1,024 true color video display adapter 128 MB or greater, Microsoft® Direct3D®-capable workstation-class graphics card; Pixel Shader 3.0 or greater required for 3D modeling
- ► Internet Explorer 7.0 or later

32-Bit AutoCAD 2013 for Windows

▶ For Windows Vista or Windows 7: Intel® Pentium® 4 or AMD Athlon® dual-core processor, 3.0 GHz or higher with SSE2 technology

▶ For Windows XP: Intel Pentium 4 or AMD Athlon dual-core processor, 2.0 GHz or higher with SSE2 technology

64-Bit AutoCAD 2013 for Windows

▶ AMD Athlon 64 with SSE2 technology, AMD Opteron® processor with SSE2 technology

▶ Intel® Xeon® processor with Intel EM64T support and SSE2 technology

▶ Intel Pentium 4 with Intel EM64T support and SSE2 technology

64-Bit AutoCAD 2013 for Mac

▶ Apple® Mac® Pro 4,1 or later; MacBook® Pro 5,1 or later (MacBook Pro 6,1 or later recommended); iMac® 8,1 or later (iMac 11,1 or later recommended); Mac® mini 3,1 or later (Mac mini 4,1 or later recommended); MacBook Air® 2,1 or later; MacBook® 5,1 or later (MacBook 7,1 or later recommended)

▶ Mac OS® X v10.6.4 or later; Mac OS X v10.5.8 or later

▶ 64-bit Intel® processor

▶ 3 GB of RAM (4 GB recommended)

▶ 2.5 GB of free disk space for download and installation (3 GB recommended)

▶ All graphics cards on supported hardware

▶ $1{,}280 \times 800$ display with true color ($1{,}600 \times 1{,}200$ with true color recommended)

▶ U.S., U.K., or France keyboard layout

▶ Apple® Mouse, Apple Magic Mouse, Magic Trackpad, MacBook® Pro Trackpad, or Microsoft®-compliant mouse

▶ Mac OS X–compliant printer

What Is Covered in This Book

AutoCAD 2013 and AutoCAD LT 2013 Essentials is organized to provide you with the knowledge needed to master the basics of computer-aided design. The book's Web page is located at www.sybex.com/go/autocad2013essentials, where you can download the sample files used in each chapter.

Chapter 1: Getting Started   You'll take a tour of the user interface and learn to identify each of its parts by name. Chapter 1 is essential reading as you'll need to know the difference between workspaces, ribbon tabs, toolbars, panels, palettes, status toggles, and so on to understand the terminology used by your colleagues and in the rest of this book. In addition, you'll learn about how to match your industry's standard units to the drawings you'll be creating.

Chapter 2: Basic Drawing Skills   Learn how to navigate a 2D drawing with Zoom and Pan so that you can zero in on areas of interest. You'll learn how to draw lines, rectangles, circles, arcs, and polygons; how to cancel, erase, and undo; and how to fillet and chamfer lines. In addition, you'll use two coordinate systems to specify the exact sizes of objects you are drawing.

Chapter 3: Using Drawing Aids   Drawing aids are something you'll want to learn how to use to create measured drawings with ease. The drawing aids covered with step-by-step exercises in this chapter include grid and snap, ortho and polar tracking, PolarSnap, running object snaps, the From snap, and object snap tracking.

Chapter 4: Editing Entities   This chapter teaches what you'll probably be doing most of the time in AutoCAD: editing the basic entities that you've drawn to make them conform with your design intent. Editing commands covered include Move, Copy, Rotate, Scale, Array, Trim, Extend, Lengthen, Stretch, Offset, and Mirror. In addition to these commands, you'll learn an alternative method for editing entities called grip editing.

Chapter 5: Shaping Curves   The landscape exercise in this chapter teaches you how to create complex curves with NURBS-based splines, curved polylines, and ellipses. By the end, you'll be able to shape curves to create almost any curvilinear form imaginable.

Chapter 6: Controlling Object Visibility and Appearance   You'll learn how to hide and reveal objects with properties and layers. Layers are essential to managing the complexity of design, and you'll use many different layer tools in this chapter's step-by-step exercises.

Chapter 7: Organizing Objects   By combining entities such as lines, polylines, circles, arcs, and text into blocks and/or groups, you can more efficiently manipulate more complex objects such as chairs, mechanical assemblies, trees, or any other organizational designation appropriate to your industry. You'll learn how to create and work with blocks and groups in this chapter.

Chapter 8: Hatching and Gradients   In this chapter, you'll flood bounded areas with solid fill, hatch patterns, and/or gradients to indicate transitions between materials and to improve the readability of drawings in general.

Chapter 9: Working with Blocks and Xrefs   You'll learn how to access content from other files in the current drawing in this chapter. You'll also understand the important distinction between inserting and externally referencing content. In addition, you'll store saved content on tool palettes for simplified reuse.

Chapter 10: Creating and Editing Text   The written word is undeniably a part of every drawing. This chapter teaches you how to create both single- and multi-line text, how to edit any text, and how to control its appearance through text styles and object properties.

Chapter 11: Dimensioning   You'll learn how to annotate drawings with specific measurements known as dimensions in this chapter. In addition to learning how to control measurements' appearance with dimension styles, you'll create linear, aligned, angular, and radius dimension objects.

Chapter 12: Keeping in Control with Constraints   This chapter teaches you how to add geometric and dimensional constraints to objects so that their ultimate form is controlled by mathematical formulas. The formulas in the examples are as simple as adding two dimensions or calculating the diameter of a circle from its radius.

Chapter 13: Working with Layouts and Annotative Objects   AutoCAD has two environments, which you'll learn about in this chapter on layouts: modelspace and paperspace. You'll create floating viewports to display the contents of modelspace in the paperspace of a layout. In addition, you'll create annotative styles and objects that always display the proper height no matter which viewport or annotation scale is selected.

Chapter 14: Printing and Plotting   From plotter drivers to plot style tables and page setups, you'll learn the intricacies of creating printed output to scale in AutoCAD. You'll plot in both modelspace and paperspace, and you will even create electronic output that can be shared on the Internet.

Chapter 15: Storing, Presenting, and Extracting Data   Attributes, fields, and tables are the subjects of this chapter on managing data. You'll learn how to embed nongraphical data in blocks, how to link to that data dynamically in text fields, and finally how to display and format this same data in an organized fashion in spreadsheet-like tables.

Chapter 16: Navigating 3D Models   In this chapter, you'll learn how to change your point of view while working on 3D models using the ViewCube, the Orbit tool, and SteeringWheel technology. In addition, you'll compose and save perspective views with cameras to help you visualize 3D models with added realism.

Chapter 17: Modeling in 3D   You'll learn the basics of surface, solid, and mesh modeling in this chapter by building the 3D geometry you navigated in the previous chapter. Each 3D toolset has its strengths and limitations, and you'll learn to use tools in each category to get the job done.

Chapter 18: Presenting and Documenting 3D Design   By assigning realistic materials, inserting artificial and natural light sources, and rendering the scene, you'll create realistic computer-generated imagery in this chapter. By approaching the final render in a series of ever more realistic test renders, you'll hone in on photo-realistic output in stages. You'll also learn how to project 2D plans, sections, and detail drawings from a model so that you can dimension and document 3D designs.

Appendix: Autodesk AutoCAD 2013 Certification   The appendix contains information about how to prepare for Autodesk certification exams using this book. The tables point you to the chapters where you'll find specific examples giving you practical experience with the topics covered in the exams.

The Essentials Series

The *Essentials* series from Sybex provides outstanding instruction for readers who are just beginning to develop their professional skills. Every *Essentials* book includes these features:

▶ Skill-based instruction with chapters organized around projects rather than abstract concepts or subjects.

▶ Suggestions for additional exercises at the end of each chapter, where you can practice and extend your skills.

▶ Digital files (via download) so that you can work through the project tutorials yourself. Please check the book's web page at www.sybex .com/go/autocad2013essentials for these companion downloads.

Certification Objective
The certification margin icon will alert you to passages that are especially relevant to AutoCAD 2013 certification. See the certification appendix and www.autodesk.com/certification for more information and resources.

CHAPTER 1

Getting Started

As you begin this book on AutoCAD®, I'm reminded of a quote by Chinese philosopher Lao-Tzu: "A journey of a thousand miles begins with a single step." In much the same way, learning AutoCAD is something anyone can do by taking it one step at a time. And I promise that AutoCAD is much easier than walking a thousand miles!

By buying this book, you have already taken the first step in this journey. When you finish, you will have a solid understanding of AutoCAD.

▶ **Exploring the AutoCAD 2013 for Windows User interface**

▶ **Setting drawing units**

Exploring the AutoCAD 2013 for Windows User Interface

> **AutoCAD for Mac has a user interface that is customized to the Mac experience. Although the Mac user interface is not covered in this book, its commands and capabilities are similar to those in AutoCAD for Windows.**

Autodesk has recently released new versions of AutoCAD, including AutoCAD® 2013 and AutoCAD LT® 2013. The two Windows versions look nearly identical and function in almost the same way. The main difference between them is that AutoCAD LT doesn't support automation and some of the advanced 3D functions. The Mac version looks a bit different than its Windows cousins, but it functions nearly identically to AutoCAD for Windows, albeit with a slightly reduced set of features. Although this book was written using AutoCAD 2013 running on Windows XP Professional, you can use it to learn any of the current versions of AutoCAD.

Exploring the Graphical User Interface

Before you can use AutoCAD, you'll need to familiarize yourself thoroughly with its graphical user interface (GUI). The AutoCAD 2013 (for Windows) user interface is shown in Figure 1.1.

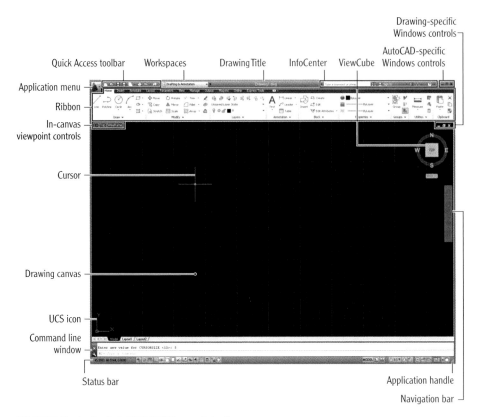

Drawing-specific Windows controls

AutoCAD-specific Windows controls

Quick Access toolbar   Workspaces   Drawing Title   InfoCenter   ViewCube

Application menu

Ribbon

In-canvas viewpoint controls

Cursor

Drawing canvas

UCS icon

Command line window

Status bar

Application handle

Navigation bar

FIGURE 1.1 AutoCAD 2013 user interface

Let's now step through the basic user interface for AutoCAD:

Certification Objective

1. Click the Application menu. Type **polygon**, and observe that the text appears in the search box at the top of the Application menu. The search results (see Figure 1.2) list many related AutoCAD commands. Search is useful when you're not sure how to access a command in the interface or what its exact name is.

2. Click the red X at the extreme right edge of the search box to make the initial Application menu interface reappear. Here you can create new or open existing drawings, export or print drawings, and more. Hover the cursor over Open, and then click Drawing (Figure 1.3).

FIGURE 1.2 Searching for commands in the Application menu

Certification
Objective

FIGURE 1.3 Opening a drawing from the Application menu

3. Select the following sample file, and click Open in the Select File dialog box:

```
C:\Program Files\Autodesk\AutoCAD 2013\Sample\
Sheet Sets\Manufacturing\VW252-02-0142.dwg
```

If you are using AutoCAD LT, open any of the sample files located under `C:\Program Files\Autodesk\AutoCAD LT 2013\Sample`. The Sheet Set Manager palette appears when the sample file is opened (see Figure 1.4). This palette automatically appears when you open any drawing that's a part of a sheet set. AutoCAD has many palettes to organize tools and reusable drawing content.

Sheet sets are not available in AutoCAD LT, and they are an optional feature in AutoCAD.

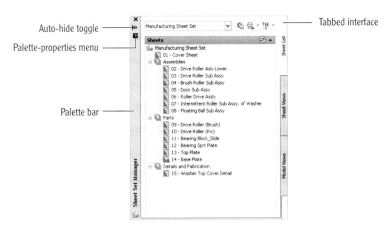

FIGURE 1.4 Opening a sample drawing reveals this palette.

Drag floating palettes to a secondary monitor to maximize the drawing area on your primary monitor.

4. Click the Sheet Views tab along the right edge of the Sheet Set Manager, and observe that tabs provide a means of accessing additional interface content. In its present state, the Sheet Set Manager is a floating palette. Drag its palette bar, and relocate it on screen.

5. Click the Auto-hide toggle, and watch the palette collapse to its vertical palette bar; this saves space on screen. Hover the cursor over the palette bar, and watch the whole palette reappear so that you can access its content. Now toggle Auto-hide off.

6. Click the palette properties menu and select Anchor Left. The Sheet Set Manager palette is docked along the left edge of the user interface (see Figure 1.5). There are many options you can use to organize the user interface to match the way you work.

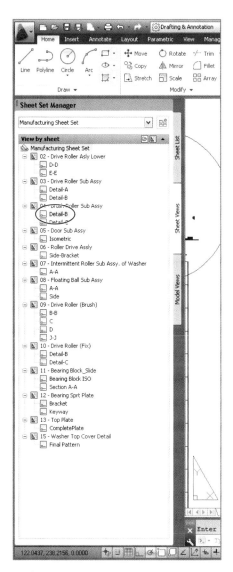

FIGURE 1.5 Docking a palette

7. Double-click Detail-B under 04 – Brush Roller Sub Assy in the Manufacturing sheet set. A new drawing appears in the drawing window.

8. Click the Open button in the Quick Access toolbar. Select any drawing in the Manufacturing folder and click Open. If you are using AutoCAD LT, open any other sample file.

The Quick Access toolbar is a convenient way to open drawings, especially when you're not using the Sheet Set Manager.

Certification
Objective

9. Click the Quick View Drawings button in the application status bar (see Figure 1.6). Move the cursor over the first drawing, and observe that two smaller views appear above it. These are the highlighted drawing's spaces. Move the cursor over Model, and its view will enlarge. Click the model view icon to go there immediately. Use Quick View to navigate through open drawings and their spaces.

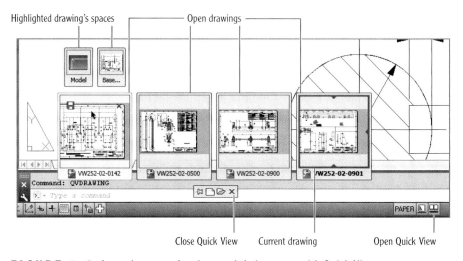

FIGURE 1.6 Accessing open drawings and their spaces with Quick View

AUTOCAD DRAWING SPACES

AutoCAD has two types of drawing spaces: paper and model. Paperspace is a two-dimensional area analogous to, and having the dimensions of, a sheet of paper. Various sizes of "paper" can be created in individual layouts (see Chapter 13, "Working with Layouts and Annotative Objects"). Modelspace, on the other hand, is a single three-dimensional volume where everything is drawn in actual size. Modelspace is typically scaled down in viewports and displayed in paperspace. Most of the drawing you will do in AutoCAD will be in modelspace. Both paper- and modelspaces are saved in the same drawing file.

Exploring Workspaces

AutoCAD workspaces (not to be confused with drawing spaces) are stored sets of user interface controls, which include menus, toolbars, palettes, and the ribbon. People use workspaces to configure the interface quickly for the task at hand. Let's take a brief look at the workspaces in AutoCAD:

1. Select the AutoCAD Classic workspace from the drop-down menu on the Quick Access toolbar. The user interface changes dramatically (see Figure 1.7). The AutoCAD Classic workspace makes AutoCAD look similar to how it did in 2008 and earlier.

Although longtime users might feel more comfortable with the AutoCAD Classic interface, there are many advantages to using all the workspaces.

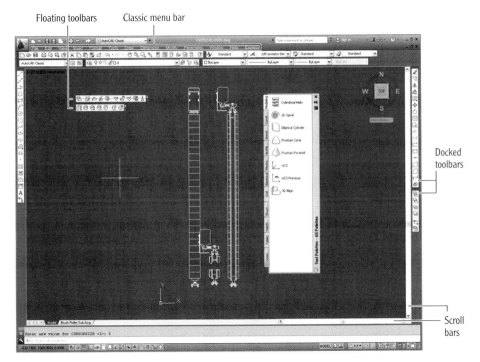

FIGURE 1.7 AutoCAD Classic workspace

2. Drag a docked toolbar out from the edge of the screen and convert it into a floating toolbar. Select Tools ➢ Toolbars ➢ AutoCAD ➢ Dimension from the Classic menu bar. Drag the Dimension floating toolbar to any edge of the screen and dock it.

Certification
Objective

Certification
Objective

3. Position the cursor over a docked toolbar button and right-click; a toolbar context menu appears. Select Object Snap from this menu (Figure 1.8).

FIGURE 1.8 Using the context menu to open toolbars

> Context menus appear when you right-click certain items. What appears in the menu depends on the context of what you right-click on.

4. Right-click in the drawing window, and you'll see a different context menu. Right-clicking over most items, from the tool palettes to the status bar buttons, brings up other unique context menus. In the Classic workspace, right-clicking is the means for accessing numerous context-sensitive menus throughout the user interface.

The AutoCAD Ribbon

> The ribbon doesn't appear in the AutoCAD Classic workspace.

AutoCAD has so many toolbars, palettes, and menus that finding the right tool for the job can seem like a job in itself. The ribbon is therefore an important feature that was introduced to AutoCAD 2010. Autodesk adopted Microsoft's ribbon standard to organize the ever-increasing number of toolbars in a single palette, making tools much easier to find. Now let's explore the various ribbon modes and identify the user interface elements of each mode.

Certification
Objective

1. Choose the 3D Basics workspace from the drop-down menu in the Quick Access toolbar. The ribbon replaces all the Classic menus and toolbars (see Figure 1.9). Close the Tool Palettes and the Online floating toolbar.

Tabbed interface   Minimize ribbon

Typical panel

FIGURE 1.9 The full ribbon interface

2. Click the Minimize Ribbon button, and observe that the full ribbon changes to display tabs and panel buttons (see Figure 1.10). Hover the cursor over the panel buttons. The buttons expand to reveal all the tools shown on the full ribbon.

Panel buttons —

Panel titles —

Tabs —

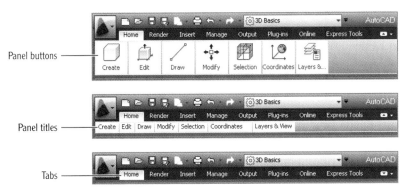

FIGURE 1.10 Ribbon modes

3. Click the Minimize Ribbon button again. The panel buttons change into panel titles. Hover the cursor again over the titles to reveal each panel's tools.

4. Click the Minimize Ribbon button once again. Hovering the cursor over the tabs doesn't have any effect. Click the Home tab to reveal the full panel temporarily. It disappears after you move the cursor away.

5. Click the Minimize Ribbon button one last time. The full ribbon interface is restored.

6. Click the Create button at the bottom of the Create panel to reveal additional tools. Hover the mouse over one of the tools to display a tooltip that identifies the tool and describes its function. Holding the

Certification
Objective

◀

I recommend using the full ribbon interface until you learn the location of all the tools. Use one of the minimized modes to save space on the screen.

cursor still a while longer reveals either a drawing or a video (without audio) that visually demonstrates what the tool does (see Figure 1.11).

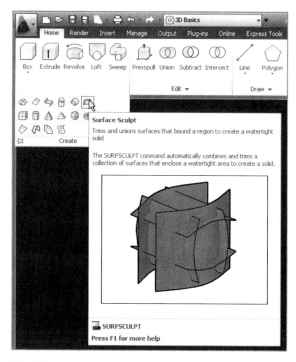

FIGURE 1.11 Tooltip and video

AutoCAD is based on commands. If you know the name of a command, you can type it instead of finding it in the GUI.

7. Observe that the bottom of the tooltip shown in Figure 1.11 reveals the command name (SURFSCULPT in this case). The ribbon, menus, toolbars, and palettes are all graphical alternatives to typing commands.

8. Press and release the Alt key. Keytips appear on the ribbon (see Figure 1.12). Pressing any of the letter combinations activates that part of the GUI. Type **IN**, and observe that the Insert tab is selected without moving the cursor.

FIGURE 1.12 Keytips allow you to press keys to manipulate the ribbon with the keyboard.

9. Press the F2 key to open the AutoCAD Text window. The bottom line, Command:, is called the *command line*. It is the active line where commands appear, regardless of whether they are typed or triggered from the GUI. The complete history of commands scrolls upward as new commands are entered. Close the AutoCAD Text window. Three lines of this command history appear at the bottom of the user interface, just above the application status bar.

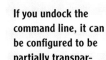

If you undock the command line, it can be configured to be partially transparent and to show a number of lines of prompt history.

10. The application status bar contains a coordinate readout on the left, a number of status toggle buttons, and various items, as shown in Figure 1.13. Toggle off all the status bar toggles so that none of their icons are highlighted in blue. Click the application status bar menu, and deselect Clean Screen; its button disappears. You can control which buttons appear using this menu.

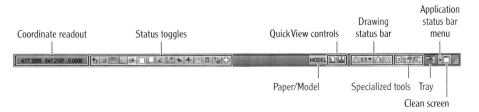

FIGURE 1.13 Application, drawing status bars, and the tray

11. Type **POL**, and observe how the command line's AutoComplete feature highlights commands in alphabetical order as you type (see Figure 1.14). Use the arrow keys to move up or down through the list, and press Enter when you find the command for which you are looking instead of typing the entire word. (Note: Some commands and system variables can be quite lengthy.)

To cancel a current command, press the Esc key.

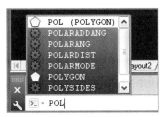

FIGURE 1.14 Command line's AutoComplete feature

12. Take a look at the InfoCenter at the top right of the screen (see Figure 1.15). This is where you connect to Autodesk and the larger community. Click in the search field and type **solid**.

FIGURE 1.15 InfoCenter

13. Click the binoculars icon on the right of the search field, and the AutoCAD Exchange dialog box appears. Multiple online books are searched and relevant results appear in the left panel. The description of the SOLID command appears in the right panel.

14. Click the Help button on the right edge of the InfoCenter. The Help Table of Contents page opens in your browser. All AutoCAD documentation is accessible through this interface.

Setting Drawing Units

Before you start drawing, it's important to decide what one drawing unit represents in the real world. Architects in the United States typically equate one drawing unit with one inch in AutoCAD. You need to choose a unit type that matches your country's industry standard.

Architectural   As the name suggests, most American architects will choose this type, which displays units in feet and inches. For example, 12 feet, 6½ inches is typed as **12′6-1/2″**. The hyphen is used to separate inches from fractions of an inch rather than feet from inches.

Decimal   Metric users should select this type. One decimal unit can be equal to one millimeter, one centimeter, or any metric unit.

Engineering   Like the architectural type, engineering units feature feet and inches, but the inches are represented in decimal form—for example, 126.500.

Fractional   American woodworkers often prefer to set AutoCAD drawings in fractional units of inches because that is how their work is normally reckoned. For example, 12 feet, 6½ inches reads 150-1/2″ in fractional units.

Scientific   For example, 12 million parsecs reads 12.000E+06 in scientific units, where 12.000 indicates 12 accurate to a precision of three decimal places and E+06 indicates the exponential function to the sixth power, or one million.

Let's set the AutoCAD drawing units:

1. Click the New button on the Quick Access toolbar. Click the arrow button next to the Open button in the Select Template dialog box, and choose Open With No Template – Imperial (see Figure 1.16).

Certification Objective

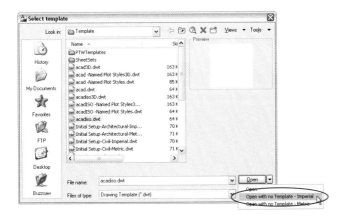

FIGURE 1.16   Opening a drawing with no template

2. Type **UN**, and press Enter to bring up the Drawing Units dialog box (see Figure 1.17). UN is the command alias (abbreviation) of the UNITS command. Most commands have aliases that minimize typing.

You can press Enter or the spacebar to enter commands (command names never have spaces). Commands and their options can be typed in upper or lowercase.

FIGURE 1.17   Setting drawing units

3. Select Architectural from the Type drop-down menu. We're using Architectural in this book, but you should select the unit type that fits your industry when working professionally. Metric users should select Decimal length units.

4. Click the Length Precision drop-down menu, and select 1/8″ (or 0 for metric). Set Angle Type to Decimal Degrees and Angle Precision to 0.00 (two decimal places).

5. Click the Insertion Scale drop-down menu, and select Inches (or Centimeters for metric). Click OK to close the Drawing Units dialog box.

THE ESSENTIALS AND BEYOND

You have had a brief overview of the user interface and learned how to control the look and feel of AutoCAD to suit your working style and needs. In addition, you've learned how to create a new drawing and set the drawing units, and you're ready to get started on the business of drawing.

ADDITIONAL EXERCISES

▶ *Drawing templates* are drawing files that store styles, layers (which you will learn about in Chapter 6, "Controlling Object Visibility and Appearance"), and settings that you want to keep consistent in every drawing you create. Set up the drawing units according to the way you work, and save a new template file (. dwt). Then create a new drawing file (. dwg) based on your template, and verify that the units are as expected. As you learn more about styles, layers, and settings later in this book, you can add your preferences to this template file. Be aware that templates do not affect preexisting drawings.

CHAPTER 2

Basic Drawing Skills

This chapter teaches you how to draw basic shapes, such as lines, rectangles, circles, arcs, and polygons. You will learn how to correct mistakes, navigate two-dimensional space, and use coordinate systems to draw accurately. In addition, you'll perform your first editing tasks by joining existing lines in straight, rounded, or angled intersections.

▶ **Navigating 2D drawings**

▶ **Drawing lines and rectangles**

▶ **Canceling, erasing, and undoing**

▶ **Using coordinate systems**

▶ **Drawing circles, arcs, and polygons**

▶ **Filleting and chamfering lines**

Navigating 2D Drawings

You can change the uniform background color using the OPTIONS command's Display tab and Colors button.

▶

Unlike image-editing programs where zooming in results in blurry, pixilated images, you can zoom in forever in AutoCAD® without suffering any loss in quality. However, to avoid getting lost in space, you'll need to learn how to navigate with a variety of pan and zoom tools that you'll explore here.

1. Go to the book's web page at www.sybex.com/go /autocad2013essentials, and browse to Chapter 2. Get the file Ch2-A.dwg or Ch2-A-metric.dwg, and open it in AutoCAD (see Figure 2.1).

Certification Objective

2. Click the arrow under the Zoom Extents button on the Navigation bar to open the Zoom flyout menu, and select Zoom In. The Zoom In button replaces the original button (which was Zoom Extents) on the Navigation bar. The last used tool appears on top. Click the Zoom In icon again, and the view is magnified by another factor of 2.

Instead of changing the size of objects, Zoom merely increases the magnification on the canvas.

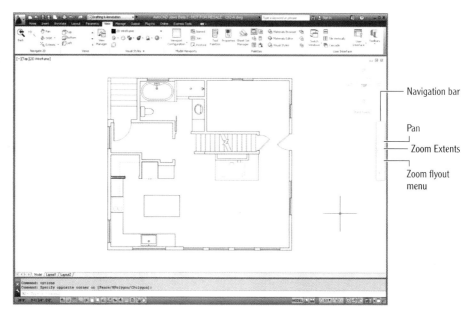

Navigation bar

Pan

Zoom Extents

Zoom flyout menu

FIGURE 2.1 House sample file

3. Click Pan in the Navigation bar, drag the mouse from left to right, and then press Enter to end the command.

4. For an alternative method, press and hold the mouse wheel and pan the drawing to center the refrigerator on the canvas (as shown in Figure 2.2).

5. Select the Drafting & Annotation workspace if it is not already selected, and then select the View tab in the ribbon. Click the bottom menu arrow in the Navigate 2D panel, and select Zoom Realtime (see Figure 2.3). Drag up in the document window to zoom in until the refrigerator fills the screen, and then press Esc.

6. Pan to the lower-left corner of the refrigerator using the scroll bars at the edges of the document window. If your scroll bars are not visible, drag the mouse wheel to pan. (You can turn on the scroll bars with the OPTIONS command.)

7. Select Zoom Window from the Navigate panel on the View tab. Click points A and B, as shown in Figure 2.4. The area of the rectangle you draw is magnified to fill the canvas.

There are many methods for executing commands in AutoCAD so that you can find your favorite ways of working and become more efficient.

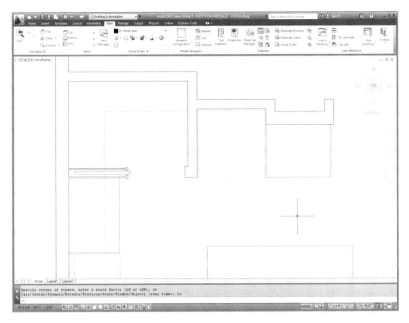

FIGURE 2.2 Navigating to focus on the refrigerator

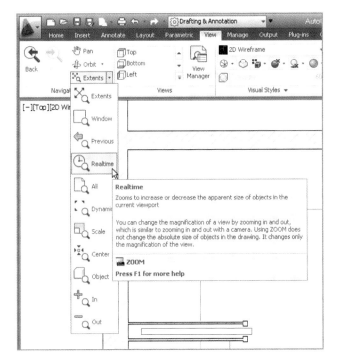

FIGURE 2.3 Zoom tools on the Navigate 2D panel of the View tab of the ribbon

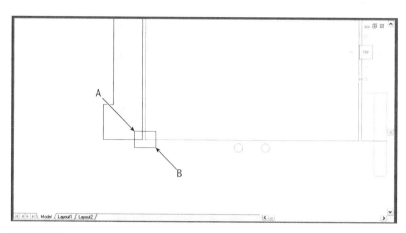

FIGURE 2.4 Zooming into a window

8. Roll the mouse wheel forward to zoom in further, and drag the mouse wheel if necessary to reveal the object in the lower-left corner of the refrigerator (see Figure 2.5).

FIGURE 2.5 Secret text in the lower-left corner of the refrigerator

It's not good practice to create infinitesimally small text objects; this was done only to demonstrate the infinite zoom capability of AutoCAD.

9. Type **Z**, and press the spacebar (Z is the command alias for the ZOOM command). Read the prompt in the Command window or press the Down Arrow key to see the menu in the drawing area:

```
ZOOM
Specify corner of window, enter a scale
factor (nX or nXP), or [All/Center/Dynamic/
Extents/Previous/Scale/Window/Object] <real time>:
```

You are looking at the roots of AutoCAD in the form of command-line options. This interface was invented before the rest of the GUI, and remarkably it not only still functions but is also a very efficient means of working with AutoCAD. Execute any of the options shown in square brackets by typing the capitalized letter. The option in angled brackets (real time in this case) executes by default if you press Enter without typing anything.

10. Type **P**, and press Enter to execute Zoom Previous. Press Enter again to repeat the previous command (ZOOM), type **P**, and press Enter again. Repeat this process until you can see the entire refrigerator again.

11. To see everything that has been drawn, you use Zoom Extents. Double-click the mouse wheel to use Zoom Extents.

12. Position the cursor over the bathroom sink, and roll the mouse wheel forward to zoom in. Notice that the view stays centered on the sink without having to pan (see Figure 2.6). Drag the mouse wheel to make slight panning adjustments if necessary to center the target object on the screen.

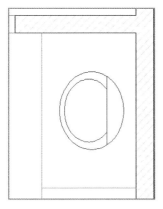

FIGURE 2.6 Directing navigation by positioning the cursor over the bathroom sink while zooming

Navigation should become second nature to you so you don't have to think much about it and can focus on drawing.

13. Practice zooming into the kitchen sink, the stove, and the bathtub using the various methods shown in this section. Leave the drawing file open for work in the next section.

Drawing Lines and Rectangles

The drawing commands you'll probably use the most in AutoCAD are LINE and RECTANGLE. You will begin by drawing some lines and rectangles without worrying yet about entering measurements.

Drawing Lines

Lines are the backbone of AutoCAD. Let's begin drawing lines.

1. In Ch2-A.dwg or Ch2-A-metric.dwg, zoom into the living room at the lower right of the floor plan so that empty space fills the canvas.

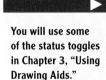

You will use some of the status toggles in Chapter 3, "Using Drawing Aids."

2. Turn off all status toggles in the application status bar. Status toggles are highlighted in blue when they are on and appear in gray when they are off (see Figure 2.7).

F I G U R E   2 . 7   All status toggles shown are as off.

3. Type **L**, and press Enter. Click two arbitrary points to define a line object. Observe the flexible segment (called a *rubberband*) connecting the cursor with the second point you clicked (see Figure 2.8).

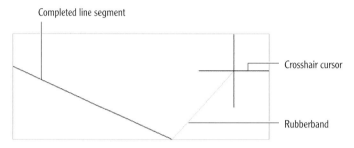

F I G U R E   2 . 8   Drawing a line

4. Click another point to draw your second segment. The prompt in the Command window reads:

```
Specify next point or [Close/Undo]:
```

Type **U**, and press Enter. The last point you clicked is undone, but the rubberband continues to be connected to the cursor, indicating that you can keep drawing lines.

5. Click two more points, and then type **C** and press Enter to create a closing segment between the first and last points. The close option automatically terminates the Line command.

6. Press the spacebar (or Enter) to repeat the last command. Click two arbitrary points to create a single line segment. Right-click to open the context menu, and then select Enter with a left-click to complete the Line command.

7. Open the Application menu and click the Options button at the bottom. Click the User Preferences tab in the Options dialog box that appears. Under the Windows Standard Behavior section, select Right-Click

Customization and then, in the new dialog box, select Turn On Time-Sensitive Right-Click (see Figure 2.9). Click Apply & Close, and then click OK in the Options dialog box.

Time-Sensitive Right-Click is just that: an option. Try it out to see if you find drawing lines in this way more efficient.

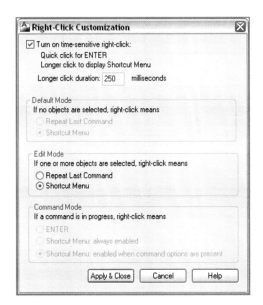

FIGURE 2.9 Turning on Time-Sensitive Right-Click for more efficient drawing

8. Select the Home tab in the ribbon, and click the Line tool in the Draw panel. Click two points, and draw another line. This time, right-click quickly to terminate the Line command.

9. Right-click again to repeat the last command, and then click two points on the canvas. Next, slowly right-click (holding down the right mouse button for longer than 250 milliseconds, to be precise), and you'll see the context menu shown in Figure 2.10. Left-click, and press Enter from this menu to complete the Line command.

FIGURE 2.10
This context menu appears when you hold down the right mouse button longer than 250 milliseconds.

Drawing Rectangles

Line segments are treated as individual objects, whereas the four line segments comprising a rectangle are treated as a single entity. Although rectangles can obviously be drawn with the Line command, specialized commands such as RECTANGLE are more efficient for constructing specific shapes, and they offer more options. Let's experiment now with this feature.

Certification Objective

1. Click the Rectangle tool in the Draw panel, and then click two opposite corner points on the canvas. The command automatically terminates when the rectangle is drawn.

Pay close attention to the prompts in the Command window to see what options are available and/or what specific input is requested at each step.

2. Press Enter to repeat the last command. This time pay attention to the prompts in the Command window:

```
Specify first corner point or
[Chamfer/Elevation/Fillet/Thickness/Width]:
```

3. Click the first corner point in the document window. A new prompt appears:

```
Specify other corner point or
[Area/Dimensions/Rotation]:
```

4. Click the other corner point and the command is finished. You had the opportunity to execute a number of options before you clicked the first point, and again more options appeared after you clicked the first point but before the second point terminated the command.

5. Type **RECTANG** (the command alias for the RECTANGLE command), and press the spacebar. Type **F**, and press Enter to execute the Fillet option. The command prompt reads as follows:

```
Specify fillet radius for rectangles <0.0000>:
```

Do not type cm when using metric units; input numbers only.

6. Type **2″** (or **5** for metric), and press Enter. Units are drawing-specific, so you must use the UNITS command and select Architectural to input feet or inches if you are using a generic or metric template.

7. Click two points to draw the rectangle. The result has filleted corners (see Figure 2.11).

8. Draw another rectangle, and observe that it also has rounded corners. Some options such as the fillet radius are sticky; they stay the same until you change them. Zero out the Fillet option by pressing

the spacebar, typing **F**, pressing Enter, typing **0**, and pressing Enter again. Click two points to draw a sharp-edged rectangle.

9. Save Ch2-A.dwg or Ch2-A-metric.dwg by clicking the Save button in the Quick Access toolbar.

First click

Second click

FIGURE 2.11 Rectangle drawn using its Fillet option

DRAWING RECOVERY MANAGER

Occasionally something goes wrong with AutoCAD and it crashes. The next time you launch AutoCAD, the Drawing Recovery Manager will automatically appear, allowing you to recover damaged drawings that were open (and possibly corrupted) when the program unexpectedly came to a halt.

Canceling, Erasing, and Undoing

Making mistakes in AutoCAD is entirely acceptable if you know how to cancel, erase, and/or undo what you've done wrong. The following exercise will show you how to do all three:

1. Type **L**, and press Enter. Click two points on the canvas, and then press the Esc key; the LINE command is terminated but the single segment you just created remains. The Esc key will get you out of any running command or dialog box.

2. Type **E**, and press the spacebar. Click the line created in step 1, and then right-click; the segment is erased.

   Certification
   Objective

3. Click the Line tool in the Draw panel, click four points on the canvas (making three segments), and then right-click to finish the LINE command.

4. Click each of the segments, one at a time. Blue grips appear on the lines' endpoints and midpoints (see Figure 2.12). Grips are used for editing, and you'll learn more about them in Chapter 4, "Editing Entities." In the meantime, it's helpful to know that if you press the Delete key, the lines are gone.

The virtually unlimited number of undo and redo actions in AutoCAD means that it is a very forgiving program. However, you can't undo past the point when you opened an existing file; in other words, undo and redo actions are not stored in the file but in volatile RAM.

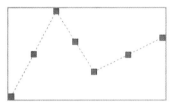

FIGURE 2.12 Selecting lines before deleting them

FIGURE 2.13 Undo and Redo

5. Click the Undo arrow on the Quick Access toolbar (see Figure 2.13). The lines you deleted in step 4 reappear.

6. Click the Redo button, and the lines disappear again.

7. Undo again and, without issuing any command, click two points around the same three lines to create a selection window completely surrounding them. Press the Delete key to erase the selected objects.

8. Click the Undo button's menu arrow. A list of all the commands you've issued in this session appears. Select the bottom item in the list to undo all the way back to the moment when you opened Ch2-A.dwg or Ch2-A-metric.dwg.

Using Coordinate Systems

Certification Objective

AutoCAD uses the same Euclidean space you learned about in Geometry class—but don't panic, I don't expect you to remember any theorems! You can draw objects in Euclidean space using the following coordinate systems: Cartesian, polar, cylindrical, and spherical. (The last two are rarely used, so they won't be covered in this book.)

Cartesian coordinates are useful for drawing rectangles with specific length and width measurements. Polar coordinates are used most often for drawing lines with specific lengths and angles, with respect to horizontal. Once you learn coordinate system syntax, you can use the systems interchangeably to draw accurately in any context.

In the Cartesian system, every point is defined by three values, expressed in terms of distances along the x-, y-, and z-axes. In two-dimensional drawings, the z-coordinate value of all objects is 0, so objects are expressed solely in terms of x- and y-coordinates (see Figure 2.14).

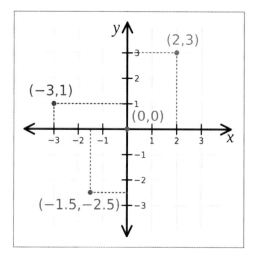

FIGURE 2.14 Cartesian two-dimensional coordinates

Using Absolute Coordinates

Coordinates can be *absolute* or *relative*, no matter which coordinate system is used. Let's first focus on drawing a line using absolute coordinates.

1. If it's not already open, open Ch2-A.dwg or Ch2-A-metric.dwg.

2. Click the Line tool on the Draw panel. The prompt in the Command window reads:

   Specify first point:

   Type **0,0** and press Enter. The origin point of Euclidean space has coordinates 0 in x and 0 in y, which is written as 0,0.

3. Now the prompt in the Command window reads:

   Specify next point or [Undo]:

   Type **3′,0** (or **90,0** in metric), and press Enter. Right-click to finish the LINE command. You drew a line measuring 3′ (or 90 for metric) horizontally along the x-axis.

Certification
Objective

Using Relative Coordinates

Calculating where every object is in relation to the origin point (which is what absolute coordinates require) would be far too cumbersome in practice. Therefore, relative coordinates are used more frequently. Let's explore how to use them:

Certification
Objective

1. Click the Line tool on the Draw panel. Click an arbitrary point in the middle of the living room. The coordinates of the point you clicked are unknown; thankfully, you won't ever need to find out what they are.

2. Type @3',0 (or @90,0 in metric), and press Enter twice. Another 3' (or 90 for metric) line has now been drawn horizontally. The @ symbol tells AutoCAD to consider the previous point as the origin point, relatively speaking.

3. Press Enter to repeat the last command. You'll see the prompt:

   Specify first point:

4. Right-click in the drawing canvas, and hold (for longer than 250 milliseconds) to open the context menu. Select the first coordinate value from the Recent Input menu (see Figure 2.15). You will use the last point entered as the first point in a new line. A rubberband connects the right end of the horizontal line to the cursor.

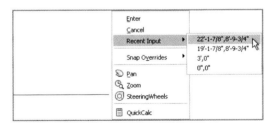

FIGURE 2.15 Drawing a new line from the end of the previous line

5. Type @0,6' (or @0,180 in metric), and press Enter. A line measuring 6' (or 1.8m) is drawn vertically along the y-axis.

6. Type @-3',0 (or @-90,0 in metric), and press Enter. Type @0,-6' (or @0,-180 in metric), and press Enter twice to complete a rectangle.

7. Click the Erase tool on the Modify panel (of the Home tab); select all four lines you just drew and right-click.

8. It's very efficient to use RECTANGLE with Cartesian coordinates. Click the Rectangle tool on the Draw panel, and then click an arbitrary point at the bottom of the living room. The prompt reads:

```
Specify other corner point or [Area/Dimensions/Rotation]:
```

9. Type **@3',6'** (or **@90,180** in metric), and press Enter. The same rectangle that you more laboriously drew with lines is already done.

Using Polar Coordinates

Polar coordinates are another useful way of measuring Euclidean space. In polar coordinates, points are located using two measurements: the distance from the origin point and the angle from zero degrees (see Figure 2.16). East is the default direction of zero degrees.

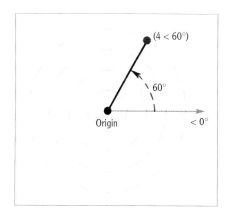

FIGURE 2.16 Polar coordinates

Let's explore how to use polar coordinates:

1. Click the Line tool on the Draw panel. Click an arbitrary first point in the living room, and then type **@3'<45** (or **@90<45** in metric) and press Enter to end the LINE command. You have drawn another 3' (or 90 for metric) line using relative polar coordinates.

2. Press Enter to repeat the last command. Click an arbitrary first point, move the cursor up and to the left, type **3'** (or **90** for metric), and press Enter twice. A 3' (or 90 for metric) line is drawn at an arbitrary angle.

By default, zero degrees is toward the East, or right side of the canvas. In addition, positive angles are typically measured counterclockwise from East. These defaults can be set in the UNITS command.

The less than symbol (hold Shift and press the comma key) represents angular measure in AutoCAD. Think of the < symbol as the representation of an angle.

SPECIFYING ANGLES WITH THE CURSOR

Direct distance entry is the relative method of using the cursor to determine an angle, rather than typing in a specific number of degrees following the < symbol. Direct distance entry is most efficiently used with Ortho and/or Polar modes, which you'll learn about in Chapter 3.

3. Press **L**, and then press the spacebar. Click an arbitrary first point, type **@4'<180** (or **@120<180** in metric), and press Enter. The line is drawn to the left from the first point because 180 degrees is the same direction as angle zero but leads in the opposite direction.

4. Type **@3'<–90** (or **@90<-90** in metric), and press Enter. Negative angles are measured clockwise from angle zero by default. Press **C** and then Enter to close the 3:4:5 triangle you've just drawn.

5. Type **UCSICON**, and press Enter. *UCS* stands for *user coordinate system*. You, the user, can change the coordinate system's orientation. Type **on**, and press Enter. An icon indicating the directions of the positive x- and y-axes is displayed in the lower-left corner of the canvas (see Figure 2.17).

FIGURE 2.17
UCS icon in the default orientation

FIGURE 2.18
Rotating the UCS about its z-axis

6. Type **UCS**, and press Enter. The prompt in the Command window reads as follows:

```
Specify origin of UCS or [Face/NAmed/Object/
Previous/View/World/X/Y/Z/ZAxis] <World>:
```

There is much you can do with the UCS, but here you will simply rotate the UCS about its z-axis (the axis coming out of the screen). Type **Z**, and press Enter.

7. Type **90**, and press Enter to rotate the coordinate system. Observe the UCS icon has changed to reflect the new orientation (see Figure 2.18).

AutoCAD® LT® has only one coordinate system that cannot be changed. AutoCAD LT users can skip ahead to the next section.

8. Type **PLAN**, and press Enter. The prompt in the Command window reads:

```
Enter an option [Current ucs/Ucs/World] <Current>:
```

The option in the angled brackets, <Current>, is what you want, so press Enter to make this selection. The house is reoriented with respect to the current UCS (see Figure 2.19). Notice that the ViewCube's compass directions are rotated (North is now to the right).

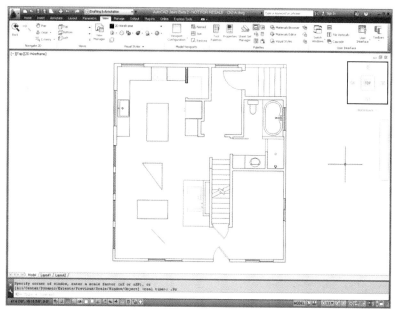

FIGURE 2.19 Reorienting the drawing to the xy plane of the UCS

ROTATING THE PLAN TO MATCH THE UCS

User coordinate systems are usually associated with 3D modeling, but there is one transformation especially useful for 2D drafting: rotation about the z-axis. If you are drawing a building wing or mechanical part that is at an angle with respect to horizontal (especially when the angle isn't an increment of 90 degrees), try rotating the UCS's z-axis and then use the PLAN command to reorient the drawing to the new horizontal.

9. Click the Line tool on the Draw panel. Click an arbitrary first point in the living room, and then type **@3'<45** (or **@90<45** in metric), and press Enter to end the LINE command. You have drawn another 3' (or 90

for metric) line using relative polar coordinates (the same as step 1). However, this time the new line has a different orientation with respect to the original line and the rest of the house (see Figure 2.20).

10. To restore the current coordinate system to its original state, called the *world coordinate system (WCS)*, type **UCS** and press Enter twice. Then type **PLAN**, and press Enter twice more. The plan is oriented to the WCS as it was initially. Observe that North is up again in the ViewCube.

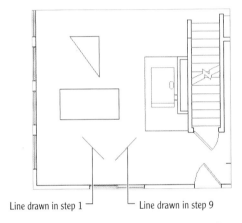

Line drawn in step 1 ⎯⎯⎯   ⎯⎯ Line drawn in step 9

FIGURE 2.20 Angles are relative to the coordinate system in which they are drawn. Both lines were drawn at a 45-degree angle but in different coordinate systems.

Drawing Circles, Arcs, and Polygons

Arcs are sections of circles. Polygons are regular figures made of straight segments such as a triangle, square, pentagon, or hexagon. A polygon with a large number of segments may look like a circle but is fundamentally different.

There are many options for creating circles, arcs, and polygons. AutoCAD provides these options to make it easier to create accurate shapes based on all the types of geometric situations that typically arise in drawings.

Creating Circles

Let's draw some circles on the kitchen stove to represent the burners:

1. Zoom into the stove in the kitchen. Two of the burner circles are missing, and you will draw them.

FIGURE 2.21
Making the Equipment
layer current

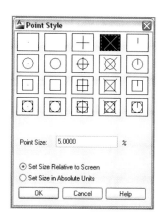

FIGURE 2.22 Changing
the point style so that points
are more visible

FIGURE 2.23
Object Snap context menu

Drawn objects
appear on whichever
layer is current.
Think of layers as
invisible sheets of
tracing paper that
you draw on. You'll
learn more about
layers in Chapter 6,
"Controlling Object
Visibility and
Appearance."

2. On the Home tab, take a look at the Layer drop-down menu in the
Layers panel, and observe that Furniture is the current layer (because
you see its name without having to open the drop-down). Open the
Layer drop-down menu, and select Equipment as the current layer
(see Figure 2.21).

3. You will use preexisting points as guides in drawing the burners.
However, the points are difficult to see right now because they are
represented as single pixels. Expanad the Utilities panel on the Home
tab, and select Point Style. In the Point Style dialog box, select the
X icon and click OK (see Figure 2.22).

Drawing objects
close by eye is not
good enough in
AutoCAD. Always
use object snaps
to connect objects
precisely.

4. Click the Circle tool on the Draw panel. Before you click a center point,
hold down Shift and right-click to open the Object Snap context menu
(see Figure 2.23).

Certification
Objective

5. Select Node from the context menu, and then click point A, as shown
in Figure 2.24. The prompt in the Command window reads:

```
Specify radius of circle or [Diameter] <0'-0">:
```

Type **3″** (or **8** in metric), and press Enter to create a circle with a
radius of 3″ (or 8 for metric). Note that typing the inch symbol is not
necessary. Never type **m**, **cm**, or **mm** to represent metric units.

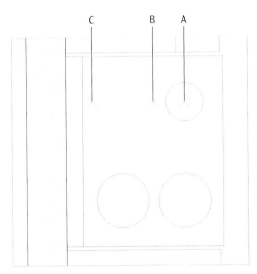

FIGURE 2.24 Drawing a circle by locating its center using node snap

6. Right-click to repeat the last command. The prompt in the Command window reads:

```
Specify center point for circle or
[3P/2P/Ttr (tan tan radius)]:
```

Type **2P** to indicate the two-point option, and press Enter. Hold down Shift, and right-click to open the Object Snap context menu. Select Node, and then click point B, as shown in Figure 2.24.

7. Hold Shift again, right-click, and choose Node. Click point C, as shown in Figure 2.24, and the CIRCLE command is completed.

8. Click the arrow under the Circle tool in the Draw panel, and select 3-Point. Shift+right-click, and select Tangent. Click the circle you drew in the previous step.

9. Hold Shift, right-click again, and type **G**. Notice that this letter is underlined in the word Tangent in the context menu (refer to Figure 2.23). Click the circle on the bottom left.

10. Type **TAN**, press Enter to invoke the Tangent object snap, and click the circle on the lower right. You can type the first three letters of any object snap as an alternative to using the context menu. AutoCAD draws a circle precisely tangent to the three others (see Figure 2.25).

11. Erase the three-point objects and the last circle you drew to leave the four burners of the stove.

Object snaps listed in the context menu must be selected each time they are used. You will learn how to set up running object snaps in Chapter 3.

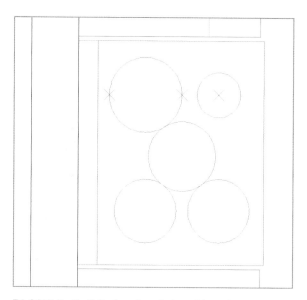

FIGURE 2.25 Drawing circles with various options

Creating Arcs

Arcs have more options than circles because of the complexities of the geometric situations in which arcs can be drawn. In the next set of steps, you will use one such arc option to draw a door swing:

1. Zoom into the bathroom. The bathroom door needs an arc to represent the way it swings.

2. Select Doors from the Layer drop-down menu in the Layers panel.

3. Click the Arc tool's drop-down flyout menu in the Draw panel, which is indicated by the arrow under the word Arc. Select Center, Start, End. This is the sequence in which information must be entered.

   Certification Objective

4. Type **INT**, press Enter to invoke the Intersection object snap, and click the center point A in Figure 2.26.

5. Hold Shift and right-click. Select Endpoint from the context menu, and click the start point B (shown in Figure 2.26).

6. Hold Shift and right-click, type **END**, and click the arc endpoint C (shown in Figure 2.26). The arc appears, and the command is completed.

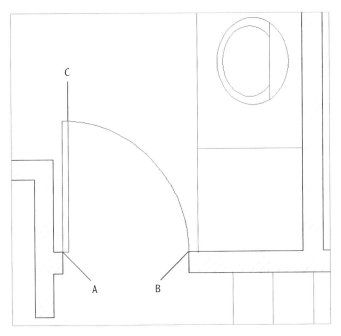

FIGURE 2.26 Drawing a door swing with an arc option

CONTROLLING ARC AND CIRCLE SMOOTHNESS

Arcs and circles are defined with perfect curvature in AutoCAD, but sometimes they appear blocky on screen. The system variable VIEWRES controls how smoothly arcs and circles are drawn on screen. Adjust this on the View tab under the Visual Style panel's expansion menu. Set the resolution to the maximum VIEWRES value by typing **VIEWRES**, pressing Enter twice, typing **20000**, and pressing Enter again. Type **REGEN**, and press Enter to make this change take effect on screen.

Drawing Polygons

When you want to draw triangles, squares, pentagons, or any figure having equally sized edges, use the POLYGON command. You can draw these shapes inside or outside a circle, or specify the edge length, as shown in the following steps:

1. Select the Home tab if it's not already active. Make the Furniture layer current by selecting it from the Layer drop-down menu in the Layers panel.

2. Zoom into the living room.

3. Click the Rectangle tool's drop-down flyout, and select the Polygon tool. The prompt in the Command window reads:

```
Enter number of sides <5>:
```

4. Type **4**, and press Enter to draw a square.

5. The command prompt now reads:

```
Specify center of polygon or [Edge]:
```

Type **E**, and press Enter to specify an edge length and direction. Click a point somewhere in the living room as the first endpoint of the edge, and type **@2'<0** (or **@60<0** in metric) to specify the second endpoint of the edge relative to the first one, using polar coordinates in this case. A 2' (or 60 for metric) square appears.

6. Type **POL**, and observe that, as you type, the AutoComplete menu appears above the command line suggesting commands and system variables (see Figure 2.27). Press the down arrow until POLYGON is highlighted and press Enter.

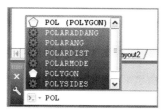

FIGURE 2.27 A menu suggesting commands and system variables appears as you type.

7. Type **6**, and press Enter to draw a hexagon. Click a point in the living room where you want to center the hexagon. The prompt now reads:

```
Enter an option [Inscribed in circle/
Circumscribed about circle] <I>:
```

8. Press Enter to accept the default Inscribed In Circle option.

9. Type **1'** (or **30** in metric) as the radius of the circle and press Enter. A hexagon fitting inside a 1' (or 30 for metric) radius circle appears.

Filleting and Chamfering Lines

Fillet and Chamfer are tools that create transitions between objects. *Fillet* creates arcs and *Chamfer* creates lines. Fillet is most commonly used for a purpose for which it probably wasn't designed—joining separate lines so that they intersect at their endpoints, without creating arcs at all.

Joining Nonparallel Lines

Fillet and Chamfer can be used to join lines that are crossing as well as lines that don't meet. Chamfer doesn't work on parallel lines at all, but Fillet will create a half circle connecting the endpoints of parallel lines, regardless of the fillet radius. Let's explore the FILLET and CHAMFER commands:

1. Draw two lines. It doesn't matter what size they are or what angle is between them, as long as the lines aren't parallel.

2. Press the F12 key to toggle *dynamic input* on, an optional mode that displays command-line options on the canvas. Position the cursor on the canvas, and type **CHA**, the command alias for the CHAMFER command, and the AutoComplete window appears on the canvas rather than in the Command window.

3. Press Enter, and then press the Down Arrow key to expand the command's options on screen.

4. Press the down arrow three more times, and press Enter to select the Distance option in the Dynamic Input display (see Figure 2.28). Type **1′** (or **30** for metric), and press Enter twice to input equal first and second distances equal to 1′.

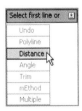

F I G U R E   2 . 2 8
Displaying a command-line
option on the canvas
with dynamic input

5. Click one line and then hover the cursor over the second line; you'll see a preview of the chamfer that will be created. Click the second line to perform the chamfer and complete the command. (The chamfer is shown in the middle of Figure 2.29.)

Fillet and chamfer previewing works only if When A Command Is Active is selected on the Selection tab of the Options dialog box. This option should be selected by default.

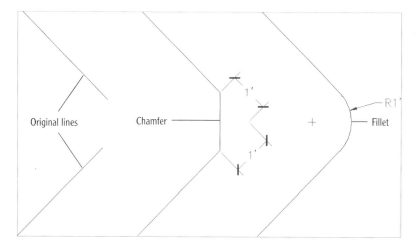

FIGURE 2.29 Chamfered and filleted lines

6. Draw two more noncrossing and nonparallel lines.

Certification
Objective

7. Type **F**, and press Enter to execute the FILLET command. Press the down arrow, and choose Radius from the Dynamic Input display. Type **1′** (or **30** for metric), and press Enter.

Fillet radius and chamfer distances are sticky; they stay the same until you change them.

8. Click the first line, and then hover the cursor over the second line; the fillet preview shows on screen. Click the second line to commit to that particular radius. (This fillet is shown at the right of Figure 2.29.)

Joining Crossed Lines

When lines cross, there are multiple fillet and chamfer possibilities on different sides of the intersection. In the case of crossing lines, you must select the lines on the portions that you want to keep, as shown in these steps:

1. Draw two lines that cross.

2. Type **F**, and press Enter. Press the down arrow to access the Dynamic Input display, and select Radius. Type **0**, and press Enter. Now Fillet will not create an arc at all.

3. Click the points A and B, as shown in Figure 2.30. The lines are joined at their endpoints, and the remaining portions of the lines beyond their intersection point are trimmed away.

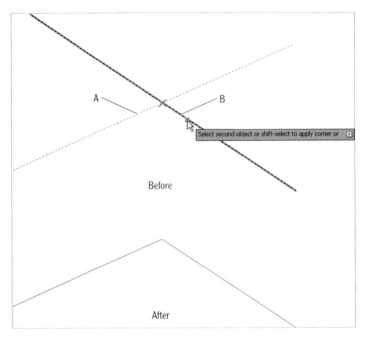

FIGURE 2.30 Filleting lines with a zero radius joins them together precisely.

4. Click the Save As button on the Quick Access toolbar. Type **Ch2-B.dwg** or **Ch2-B-metric.dwg** as the filename. The end file is provided on Chapter 2's download page at www.sybex.com/go/autocad2013essentials for your convenience.

THE ESSENTIALS AND BEYOND

This chapter covered the mechanics of drawing many basic object types, including lines, circles, arcs, and polygons. You learned how to navigate 2D drawings in a variety of ways. By learning how to cancel, erase, and undo, you won't be afraid to make mistakes in AutoCAD. In addition, we explored how coordinate systems make accurate drawing possible. Finally, you altered existing lines with Fillet and Chamfer, and learned how to join lines by using a zero fillet radius.

ADDITIONAL EXERCISE

▶ Explore the Donut and Solid commands on your own. Unlike most AutoCAD drawing tools, these older commands produce objects that have two-dimensional solidity. Refer to Help in AutoCAD if you need further information.

CHAPTER 3

Using Drawing Aids

The drawing aids in AutoCAD® are like the triangles, compasses, and engineering scales of traditional drafting. Drawing aids are essential modes and methods of entering data that, once mastered, allow you to create measured drawings with ease. I highly recommend learning all of the drawing aids, because they will make you a more productive draftsperson. Most drawing aids can be toggled on or off from the application status bar. Additional settings and dialog boxes are accessible by right-clicking the individual status bar toggles.

▶ **Grid and Snap**

▶ **Ortho and Polar Tracking**

▶ **PolarSnap**

▶ **Running object snaps**

▶ **From snap**

▶ **Object Snap Tracking**

Grid and Snap

**Certification
Objective**

The most basic drawing aid, *Grid,* makes AutoCAD's canvas look like graph paper. You can adjust the grid's measured size and the spacing of its major lines to simulate many types of graph paper.

Snap constrains your ability to draw objects so that they automatically start and end precisely at grid intersections. Grid and Snap are most helpful when used together so that you can draw objects that snap to the grid. Figure 3.1 shows some of the status bar toggles that you'll be learning about in this chapter.

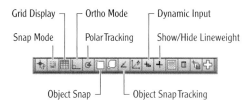

FIGURE 3.1 Various status bar toggles

1. Click the New button on the Quick Access toolbar.

2. Choose the `acad.dwt` Imperial template (or `acadiso.dwt` metric template) from the Select Template dialog box and click Open.

Grid spacing is usually equal to or an increment of the snap interval.

3. Right-click the Grid Display toggle on the status bar, and choose Settings from the context menu. Change Grid X spacing to 1″ (or 10 mm), and press Tab; Grid Y spacing updates with the same value. Set Major Line Every to 12 for Imperial (or 10 for metric) so that you'll see darker grid lines every foot. Notice that Snap spacing is set to 1/2″ (or 10 mm) by default. Select Snap On, and verify that the Grid Snap radio button is selected in the Snap Type area (see Figure 3.2). Click OK.

FIGURE 3.2 Setting up grid spacing and toggling on Snap

4. Click the Line tool in the Draw panel on the ribbon's Home tab. Click the first point near the lower-left corner of the canvas at the intersection of major grid lines (darker lines). Click the second point 2′ (or 600 mm) above the first point by clicking the second intersection (or sixth

intersection in metric) of major grid lines. Right-click to end the LINE command. It's very difficult to see the line because the grid obscures it.

5. Click the Show/Hide Lineweight icon in the status bar so that the button is highlighted in blue. It's difficult to see the line because the default lineweight display is too thin.

6. Right-click the Show/Hide Lineweight icon, and choose Settings from the context menu. Open the Default drop-down list, select 0.016″ (or 0.40 mm) (see Figure 3.3), and click OK. The line you drew in step 4 is displayed thicker so that it's more visible against the grid.

You'll learn how to control line-weight with lay-ers in Chapter 6, "Controlling Object Visibility and Appearance."

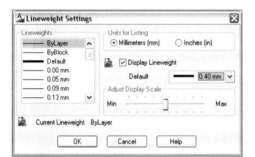

FIGURE 3.3 Adjusting the default lineweight settings

7. Type **L**, and press Enter twice to continue drawing from the last point clicked. Toggle Grid Display off and Dynamic Input on in the status bar. Move the cursor horizontally to the right from the point at which the rubberband is anchored. Notice that 1/2″ (or 10 mm) increments are all that show up on screen; this is due to Snap. Snap can be used independently of the grid; the grid is merely a visual drawing aid. Click on the drawing canvas when the dynamic input value reads 2′-0″ (or 600 mm), as shown in Figure 3.4. Leave the file open for work in the next section.

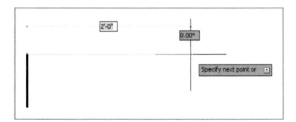

FIGURE 3.4 Using Snap with Dynamic Input to gauge distances without typing

steps, you will learn several efficient selection methods that you can use at any `Select objects:` prompt, which appears in every editing command.

Black on white is easier to see in a book but AutoCAD has a dark background by default. You can change the background color on the Display tab of the OPTIONS command.

1. Go to the book's web page at www.sybex.com/go/autocad2013essentials, browse to Chapter 4, get the file Ch4-A.dwg (or Ch4-A-metric .dwg)—a fictitious office building—and open it (see Figure 4.1).

2. Zoom into Stair A in the building core.

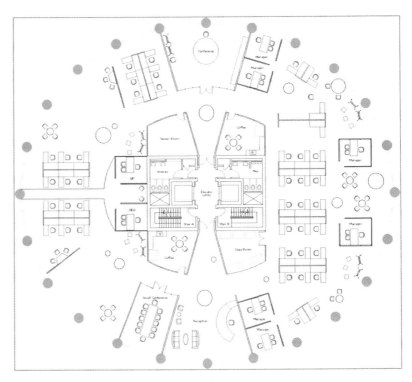

FIGURE 4.1 Office building start file

3. Click the Erase tool in the Modify panel on the Home tab of the ribbon. The prompt in the Command window reads as follows:

   `Select objects:`

   This is the same way almost every command begins—with the opportunity to create a selection set.

Certification Objective

4. Click point A and then B, as shown in Figure 4.2. Observe that a transparent *implied window* appears between these points. The objects that are selected are only those completely contained within the borders

of the blue window. This particular selection includes the stair arrows, handrails, and three lines representing stair treads near the break lines.

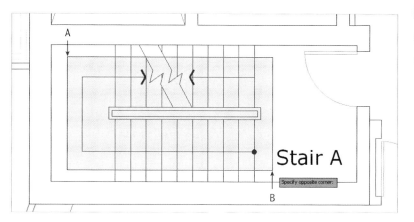

FIGURE 4.2 Drawing an implied window

You can draw implied windows either with a click and a click, or a click and drag.

5. Type **R** (for Remove), and press Enter. The command prompt reads as follows:

```
Remove objects:
```

6. Click point A and then B, as shown in Figure 4.3. When you click the first point on the right (A) and move the cursor to the left (at B), a transparent green *crossing window* appears between the points. Whatever the green window crosses is selected. The crossing selection removes the handrail and two of the stair treads because the selection was made at the Remove objects: prompt.

Certification
Objective

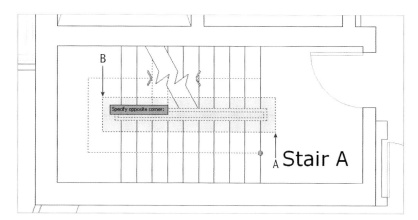

FIGURE 4.3 Drawing a crossing window to remove objects from the selection set

7. Click point A and then B, as shown in Figure 4.4. This implied window selects the short line segment trapped in the break line and removes it from the selection set.

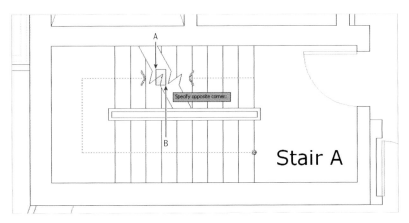

FIGURE 4.4 Removing a short line from the selection set with an implied window

8. Type **A** (for Add), and press Enter. The command prompt again reads as follows:

```
Select objects:
```

9. Click each of the break lines to add them to the selection set. All of the break line segments are selected in two clicks because the break lines are polylines.

10. Hold Shift, and click the break lines again. They are removed from the selection set without being at the Remove objects: prompt.

11. Press Esc to cancel the ERASE command.

Creating a Selection Set Before Deciding on a Command

In addition to creating a selection set at any Select objects: prompt, you can create a selection set first and then decide which command to use afterward. (Additional dynamic input prompts are available on screen when you select objects first.) Let's explore these additional selection methods:

1. If the file is not already open from performing the previous step, go to the book's web page, browse to Chapter 4, download the file Ch4-A.dwg (or Ch4-A-metric.dwg), and open it.

2. Toggle on Dynamic Input mode in the status bar.

3. Click point A, as shown in Figure 4.5. Press the Down Arrow key to expand the dynamic input menu on screen. Select WPolygon.

The related CPolygon option creates a polygonal crossing window, shown in transparent green. The Fence option allows you to draw a multi-segmented line that selects whatever it crosses.

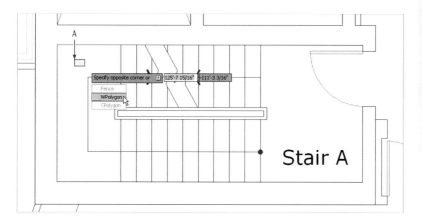

FIGURE 4.5 Selecting WPolygon selection mode from the dynamic input prompt

4. Click points B through H, as shown in Figure 4.6. The transparent blue polygon you are drawing functions the same as an implied rectangular window; the difference is the polygonal window offers more flexibility as you have the power to shape it. Only those objects completely contained within the borders of the blue window will be selected.

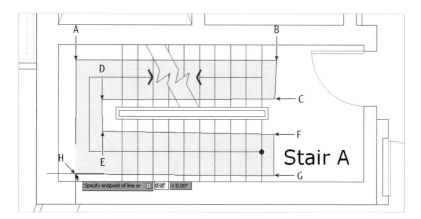

FIGURE 4.6 Drawing a polygonal implied window to create a selection set

5. Press Enter to make the selection. Square blue dots appear on the selected objects—these are called *grips*, and you will learn to use them later in this chapter. Press Esc to deselect.

 6. Toggle on Ortho mode in the status bar. Without being concerned with measurements or accuracy, draw a line under the word Stair, a circle around the letter A, and a rectangle around the entire section, in that order (see Figure 4.7).

FIGURE 4.7 Drawing a few objects to learn about the selection buffer

7. Type **SELECT**, and press Enter. Select the circle and the line and press Enter. The SELECT command is used merely to make a selection. The grips for the circle and line appear; press Esc to deselect.

 8. Click the Erase icon on the Modify panel. At the Select objects: prompt, type **P** (for Previous) and press Enter. The circle and line are selected because they comprise the set of objects that was selected previously. Press Enter again to delete these objects.

9. Press the spacebar to repeat the last command (ERASE). Type **L** (for Last), and press Enter. The rectangle is selected because it was the last object you created. There can only be one last object. Press Enter again to delete the rectangle.

10. Toggle on Selection Cycling in the status bar.

11. Click the dot at the end of the stair direction line (shown in Figure 4.8). This dot is at the confluence of the horizontal stair direction line and the vertical tread line. When selection cycling is on, you are presented with the Selection dialog box whenever your selection is ambiguous. Hover the cursor over the items in the list and each one's grips are highlighted on the drawing canvas. Select the line in the list that highlights grips on the stair direction line as shown in Figure 4.8 and then press Esc.

12. Press Ctrl+W to toggle selection cycling off.

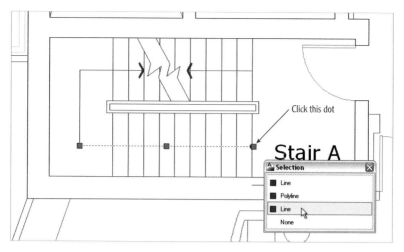

FIGURE 4.8 Selection cycling

13. Select one of the vertical tread lines in Stair A by clicking on it. Right-click, and choose Select Similar from the context menu that appears. All lines on the same layer are selected (see Figure 4.9). Other object types on the same layer remain unselected because they were not similar enough. Press Esc.

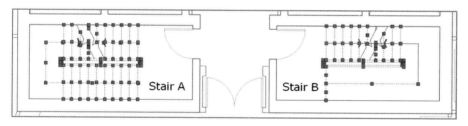

FIGURE 4.9 Selecting similar objects en masse

SELECTING SIMILAR OBJECTS

Type **SELECTSIMILAR**, press Enter, type **SE**, and press Enter again to open its settings dialog. Here you can select criteria to determine which object properties must match in order to be selected by this useful command: color, layer, linetype, linetype scale, lineweight, plot style, object style, or name.

Move and Copy

MOVE and COPY are the most commonly used commands in AutoCAD. As you'll see in the following steps, they are very similar in that they both require a distance and a direction to indicate where you plan to displace the selected objects.

1. If the file is not already open from performing the previous step, go to the book's web page, browse to Chapter 4, download the file Ch4-A.dwg (or Ch4-A-metric.dwg), and open it.

2. Pan to the upper-right quadrant of the building, and zoom into the furniture grouping that needs to be filled in.

3. Click the chair that is not in front of a desk to select it. Position the cursor over the selected chair, but not over its grip. Drag the chair to move it closer to the upper desk, as shown in Figure 4.10.

The disadvantage to moving by dragging is that the displacement is unmeasured, and you can't use Object Snap to maintain accuracy.

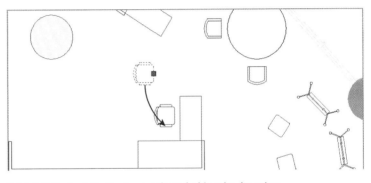

FIGURE 4.10 Moving a selected object by dragging

4. To position the chair more precisely, click the Move tool in the Modify panel. Select the chair you just moved in the previous step and press Enter. The command prompt reads as follows:

```
Specify base point or [Displacement] <Displacement>:
```

Certification Objective

5. Right-click the Object Snap toggle in the status bar, and choose Midpoint from the context menu if it is not already selected. Click the base point at the midpoint of the front of the chair (point A in Figure 4.11).

6. Click the second point, B, as shown in Figure 4.11. The chair is moved precisely to the midpoint of the desk edge.

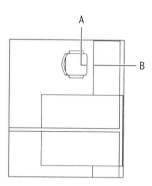

FIGURE 4.11 Selecting the base point for a move

7. Press the spacebar to repeat MOVE. Type **P**, and press Enter twice to select the same chair again. Press Enter once more to accept the default option <Displacement>. In Displacement mode, the first point is the origin point. Any coordinates you enter are relative to the origin, so typing the @ symbol is unnecessary. Type **4<180** (or **10<180** in metric) and press Enter.

Certification Objective

8. Click the Copy tool in the Modify panel. Select the chair you just moved and press Enter. Select the midpoint of the desk (point B in Figure 4.11) as the base point, and then click the midpoint of the corresponding mirror image desk below in the same furniture group as the second point. Press Enter to end the COPY command.

9. Press the spacebar to repeat the previous command, select both desks and chairs with crossing windows, and press Enter. Select point A in Figure 4.12 as the base point and point B as the second point. Press Esc to end the command.

Certification Objective

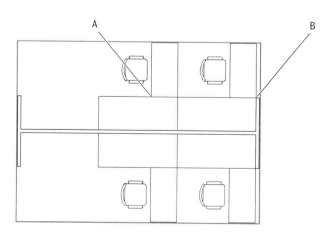

FIGURE 4.12 Copying multiple items

10. Pan over to the Conference room. To copy an array of chairs along the left wall, you will rotate the user coordinate system (UCS) to match the orientation of the wall. Type **UCS**, and press Enter. Select the Object option by typing **OB** and press Enter. Select the inner left wall line and watch as the crosshair cursor changes to match the angle of the wall (see Figure 4.13).

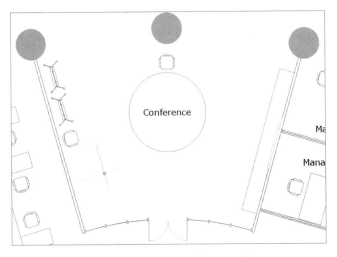

FIGURE 4.13 Reorienting the UCS to an object

11. Type **CO** (for Copy), and press Enter. Select the chair that is against the left wall of the Conference room and press Enter. Click an arbitrary base point by clicking in the empty space of the Conference room. Toggle on Polar Tracking on the status bar if it is not already on.

12. Move the cursor down along the direction of the wall, type **A** (for Array), and press Enter. The command prompt reads as follows:

```
Enter number of items to array:
```

Type **5**, and press Enter. Type **F** (for Fit), and press Enter. Move the cursor downward, and observe that five ghosted chairs appear. When the spacing looks right, click in the document window to complete the array and press Enter. Figure 4.14 shows the result.

13. Type **UCS**, and press Enter twice to accept the default option of World. The crosshair cursor returns to its default orientation.

14. Save your work as **Ch4-B.dwg** (or **Ch4-B-metric.dwg**).

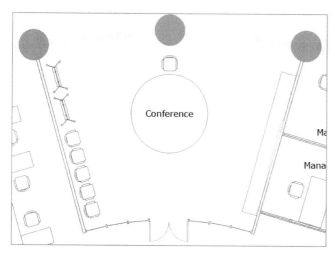

FIGURE 4.14 Copying chairs in an array

Rotate and Scale

The ROTATE and SCALE commands are obviously essential to drawing; each requires a base point to indicate the center from which objects are transformed. Numerically speaking, you typically rotate by degrees or scale by percentages about base points. On the other hand, you can avoid using numbers entirely by choosing the Reference options, which let you rotate or scale selection sets in relation to other objects. Let's rotate and scale objects.

1. If the file is not already open from performing the previous step, go to the book's web page, browse to Chapter 4, download the file Ch4-B.dwg (or Ch4-B-metric.dwg), and open it.

2. Navigate to Reception at the bottom of the floor plan. Click the Rotate button in the Modify panel, select the upper chair, and press Enter. The command line reads as follows:

    Specify base point:

    Click a point in the center of the chair; you don't need to snap this point because an approximation is good enough at this point.

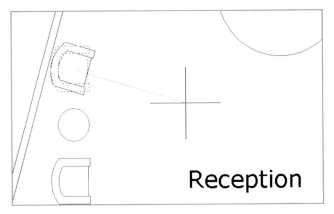

3. Toggle off Polar Tracking (and Ortho if it is on) in the status bar. Move the cursor around the point, and observe that a rubberband line connects the base point to your cursor and a ghosted image of the chair is superimposed over the original chair representation. Move the cursor until the rubberband aligns more or less perpendicularly to the wall behind the chair (see Figure 4.15) and click.

FIGURE 4.15 Rotating a chair by visually estimating the angle

4. Click the chair that you just rotated to select it without issuing an explicit command. Hold the Ctrl key, and repeatedly press the arrow keys to nudge the selected object a few pixels at a time. Nudge the chair so that it is a similar distance from the wall and the round table as compared to the other armchair in Reception. Press Esc to deselect all.

5. Zoom out and focus on the upper-left quadrant of the building. Type **CO** (for Copy), and press Enter. Select the furniture group shown in Figure 4.16, and press Enter. Select midpoint A as the base point, and select midpoint B as the second point. Press Esc to end the command.

6. Type **RO** (for Rotate), and press Enter. Select the furniture group you just copied and press Enter. Select the same midpoint where the furniture group was attached to the midpoint of the shell window wall as the base point of the rotation. The command line reads as follows:

   `Specify rotation angle or [Copy Reference] <0.00>:`

   Type **R** (for Reference), and press Enter. Instead of specifying the reference angle with a number, you will determine the angle interactively. Type @ and press Enter to input the base point of the rotation as the base point of the reference angle.

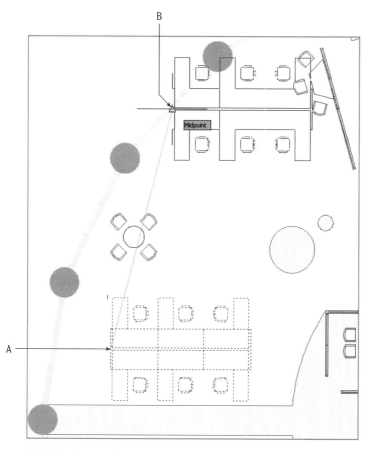

FIGURE 4.16 Copying a furniture group to a new center of rotation

7. Click endpoint A and B as shown in Figure 4.17 to specify the second point of the reference angle and the new angle. The furniture group rotates so that it is parallel and centered on the window wall.

8. Pan over to the upper-right quadrant of the building, and zoom in on the oversized round table. Click the Scale icon on the Modify panel, select the circle representing the table, and press Enter. The command line reads as follows:

```
Specify base point:
```

Snap to the center of the circle. Type **.5**, and press Enter to scale the circle down to 50 percent of its original size (see Figure 4.18).

Using the ROTATE and SCALE commands' Reference options allows you to transform with reference to other objects without having to input numerical angles or scale factors.

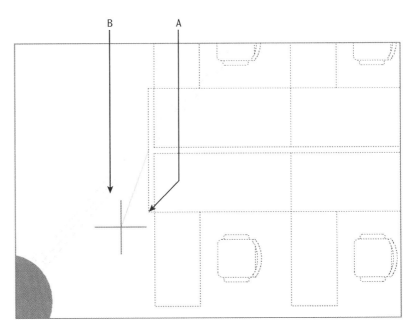

FIGURE 4.17 Rotating with the Reference option

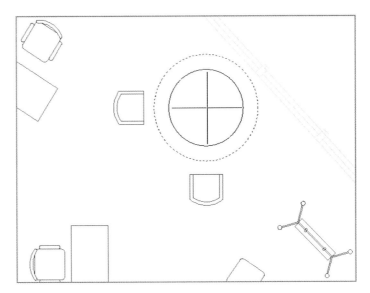

FIGURE 4.18 Scaling a circle from its center

9. Toggle on Polar Tracking on the status bar, and move the chairs closer to the table, both horizontally and vertically.

10. Save your work as Ch4-C.dwg (or Ch4-C-metric.dwg).

Working with Arrays

Arrays produce single associative objects, which you can edit at any time to alter the parameters of the array. You will learn how to create two types of associative arrays: rectangular and polar.

Rectangular Arrays

Rectangular arrays are arranged in a grid of rows (running horizontally) and columns (running vertically). Let's create a rectangular array:

1. If the file is not already open from performing the previous step, go to the book's web page, browse to Chapter 4, download the file Ch4-C. dwg (or Ch4-C-metric.dwg), and open it.

2. Instead of trying to make a rectangular array at an oblique angle, it is easier first to rotate the user coordinate system. Type **UCS**, and press Enter. Type **OB** (for Object), and press Enter. Select the top-left edge of the table in the Small Conference room. The crosshair cursor rotates to match the orientation of the conference table.

3. Click the Rectangular Array tool on the Modify panel. Select both chairs on the sides of the conference table and press Enter.

4. Change Columns to 1 and Rows to 5 on the temporary Array Creation tab that appears on the ribbon. Type **2′-4″** in the Between text box in the Rows panel (see Figure 4.19). Depending on which side of the line you selected in the previous step, you might have to enter 5 Columns and 1 Row if the UCS is 180 degrees out of phase.

5. Select the Associative toggle in the Properties panel if it is not already blue. Click Close Array on the ribbon.

6. Select one of the new chairs, and observe that all the arrayed chairs select as a unit. Change the number of Rows to 4 and Between to **3′-0″** (**90** for metric), as shown back in Figure 4.14.

7. Type **UCS**, and press Enter twice to return to the world coordinate system.

8. Save your work as Ch4-D.dwg (or Ch4-D-metric.dwg).

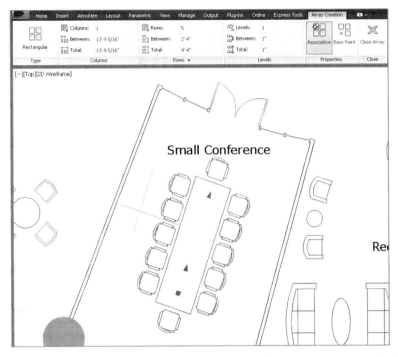

FIGURE 4.19 Creating a rectangular array by changing parameters on the ribbon

Polar Arrays

Polar arrays are used for rotating and copying objects around a common central point. Let's create a polar array:

1. If the file is not already open from performing the previous step, go to the book's web page, browse to Chapter 4, download the file Ch4-D.dwg (or Ch4-D-metric.dwg), and open it.

2. Navigate to the Conference room at the top of the plan (see Figure 4.20).

3. Type **AR** (for Array), and press Enter. Select the chair at the top of the round table, and press Enter.

4. The command prompt reads as follows:

   Enter array type [Rectangular Path Polar] <Rectangular>:

5. Type **PO** (for Polar), and press Enter.

6. Hold down Shift, and right-click to open the Object Snap context menu. Choose Center, and click the table's center to set the center point of the array.

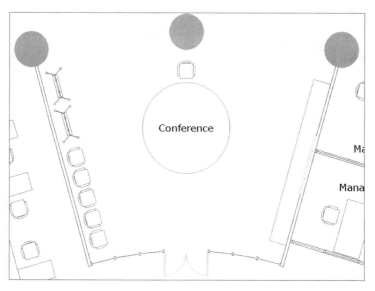

FIGURE 4.20 The Conference room

7. Type **12** in the Items text box on the ribbon. Toggle on Associative, Rotate Items, and Direction if they are not already on in the Properties panel (see Figure 4.21). Click Close Array.

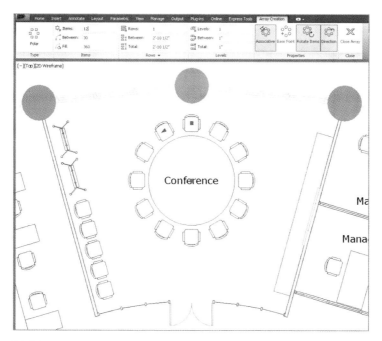

FIGURE 4.21 Creating a polar array

8. The table is a bit too large. Click the circle to select the table. Click the circle's top blue quadrant grip, and move the cursor down. Type **4′6″** (or **140** in metric) to set a new radius. Press Enter and then Esc.

9. Click any one of the chairs to select the polar array. Hover the cursor over the base point grip, and choose Stretch Radius (see Figure 4.22). Type **5′9″** (or **175** in metric); then press Enter and Esc. The chairs more closely wrap around the smaller table.

10. Save your work as Ch4-E.dwg (or Ch4-E-metric.dwg).

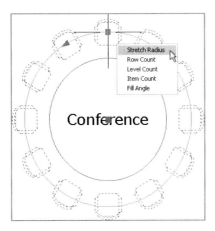

FIGURE 4.22 Editing a polar array with its grips

DIVIDE AND MEASURE

The DIVIDE and MEASURE commands do not copy objects in a rectangular grid or around a center point as does the ARRAY command. Instead, these commands are used for arraying points. Divide splits up a path into any number of evenly spaced points. MEASURE lays out points at a set distance, often leaving a remainder at the end of a path. You'll use DIVIDE in Chapter 5, "Shaping Curves."

Trim and Extend

The TRIM and EXTEND commands are opposites. You can invoke the opposite command while running either by holding down Shift. This method is especially helpful because TRIM and EXTEND are often used together:

Certification
Objective

1. If the file is not already open from performing the previous step, go to the book's web page, browse to Chapter 4, download the file Ch4-E.dwg (or Ch4-E-metric.dwg), and open it.

2. Navigate to Stair B in the building's core.

3. Click the Extend tool on the Modify panel (it is nested under Trim). Select the inner line of the bottom core wall and press Enter. This line will be the boundary edge that you will extend the stair treads to meet.

4. Create a crossing window by clicking points A and B as shown in Figure 4.23. Four tread lines are extended. Click each remaining tread line, one at a time, to extend all the stair treads to the core wall. Press Enter to end the command.

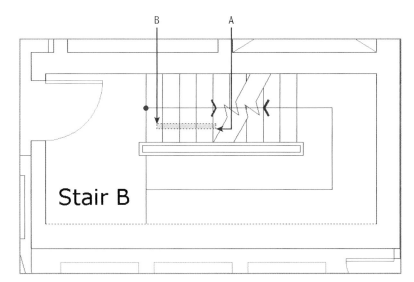

FIGURE 4.23 Extending lines with a crossing window and by selecting

5. Type **TR** (for Trim), and press Enter. Select the upper and lower hand-rail lines to act as cutting edges and press Enter. Make a crossing window in the center of the handrail to trim away all the treads that pass through the handrails, and press Enter.

6. Press Enter twice more to repeat the TRIM command, and select all edges as potential cutting edges. Then click the single tread line that extends below the break line and press Enter. Stair B should now be the mirror image of Stair A.

7. Save your work as Ch4-F.dwg (or Ch4-F-metric.dwg).

Lengthen and Stretch

The LENGTHEN and STRETCH commands are similar in how they can increase the length of objects. However, STRETCH is the more flexible of the two, allowing you to reposition interconnected objects. Let's lengthen a line and stretch a door within a wall:

1. If the file is not already open from performing the previous step, go to the book's web page, browse to Chapter 4, download the file Ch4-F.dwg (or Ch4-F-metric.dwg), and open it.

2. Navigate to the Copy Room. Notice that there is a problem with the copy machine by the door; the bottom line is drawn only halfway. Although you could use FILLET or EXTEND to fix it, type **LEN** (for Lengthen) and press Enter. The command prompt reads as follows:

   Select an object or [DElta/Percent/Total/DYnamic]:

   Type **P** (for Percent), and press Enter.

3. Type **200**, and press Enter. Click the line segment on the right side to lengthen it toward the right. The copy machine is fixed!

Certification Objective

4. Type **S** (for Stretch). The command prompt reads as follows:

   Select objects to stretch by crossing-window
   or crossing-polygon...
   Select objects:

   Implied windows won't work for STRETCH; only crossing windows or crossing polygons are acceptable. Click points A and B as shown in Figure 4.24 to select the objects to stretch and press Enter.

5. Using either Polar Tracking or Ortho mode, move the cursor down vertically, type **2′6″** (or **75** for metric), and press Enter to specify the second point. The wall, door, and swing end up more or less centered on the wall.

6. Save your work as Ch4-G.dwg (or Ch4-G-metric.dwg).

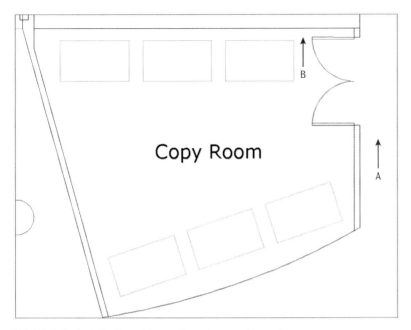

FIGURE 4.24 Stretching walls, a door, and its swing

Offset and Mirror

The OFFSET and MIRROR commands are often used to create new objects. OFFSET creates an object a set distance on one side of the original object. MIRROR creates a reversed object at a distance from the original object as determined by the position of a drawn reflection line. Let's explore these commands:

1. If the file is not already open from performing the previous step, go to the book's web page, browse to Chapter 4, download the file Ch4-G.dwg (or Ch4-G-metric.dwg), and open it.

2. Click the Offset tool in the Modify panel. The command line reads as follows:

   Specify offset distance or [Through Erase Layer] <Through>:

   Type **4**, and press Enter. Select the elliptical arc at the bottom edge of the Copy Room.

3. The command line asks you to specify a point to determine on which side of the selection to offset the new object. In this case, click anywhere above the elliptical arc and a new ellipse is created such that its curvature matches the original but is spaced 4 away. Press Enter to exit the command.

7. Press the spacebar to repeat the last command. Click point D shown in Figure 5.4, type **A** (for Arc), and press Enter.

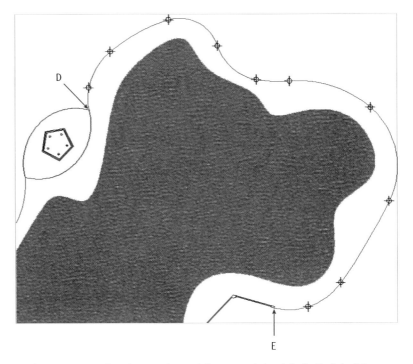

FIGURE 5.4 Drawing another polyline around the right half of the lake

8. Type **S** (for Second Point), press Enter, and snap to the node adjacent to point D.

9. Click each subsequent node around the right side of the lake until you reach point E in Figure 5.4. Press Enter.

Certification Objective

10. Type **O** (for Offset), and press Enter. Type **6** (or **2** m), and press Enter. Click the left polyline you drew around the lake in steps 1–6, and then click a point on the side of the polyline away from the lake. Click the right polyline, and click outside the lake. Click the outer arc surrounding the pentagonal structure, and then click outside the lake.

11. Click the Trim tool in the Modify panel. Press Enter to select all objects as potential cutting edges, and click the portions of the arcs that overlap in the top highlighted area in Figure 5.5. Zoom into the lower highlighted area, and trim the arcs so that they meet at their endpoints. Press Esc to end the TRIM command.

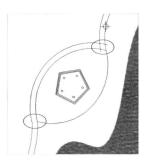

FIGURE 5.5 Trimming polylines and arcs

12. Pan over to the building at the bottom of the lake. We'd like the ends of the paths to open up to the building. Click the lower-left polyline to select it. Click the endpoint grip, move it down a short distance, and click again (see Figure 5.6). You can't get the end of the path to open up without distorting the path farther up because it's all part of the same arc segment.

Certification
Objective

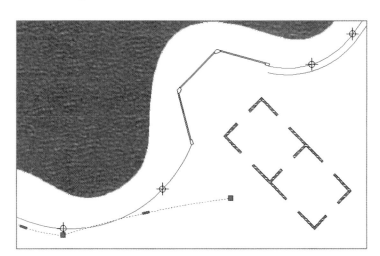

FIGURE 5.6 Adjusting an existing polyline with its grips

13. Press Esc, and then click the Undo button in the Quick Access toolbar.

14. Click the Arc tool in the Draw panel, hold Shift down and right-click, and choose Nearest from the context menu. Click points A, B, and C in Figure 5.7 to shape the arc as shown.

15. Press Enter twice to end, and restart the ARC command. Type **NEA** (for Nearest), press Enter, and click points D, E, and F in Figure 5.7.

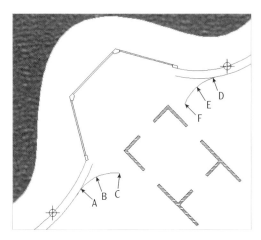

FIGURE 5.7 Drawing new short-radius arcs and snapping them along the longer existing arcs

16. Zoom in and trim away the portions of the original polylines that extend beyond the new arcs you've just drawn.

Certification Objective

17. Type **J** (for Join), and press Enter. Select all five objects that comprise the outer path (three arcs and two polylines). Press Enter, and the command line reads:

> 13 segments joined into 1 polyline

There are 13 segments if you include all the arcs that make up the two polylines. You are left with a single polyline marking the outer edge of the path.

18. Press the spacebar to repeat the JOIN command. Select the three objects along the inner edge of the path, which include two polylines and the arc above the pentagon. Press Enter, and multiple segments are joined into one polyline (see Figure 5.8).

Use JOIN to connect collinear lines even if there is a gap between them. JOIN is the antidote to BREAK.

Should You Use *JOIN* or *PEDIT*?

In previous versions of AutoCAD, objects first had to be converted into polylines and then joined using the polyline editing command called PEDIT. The streamlined JOIN command makes the older workflow unnecessary. Use it on lines, 2D and 3D polylines, arcs, elliptical arcs (sections of ellipses), and/ or helices. Multiple object types can be joined at once. The resulting object type depends on what was selected.

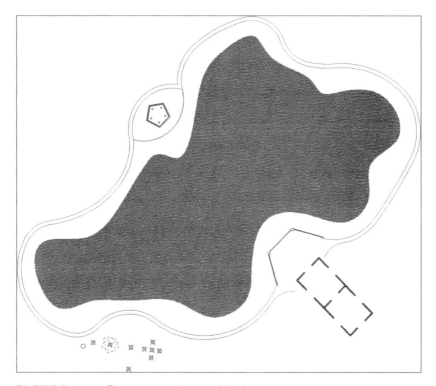

FIGURE 5.8 The curving path around the lake joined into two objects

Drawing Ellipses

AutoCAD can draw perfect ovals, which are mathematically known as *ellipses*.
Instead of stretching a cord from two pins to a moving pencil point (which is how
you draw an ellipse by hand), in AutoCAD you specify the lengths of its major and
minor axes (see Figure 5.9).

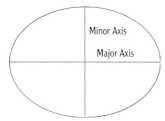

FIGURE 5.9 An ellipse's
major and minor axes

In this exercise, you will draw an ellipse and distribute shrubs along its edge:

1. Zoom into the area in the lower left where the remaining point objects are located.

2. Type **REGEN** (for Regenerate), and press Enter. The size of point objects is recalculated when the drawing is regenerated.

3. Open the Ellipse menu in the Draw panel, and choose the Center method. Click the center point, the end of the major axis, and the end of the minor axis, as shown in Figure 5.10.

4. Type **BR** (for Break), press Enter, and select the ellipse. The command prompt reads:

    Specify second break point or [First point]:

Breaking an ellipse, arc, or circle works in a counterclockwise fashion.

    Type **F** (for First Point), and press Enter. Right-click the Object Snap toggle in the status bar, and select Quadrant from the context menu. Click the quadrant point (north, south, east, or west points of any circle) opposite the point object marking the end of the major axis (see Figure 5.10), and then click the aforementioned point object itself to break the ellipse in half. The lower half of the ellipse remains, leaving an *elliptical arc*.

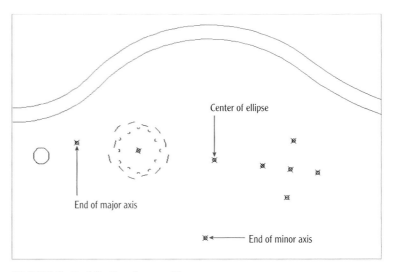

FIGURE 5.10 Drawing an ellipse

5. Type **DIV** (for Divide), and press Enter. Select the elliptical arc, and
press Enter. The command prompt reads:

Certification
Objective

```
Enter the number of segments or [Block]:
```

Type **B** (for Block), and press Enter. You'll learn more about blocks
in Chapter 7, "Organizing Objects."

6. A block called Shrub is predefined, so at the next command prompt:

```
Enter name of block to insert:
```

type **Shrub**, and press Enter.

7. Press Enter to accept the default when asked if you want to align the
block with the selected object. (It doesn't matter in this case because
the Shrub block is a circle.)

8. Type **13** (for the number of segments), and press Enter. The DIVIDE
command always creates one less point or block than the number of
segments into which the object is divided. Twelve "shrubs" appear
along the elliptical arc (see Figure 5.11).

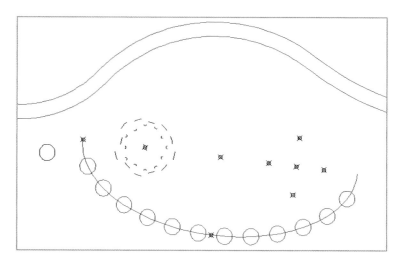

FIGURE 5.11 Dividing an elliptical arc with blocks

9. Delete the three points used in drawing the ellipse, the elliptical arc
itself, and the black circle, which is the original Shrub block. You
deleted the layout geometry and are now left with precisely positioned
shrubs.

Drawing and Editing Splines

Splines are the equivalent of a French curve in traditional drafting, used for making curves of constantly changing radii. Splines have been part of AutoCAD for many releases, but the SPLINE command was completely overhauled in AutoCAD 2011. The new splines in AutoCAD are NURBS-based curves (the same type used in Autodesk® Alias® Design Surface, Maya, 3ds Max, and many other high-end 3D programs). There are two types of NURBS curves:

▶ Those defined by control vertices (CVs), which don't lie on the curve except at its start and endpoints

▶ Those defined by fit points, which lie on the curve itself

You have more control over shaping curves with CVs, but if you want the curve to pass through specific points, or want the curve to have sharp kinks, then Fit Points mode is preferable. Fortunately, it is easy to switch between CVs and Fit Points editing modes, so you can make up your mind about which method to use to suit the situation.

Working with Control Vertices

CVs offer the most flexibility in terms of precisely shaping NURBS curves. A *control frame* connects CVs and represents the maximum possible curvature between adjacent CVs. You will now draw a CV spline around the lake:

Certification Objective

1. Toggle off Object Snap, Ortho, and Polar Tracking modes on the status bar if any of them are on. Type **SPL** (for Spline), and press Enter. The command prompt reads:

   ```
   Current settings: Method=Fit   Knots=Chord
   Specify first point or [Method Knots Object]:
   ```

   Type **M** (for Method), and press Enter.

2. The command prompt reads:

   ```
   Enter spline creation method [Fit CV] <Fit>:
   ```

   Type **CV** (for Control Vertices), and press Enter. Click the first point anywhere along the edge of the lake. Continue clicking points all the way around the lake. When you get close to the first point, type **C** (for Close) and press Enter. Click the spline you just drew to reveal its CVs (see Figure 5.12).

▶

CV curves are typically roughed-in initially and then are refined in shape immediately afterward.

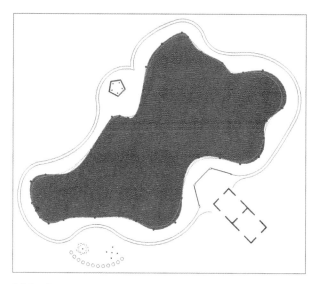

FIGURE 5.12 Drawing a rough CV spline around the lake

3. Position the cursor over a CV, and observe the multifunction grip menu. Select Stretch Vertex, move the cursor, and click to relocate that particular CV.

4. Try adding and removing vertices using the corresponding choices on the multifunction grip menu (see Figure 5.13).

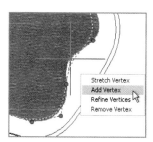

FIGURE 5.13 Adding and removing vertices from a CV spline using multifunction grips

5. Refining a vertex transforms one vertex into two adjacent vertices. Try refining vertices in areas where the curvature is changing rapidly.

6. Another way to affect the shape of a spline is to adjust the weights of individual CVs. Double-click the spline itself (rather than a CV or the control frame) to invoke the SPLINEDIT command. The prompt reads:

```
Enter an option [Open Fit data Edit vertex convert to Polyline
Reverse Undo eXit] <eXit>:
```

Type **E** (for Edit Vertex), and press Enter.

> **Vertices with higher weights pull the curve toward the control frame and vertices with weights below 1 (but above zero) push the spline farther away.**

7. The prompt now reads:

```
Enter a vertex editing option [Add Delete Elevate order
Move Weight eXit] <eXit>:
```

Type **W** (for Weight), and press Enter. Before entering a weight value, you must select the vertex in which you're interested. Zoom out until you can see all the vertices, locate the red one, press Enter repeatedly to choose the default option (Next), and move the red CV one position at a time until your chosen CV turns red.

8. Type **2**, and press Enter (see Figure 5.14). The spline will get closer to the red CV and its control frame. Type **.5**, and press Enter again; the curve moves farther away from the control frame. Type a value appropriate to your particular situation, and press Enter. We set a weight of 0.75 for the CV shown in Figure 5.14 to push it away from the control frame and more closely match the shape of the lake. The weights you need to enter depend entirely on exactly where you placed the CVs when creating the curve in step 2. Type **X** (for Exit), and press Enter. Press **X** and Enter twice more to exit SPLINEDIT fully.

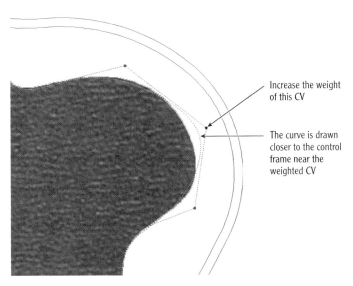

Increase the weight of this CV

The curve is drawn closer to the control frame near the weighted CV

FIGURE 5.14 Adjusting the weight of a CV

SKETCH AND REBUILD CVS

Instead of stretching, adding, removing, refining, and/or adjusting CVs, you can sketch spline curves freehand. The SKETCH command is admittedly difficult to use with a mouse, so if you have one, try using a stylus on a drawing tablet for a more natural drawing feel. Unfortunately, sketching splines usually results in an uneven distribution of CVs, but this can be rectified by using CVREBUILD. For an alternative natural drawing technique, draw splines on a tablet with SKETCH (using SPLINE in its type option) and then redistribute the resulting CVs with CVREBUILD. The CVREBUILD command's Rebuild Curve dialog box is shown here:

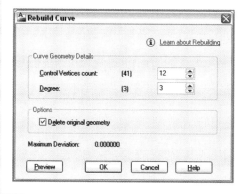

9. Continue adjusting the spline until it closely matches the outline of the lake.

10. Type **IM** (for Image), and press Enter. The External References palette appears. (You'll learn more about this palette in Chapter 9, "Working with Blocks and Xrefs.") The lake that you have been tracing is an image that you will now detach.

11. Right-click Pond in the External References palette, and choose Detach Image. Close the External References palette. Select the pond spline, and change its color to Blue in the Properties panel (see Figure 5.15). The pond is now represented by a blue curve rather than a blue image.

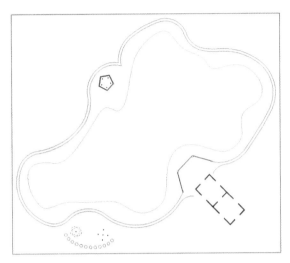

FIGURE 5.15 Pond shown as a spline rather than an image

Working with Fit Points

Fit point splines are straightforward in the sense that the fit points you click lie on (or very close to) the curve itself. Controlling the shape of a fit curve on the most basic level is a matter of adding more fit points in strategic locations. There are a few advanced options affecting the shape of a spline in between fit points (Tangent, Tolerance, Kink, and Knot Parameterization), and you will use Kink in this exercise to establish sharp points on the spline.

1. Zoom into the area at the bottom of the lake where you distributed the shrubs earlier in this chapter in an elliptical arc. More specifically, zoom into the grouping of five points. Type **REGEN**, and press Enter to regenerate the display and thus automatically resize the point objects.

2. Expand the Draw panel, and click the Spline Fit tool at the top left. Toggle on Object Snap mode in the status bar (with Node snap on), and click the top point, the point on the right, the bottom, and then the one on the left. Type **C** (for Close), and press Enter. The fit curve looks very much like a circle, although it is not perfectly round (see Figure 5.16). This will be the start of an abstract tree representation.

3. Toggle on Dynamic Input on the status bar. Select the spline you just drew, type **SPLINEDIT**, and press Enter. Choose Fit Data from the dynamic input menu. Then choose Add from the next dynamic input menu that appears.

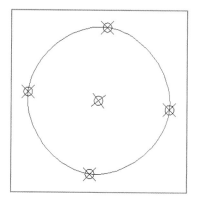

FIGURE 5.16 Snapping spline fit points to point objects

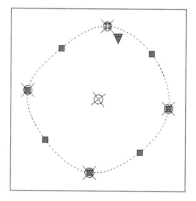

FIGURE 5.17 Adding additional fit points between the initial points

4. The prompt reads:

```
Specify existing fit point on spline <exit>:
```

Click the top point.

5. The prompt now says:

```
Specify new fit point to add <exit>:
```

This particular command requires that you snap the new fit point, so type **NEA** (for Nearest) and press Enter. Click the curve in between the top and right points. Press Enter four times to exit SPLINEDIT fully.

6. Another way to add fit points is with the multifunction grips, although this method doesn't work on the first point. To use this feature, click the spline to select it, hover the cursor over the right point, and choose Add Fit Point from the menu that appears. Hold Shift, right-click, and choose Nearest from the context menu. Click a point between the right and bottom points.

7. Repeat the previous step twice more, adding additional fit points between the bottom, left, and top points (see Figure 5.17).

8. Double-click the spline itself to invoke the SPLINEDIT command without typing. Type **F** (for Fit Data), and press Enter. The prompt reads:

```
Enter a fit data option
[Add Open Delete Kink Move Purge Tangents
toLerance eXit] <eXit>:
```

Type **K** (for Kink), and click eight points in between all the existing fit points (see Figure 5.18). Press Enter three times to exit the command fully.

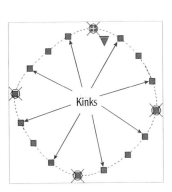

FIGURE 5.18 Adding kinks to the fit points spline

FIGURE 5.19 Abstract tree created by stretching kinks in a fit point spline

9. Click each kink grip, and move it in toward the center to create an abstract representation of a tree. Delete the five point objects that helped you lay out the tree (see Figure 5.19). If you have trouble selecting point objects, try changing their size with the DDPTYPE and REGEN commands.

Blending Between Objects with Splines

The BLEND command creates a CV spline in between two selected lines, circular or elliptical arcs, splines, or any combination of these object types. Blend curves join the endpoints of the two objects with a curve having either tangent or smooth continuity. There is a subtle difference between these types of blending.

A blend curve with tangent continuity has its control frame parallel to the control frame of the adjacent curve. A blend curve with curvature continuity not only has its control frame parallel to the control frame of the adjacent curve, but the control frames have equal lengths. In simpler terms, tangent continuity is smooth, and smooth continuity is "perfectly smooth." In the following steps, you will create blend curves with two types of curvature:

1. Pan over to the other "tree" to the left of the tree you've drawn with kinks. Type **BLEND**, and press Enter.

2. The prompt reads:

    ```
    Continuity = Tangent
    Select first object or [CONtinuity]:
    ```

    Select a flat arc and a tight arc, and the command is finished. A CV spline with tangent continuity blends between the two arcs.

3. Press the spacebar to repeat BLEND, type **CON** (for Continuity), press Enter, type **S** (for Smooth), and press Enter again. Click two adjacent arcs to create another blend curve (see Figure 5.20).

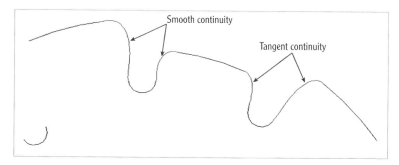

FIGURE 5.20 Blending between arcs with different types of continuity

4. Continue blending all the adjacent curves in the tree. Delete the point object at the center. Figure 5.21 shows the completed drawing.

5. Your drawing should now resemble Ch5-B.dwg (or Ch5-B-metric.dwg), which is available at this book's web page.

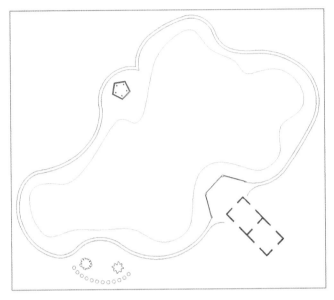

FIGURE 5.21 Completed landscape plan

THE ESSENTIALS AND BEYOND

You have learned how to shape many types of curvilinear objects in this chapter, including circular and elliptical arcs, polylines, ellipses, and CV and fit point NURBS-based splines. You've broken and joined objects, and blended smoothly between adjacent curves. In short, you now have the skills to shape just about any curve you can imagine with a fine degree of precision, which is what AutoCAD is all about.

ADDITIONAL EXERCISE

▶ Explore the HELIX command on your own. The HELIX command creates spirals and helices. You are welcome to stick with two dimensions for now and create spirals with this command. When you learn how to navigate and model in 3D (in Chapters 16 and 17), you can use this command to create springs, screw threads, or even DNA.

Controlling Object Visibility and Appearance

Layers control objects whether they are visible or hidden. All objects have properties that control their appearance—properties such as color, linetype, lineweight, and so on. The layers to which objects are assigned usually control general object properties, but these properties can be set on a per-object basis as well. This chapter explores the many AutoCAD® tools associated with layers that illustrate the importance of layers in managing the complexity of design.

▶ **Changing object properties**

▶ **Setting the current layer**

▶ **Altering the layer assignments of objects**

▶ **Controlling layer visibility**

▶ **Applying linetype**

▶ **Assigning properties by object or by layer**

▶ **Managing layer properties**

Changing Object Properties

All objects have properties controlling their appearance. When you draw a line, you are ultimately specifying its geometric properties (the start point and the endpoint). Likewise, when you draw a circle, you are just specifying its center point and radius properties. Geometric properties are the most important factor governing how objects look and in determining where the objects are in space.

7. Click the Merge tool. The command prompt reads:

> Select object on layer to merge or [Name]:

8. Click one of the brown lines in the upper portion of the reception desk and press Enter.

9. Click the violet line you changed to the Desk layer in step 5 and press Enter. The command prompt reads:

> Select object on target layer or [Name]:
> ******** WARNING ********
> You are about to merge layer "Desk-High" into layer "Desk".
> Do you wish to continue? [Yes/No] <No>:

Use the LAYDEL command to delete a layer and everything on it. Be careful, though, to avoid deleting valuable information.

10. Press **Y** (for Yes), and then press Enter to continue. The Desk-High layer is deleted, and the objects that were on it have been reassigned to the Desk layer. The LAYMRG command is done.

 11. Expand the Properties panel, and click the List tool. Pan over and select the Business Development text object by clicking on it and pressing Enter. The AutoCAD Text window appears, displaying the following property information:

> TEXT   Layer: "Title"
> Space: Model space
> Handle = 71e
> Style = "Standard"
> Annotative: No
> Typeface = Arial
> mid point, X= 193.8805 Y= 132.8080 Z= 0.0000
> height   7.5000
> text Business Development
> rotation angle   0
> width scale factor   1.0000
> obliquing angle   0
> generation normal

This list might be helpful if you were looking for a particular piece of information, but you can't edit any of the properties directly. Close the AutoCAD Text window.

Certification Objective

12. Select the View tab on the ribbon and, under Panels, click the Properties tool to open the Properties panel.

13. Select the Business Development text object you selected in step 11. Many of its properties appear in the panel (see Figure 6.4). Property values displayed on a white background are editable; those on a gray background are for your information only.

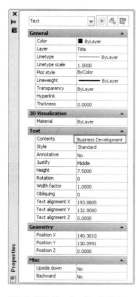

Although the LIST command shows some property information that does not appear in the Properties panel, most people prefer using the panel because much of the data is directly editable.

FIGURE 6.4 Editing a value in the Properties panel

14. Select the words "Business Development" in the Contents property, type **Marketing**, and press Enter. Press Esc to deselect the text object. The department's name has been changed. You can now close the Properties panel.

Setting the Current Layer

Objects are always drawn on the current layer, and there is only one current layer at any given time. Every drawing has at least one layer, layer 0 (zero), which is current by default when you create a new drawing.

AutoCAD has another special layer called Defpoints, which is automatically created when you add associative dimensions to a drawing (see Chapter 11, "Dimensioning").

You cannot delete or rename layer 0 or Defpoints. It's okay to draw on layer 0, but not on Defpoints.

Let's experiment with setting the current layer by drawing a few objects:

1. Using the Ch6-A.dwg (or Ch6-A-metric.dwg) file, zoom into the Manager's office. If this file is not open, find it on the book's web page.

2. Click the Rectangle tool on the Draw panel, and click a point a few inches (no need to measure) from the lower-left corner of the room. Type **@18,72** (or **@45,180** for metric) and press Enter to create a credenza in the Manager's office (see Figure 6.5).

FIGURE 6.5 Drawing furniture on layer 0

3. Select the rectangle you drew in the previous step, and change its Layer assignment to Furniture in the Quick Properties window that appears. Press Esc to deselect.

4. If you plan on drawing more than one object, a more efficient approach is to set the current layer prior to drawing, so that the new object will have the proper layer assignment automatically. Open the Layer drop-down menu in the Layers panel, and click on or to the right of the word Furniture to set this layer as current. Notice that Furniture appears "on top" when the drop-down is closed (see Figure 6.6); Furniture is now the current layer.

5. Pan over to the Marketing space.

6. Click the Rectangle tool on the Draw panel, and click a point a few inches (without measuring) from the lower-right corner of the room. Type **@-18,72** (or **@-45,180** for metric), and press Enter to create a credenza in Marketing (see Figure 6.7).

Press Shift, right-click, and choose the None object snap to override any running object snap modes whenever necessary.

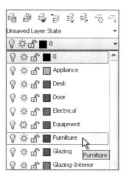

FIGURE 6.6 Setting Furniture as the current layer using the drop-down menu in the Layers panel

Current layer

Marketing

Credenza

FIGURE 6.7 Drawing another credenza on the Furniture layer

7. Select the rectangle you drew in the previous step, and verify that it is on the Furniture layer in the Quick Properties window that appears. Press Esc.

8. Pan over to the closet in Marketing. One of the lines representing shelves is missing. You will draw the missing line on the same layer as the existing shelf line.

9. Rather than selecting the existing shelf line by learning its layer name and then setting that layer as current, there is a more efficient approach. In the Layers panel, click the Make Object's Layer Current tool. Click the existing shelf line in Marketing's closet. The layer appearing at the top of the Layer drop-down menu is Millwork, which shows that it's now the current layer.

10. Toggle on Endpoint and Perpendicular running object snap modes on the status bar.

11. Click the Line tool on the Draw panel, and draw the line shown in Figure 6.8. Press Esc to end the LINE command.

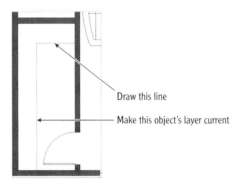

FIGURE 6.8 Drawing a line after using the Make Object's Layer Current tool

Altering the Layer Assignments of Objects

Although you have already changed the layer assignments of objects using Quick Properties, there are more efficient methods of doing so, some of which do not require you to remember a layer name. Let's explore several methods for changing the layer assignments of existing objects:

1. Using the Ch6-A.dwg (or Ch6-A-metric.dwg) file, zoom into the Manager's office. If this file is not open, find it on the book's web page.

2. Toggle off Quick Properties mode on the status bar.

3. Select the coffee table in the Marketing space. Notice that the entry in the Layer drop-down in the Layers panel changes to layer 0; this does not mean that layer 0 is current (Millwork is), only that the selected item is on layer 0.

4. Open the Layer drop-down menu, and click Furniture (see Figure 6.9) to change the layer assignment of the selected items. Press Esc to deselect.

AutoCAD 2013 shows you a preview of property changes on screen as you hover over items in the Layers drop-down menu or the Properties panel.

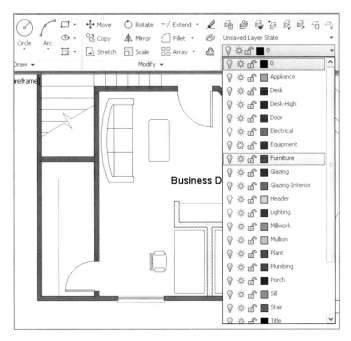

FIGURE 6.9 Changing layer assignment with the Layer drop-down menu

5. Pan over to the Lounge.

 6. Click the Match tool in the Layers panel, select the coffee table in the Lounge, and press Enter. The command prompt reads:

    Select object on destination layer or [Name]:

7. Click one of the sofas in the Lounge and press Enter; the LAYMCH command ends. The coffee table is now assigned to the same layer as the sofas (Furniture).

8. Pan to the Manager's office.

 9. Click the Match Properties tool in the Clipboard panel on the Home tab of the ribbon. Select the credenza in the Manager's office and press Enter. The command prompt reads:

Certification Objective

    Select destination object(s) or [Settings]:

10. Type **S** (for Settings), and press Enter; the Property Settings dialog box appears. You can match many properties in addition to layers with this tool (see Figure 6.10). Click OK.

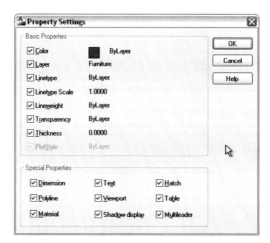

FIGURE 6.10 The Property Settings dialog box allows you to match much more than layers.

11. Click the desk in the Manager's office and press Enter; the desk turns green because it is now on the Furniture layer. Press Esc to exit the MATCHPROP command.

Controlling Layer Visibility

In traditional drafting, separate drawings would have to be made for the floor plan and the reflected ceiling plan to represent the floor and ceiling of the same space. In AutoCAD, simply displaying some layers while hiding others allows you to create some of the drawings required to describe the space graphically.

To understand better how to do this, you need to learn how to toggle layer status, isolate layers to work without distraction, and save layer states to recall the layer status of multiple layers quickly.

Toggling Layer Status

In addition to having properties such as color, linetype, lineweight, and so on, layers have states that can be toggled, including On/Off, Thaw/Freeze, and Lock/Unlock. As you'll see in the following steps, layer states control the visibility and editability of the objects assigned to layers:

1. Using the Ch6-A.dwg (or Ch6-A-metric.dwg) file, zoom into the Manager's office. If this file is not open, find it on the book's web page.

2. Expand the Layers panel, and click the Turn All Layers On tool. You now see the switches ($ symbols), downlights, and header layers. Figure 6.11 shows the result.

Washroom

Lounge

Kitchen

Reception

Manager

Marketing

FIGURE 6.11 The Small Office plan with all layers on

3. Open the Layer drop-down menu in the Layers panel, and click the Appliance layer's lightbulb icon to toggle it off. Toggle off the Desk layer as well. Click outside the Layer drop-down menu to close it.

4. Another approach to turning layers off doesn't require that you know layer names. Click the Off tool in the Layers panel, and click the following objects: sink, door, chair, plant, stairs, low wall, low wall's pattern fill, text, and the porch. Click a kitchen cabinet and the command prompt reads:

```
Layer "Millwork" is current, do you want to
turn it off? [Yes/No] <No>:
```

5. Type **Y** (for Yes), and press Enter. Press Esc to end the LAYOFF command. Figure 6.12 shows the result.

If you turn the current layer off, then anything you draw subsequently will be hidden.

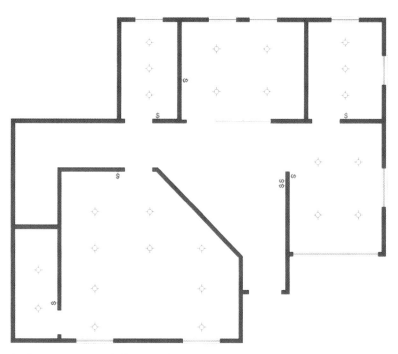

F I G U R E 6 . 1 2 Reflected ceiling plan created by toggling layers off

6. Open the Layer drop-down menu in the Layers panel, and set layer 0 as current.

7. Click Zoom Extents in the Navigation bar. Notice that there is a gap between the bottom wall of the building and the lower edge of the drawing canvas. Even though it is off, the Porch layer is still defining the extents of the drawing.

8. Open the Layer drop-down menu in the Layers panel, and freeze the Porch layer. Press Esc to close the drop-down menu.

Locking layers doesn't provide security other than disallowing selection.

9. Click Zoom Extents in the Navigation bar again. The gap disappears as the Porch layer is no longer calculated when it is frozen and therefore is no longer part of the drawing extents.

10. Expand the Layers panel, and click the Lock tool. Select one of the lights. The Lighting layer is now locked.

11. Type **E** (for Erase), and press Enter. Click on a different light, and observe a tiny padlock appear near the object (see Figure 6.13). You can't select the object because it is locked. In order to see the padlock, you must select When A Command Is Active in the Selection Preview area on the Selection tab in the Options dialog box (OPTIONS command).

FIGURE 6.13
Objects on locked layers
cannot be selected.

Isolating Layers

You can quickly isolate one or more layers to work on them without the visual clutter of all the other layers. Let's try out Isolation mode:

1. Using the Ch6-A.dwg (or Ch6-A-metric.dwg) file, zoom into the Manager's office. If this file is not open, find it on the book's web page.

2. Click the Isolate tool on the Layers panel, and then make a crossing selection through one of the windows. Press Enter and all the other layers disappear (see Figure 6.14).

FIGURE 6.14 Isolating a couple of layers for focused work

3. Expand the Layers panel, and click the Copy Objects To New Layer tool. Select each one of the nine sill lines on the inside of the building and press Enter. The command prompt reads:

```
Select object on destination layer or [Name] <Name>:
```

4. Type **N** (for Name), and press Enter. The Copy To Layer dialog box appears (see Figure 6.15). Select Header from the Destination Layer list, click OK, and press Enter. There are now nine lines on the Sill layer and nine duplicate lines on the Header layer.

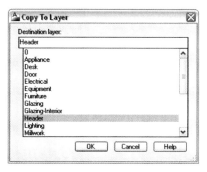

FIGURE 6.15 Selecting a layer in the Copy To Layer dialog box

5. Click the Unisolate tool on the Layers panel. The layers return to their states as they were prior to using the Isolate tool.

6. Type **LAYOFF**, and press Enter. Click one of sills on the outside of the building to turn off the Sill layer and press Enter. Open the Layer drop-down menu, and toggle on the Header layer.

7. Zoom into one of the lower windows, and click the Distance tool in the Utilities panel. Click points A and B in Figure 6.16 to measure the wall thickness. The command prompt reads:

```
Distance = 5.0000, Angle in XY Plane = 270,
Angle from XY Plane = 0
Delta X = 0.0000, Delta Y = -5.0000, Delta Z = 0.0000
```

8. Press Esc to cancel the DISTANCE command.

9. Type **O** (for Offset), press Enter, type **5** (or **12.7** for metric), and press Enter again. Click the header line in the window opening, and then click below it to offset a line on the outer edge of the wall.

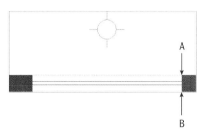

FIGURE 6.16 Measuring the wall thickness with DISTANCE

10. Continue clicking each header and a point outside the building to offset a second header line in each window opening. Press Enter to end the OFFSET command when done. The reflected ceiling plan is complete.

Saving Layer States

In this section, you will learn how to save collections of layer states for later recall. In this chapter, you have already created a reflected ceiling plan; you will now save it as a layer state so that you won't have to repeat all the work of toggling layer states in the future.

1. Using the Ch6-A.dwg (or Ch6-A-metric.dwg) file, zoom into the Manager's office. If this file is not open, find it on the book's web page.

2. Open the drop-down menu directly above the Layer drop-down (it says Unsaved Layer State by default). Select New Layer State in the drop-down menu (see Figure 6.17).

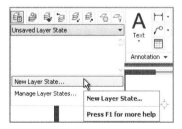

FIGURE 6.17 Saving a new layer state

3. Type **Reflected Ceiling Plan** in the New Layer State To Save dialog box and click OK. The closed drop-down now says Reflected Ceiling Plan.

4. Expand the Layers panel, and click the Turn All Layers On tool.

 5. Expand the Layers panel again, and click the adjacent Thaw All Layers tool.

Using LAYERP (Layer Previous) undoes the last set of changes to layers. This is different from UNDO, which affects more than layers.

6. Click the Freeze tool in the Layers panel, and select the following objects: light, switch, header, and computer. The layers Lighting, Electrical, Header, and Equipment are frozen. Press Enter to end the LAYFRZ command.

7. Open the Layer State drop-down menu in the Layers panel, and click New Layer State. Type **Furniture Plan** in the New Layer State To Save dialog box and click OK.

8. Open the Layer State drop-down menu, and select Reflected Ceiling Plan (see Figure 6.18). All the layer states associated with the Reflected Ceiling Plan are immediately toggled. Switch back to the Furniture Plan state, and you'll see the value in saving layer states (it saves lots of time).

FIGURE 6.18 Accessing saved layer states from the drop-down in the Layers panel

Applying Linetype

In traditional drafting, you draw short, interrupted line segments when you want to indicate what is called a *hidden line*. Hidden lines represent objects that are above the section plane. Examples, including upper cabinets, high shelves, or a roof edge, are shown as hidden because they are above an imaginary section line cutting the building horizontally.

In AutoCAD, lines are not interrupted (broken into multiple little pieces) to indicate hidden lines. Instead, continuous lines are assigned a *linetype*, and this style makes lines appear as if they are interrupted. One advantage to this is that you can adjust the scale of the line breaks without having to redraw myriad little lines. Let's explore linetype and linetype scale:

1. Using the Ch6-A.dwg (or Ch6-A-metric.dwg) file, zoom into the Manager's office. If this file is not open, find it on the book's web page.

2. Open the Linetype drop-down menu in the Properties panel, and select Other at the bottom of the menu (see Figure 6.19).

Certification
Objective

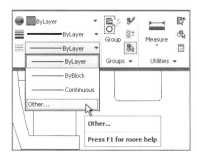

FIGURE 6.19 Accessing other linetypes

3. In the Linetype Manager dialog box that appears, click the Load button. Scroll down in the Load Or Reload Linetypes dialog box that appears, and select Hidden in the list (see Figure 6.20); then click OK. Hidden now appears in the Linetype Manager dialog box because this particular linetype style has been loaded in the drawing file; click OK to close the Linetype Manager dialog box.

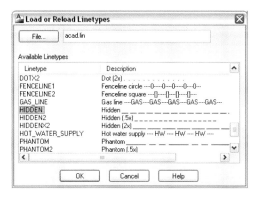

FIGURE 6.20 Loading the Hidden linetype

4. Zoom into the closet in the Marketing space, and select both lines on the Millwork layer, representing a high shelf.

5. Open the Linetype drop-down menu in the Properties panel, and select Hidden from the menu. Now the two selected lines have the Hidden linetype assigned.

6. You still don't see breaks in the lines because the linetype scale is too small by default. Type **LTSCALE** (for Linetype Scale), and press Enter. The command prompt reads:

   ```
   LTSCALE Enter new linetype scale factor <1.0000>:
   ```

7. Type **48** (or **50** for metric), and press Enter. The lines appear with breaks indicating that the shelf is above the section plane (see Figure 6.21).

The factor 50 is appropriate for 1:50 metric drawings.

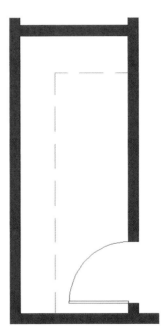

FIGURE 6.21 Hidden lines representing a high shelf in the closet

Use LTSCALE to set the linetype scale affecting the entire drawing. Higher values of LTSCALE scale linetypes smaller.

8. Select the horizontal shelf line, right-click, and choose Properties from the context menu.

9. Change Linetype Scale to **0.5** in the General section of the Properties panel (see Figure 6.22).

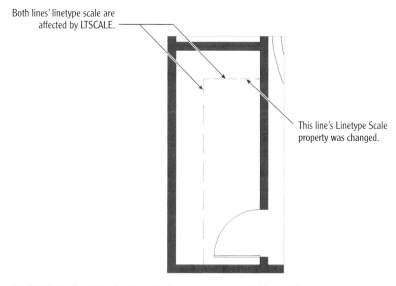

FIGURE 6.22 Adjusting the Linetype Scale property

10. Press Esc to deselect the horizontal shelf line. The breaks in the horizontal line are half as large as those in the vertical segment (see Figure 6.23). Close the Properties panel.

Alter the linetype scale of specific objects by adjusting the Linetype Scale property in the Properties panel. Lower values scale linetypes smaller.

Both lines' linetype scale are affected by LTSCALE.

This line's Linetype Scale property was changed.

FIGURE 6.23 Scaling the linetype of an individual object

Assigning Properties by Object or by Layer

Properties such as color, linetype, and lineweight are typically assigned by layer rather than by object. There is a special property value called *ByLayer* that passes control over specific properties to the properties managed by the layer to which the objects are assigned. As you'll see in these steps, using the ByLayer property is a lot easier than it sounds:

1. Using the Ch6-A.dwg (or Ch6-A-metric.dwg) file, zoom into the Manager's office. If this file is not open, find it on the book's web page.

2. Open the Linetype drop-down menu on the Properties panel, and select Hidden (see Figure 6.24). Draw a line of arbitrary length anywhere on the canvas.

FIGURE 6.24
The Properties panel settings affect all the objects you create.

3. Open the Linetype drop-down menu on the Properties panel, and select ByLayer.

4. Draw another line, and observe that it has continuous linetype.

Objects should be assigned specific colors, linetypes, or lineweights only in exceptional circumstances.

5. If you want to change the property of a specific object, use Quick Properties instead of the drop-down menus in the Properties panel. Toggle on Quick Properties mode on the status bar.

6. Select the continuous line drawn in step 2, and change its Linetype property to Hidden (see Figure 6.25).

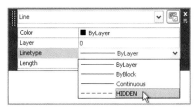

FIGURE 6.25 Changing a specific object property

7. Draw another line, and verify that it has continuous linetype.

8. Delete all three arbitrary lines you've just drawn.

Managing Layer Properties

The Layer Properties Manager is where you create layers and manage the properties that are assigned to them. Let's explore the Layer Properties Manager with a practical example:

1. Using the Ch6-A.dwg (or Ch6-A-metric.dwg) file, zoom into the Manager's office. If this file is not open, find it on the book's web page.

2. Click the Layer Properties tool in the Layers panel. The Layer Properties Manager appears (see Figure 6.26).

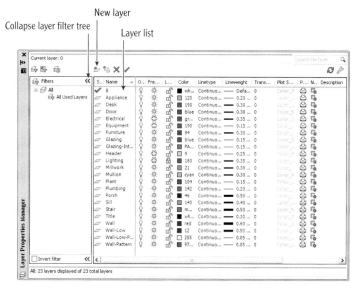

FIGURE 6.26 Layer Properties Manager

3. Click Collapse The Layer Filter Tree to save some space in the panel.

4. Click the New Layer button, type **Millwork-Upper** as the new layer's name, and press Enter.

5. Double-click the blue parallelogram next to the new layer to set it as current. Now there is a green check mark next to the Millwork-Upper layer.

6. Right-click any one of the column headers to access a context menu. Choose Maximize All Columns from this menu. Figure 6.27 shows the result: The columns are all readable.

Sorting columns is a quick way to find layers having common properties. Drag the vertical bars between columns to resize them.

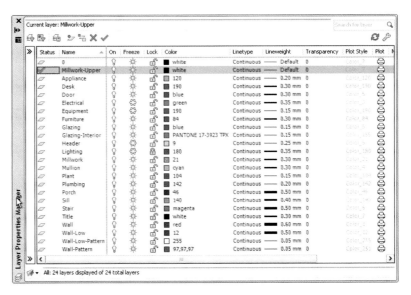

FIGURE 6.27 Maximizing the columns in the Layer Properties Manager makes them easier to read.

7. Click the Freeze column header to sort the column by that criterion (frozen state). Click the Freeze column header again to reverse the sort order. All columns are sortable.

8. Click the word Continuous in the Linetype column in the Millwork-Upper layer. In the Select Linetype dialog box that appears, choose Hidden and click OK.

9. Click Millwork-Upper's color swatch to open the Select Color dialog box. Click the larger red swatch where indicated (see Figure 6.28) and click OK.

10. Zoom into the closet in the Marketing space, and select both shelf lines. Change Layer to Millwork-Upper and Linetype to ByLayer in the Quick Properties window (see Figure 6.29). The two lines appear red with Hidden linetype. Close the Layer Properties Manager.

11. Your drawing should now resemble Ch6-B.dwg (or Ch6-B-metric.dwg), which is available among the book's download files.

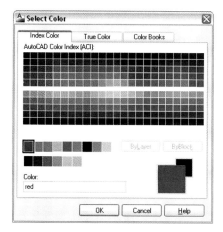

FIGURE 6.28 Selecting a layer color

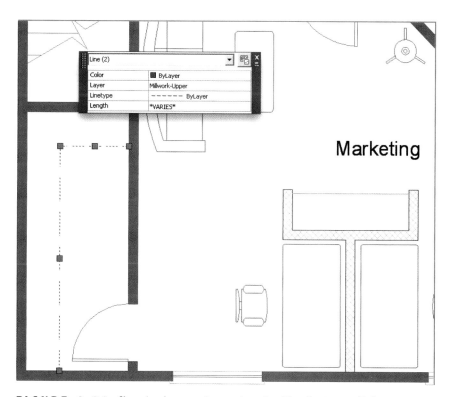

FIGURE 6.29 Changing layer assignment, and setting linetype to ByLayer

THE ESSENTIALS AND BEYOND

In this chapter, you learned how to control object visibility and how to modify object appearance with layers and properties. You learned many ways to change object properties, set the current layer, alter the layer assignments of objects, control layer visibility, apply linetypes, use the ByLayer property, and manage properties with layers. You now have a greater ability to manage design complexity.

ADDITIONAL EXERCISE

Explore layer property and group filters on your own by opening one of the sample files that ship with AutoCAD, such as:

```
C:\Program Files\Autodesk\AutoCAD 2013\Sample\
Sheet Sets\Architectural\A-01.dwg
```

Layer filters are especially useful in complex drawings where you need to manage dozens, or even hundreds, of layers.

CHAPTER 7

Organizing Objects

The fundamental entities in the AutoCAD® program are lines, polylines, circles, arcs, and text. By combining these entities into blocks and/or groups, you can manipulate more complex objects, such as chairs, mechanical assemblies, trees, or any other organizational designation appropriate to your industry.

Manipulating blocks is an efficient means of working not only because it reduces the number of items requiring selection, but also because blocks can potentially control numerous references from a single definition. In this chapter, you will learn how groups are a flexible means of organizing collections of objects, which often include blocks as members. You will also learn how to select and manipulate a group as a whole, or access the members of the group individually whenever needed.

▶ **Defining blocks**

▶ **Inserting blocks**

▶ **Editing blocks**

▶ **Redefining blocks**

▶ **Working with groups**

Defining Blocks

Before drawing and copying a series of repetitive elements, you should first define them as a block. This is because you have a higher level of organizational control over blocks than you do over individual entities. In this section, you will draw a chair and a door and then define them as blocks.

Drawing a Chair and Defining It as a Block

In the following steps, you will use the drawing skills that you've learned in previous chapters to draw a chair. Then you will convert the chair into a block definition.

1. Go to the book's web page at www.sybex.com/go/autocad2013essentials, browse to Chapter 7, get the file Ch7-A.dwg (or Ch7-A-metric.dwg), and open it (see Figure 7.1).

FIGURE 7.1 Three rooms

2. Zoom into the leftmost room above the desk.

 3. Click the Rectangle tool on the Modify panel, and then click an arbitrary point above the desk (which is represented by the blue rectangle) as the first corner point. The command prompt reads:

   Specify other corner point or [Area Dimensions Rotation]:

   Type **@18,18** (or **@45,45** for metric), and press Enter.

 4. Click the Explode tool on the Modify panel, select the rectangle you just drew, and press Enter. The single polyline is converted into four independent line objects.

 5. Click the Fillet tool on the Modify panel, type **R** (for Radius), and press Enter. Type **3″** (or **7 cm** for metric), and press Enter to set the fillet radius; then click the left and bottom edges to create an arc.

6. Press the spacebar to repeat the FILLET command. Click the bottom and right edges to create another arc. Figure 7.2 shows the result.

FIGURE 7.2 Using Fillet to round two corners

7. Expand the Modify panel, click the Join tool, select all the objects making up the chair you are drawing, and press Enter. Four lines and two arcs have now been converted into a single polyline.

8. Toggle on Ortho mode on the status bar.

9. Select the polyline you joined in step 7. Hover the cursor over the top-middle grip, and select Convert To Arc from the multifunction grip menu that appears (see Figure 7.3).

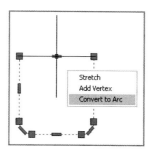

FIGURE 7.3 Converting a straight polyline segment into an arc

10. Move the cursor upward, type **3″** (or **7 cm**), press Enter, and then press Esc to clear the selection. You've created the curve of the backrest.

11. Click the Explode tool on the Modify panel, press Enter, select the chair, and press Enter again. The polyline is converted into three lines and three arcs.

12. Click the Offset tool in the Modify panel, type **2″** (or **5 cm** for metric), and press Enter. Select the arc you created in step 9 and then click a point above it on the drawing canvas to offset a new arc 2″ (or 5 cm) above. Press Enter to exit the OFFSET command.

13. Type **BLEND**, press Enter, and select the two arcs making up the backrest near their left endpoints. A spline object smoothly joins the arcs.

14. Press Enter to repeat the BLEND command, and select the two arcs near the right endpoints; another spline object is created (see Figure 7.4).

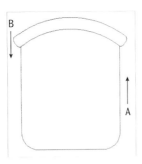

FIGURE 7.4 Blending between concentric arcs

 15. Click the Stretch tool in the Modify panel, click points A and B shown in Figure 7.4 to create a crossing window, and press Enter. Click an arbitrary point on the drawing canvas as the first point of the Stretch operation. Move the cursor downward on the drawing canvas, type **3″** (or **7 cm** for metric), and press Enter. The seat depth is reduced.

Certification Objective

 16. Select the entire chair with an implied window. Click the Create tool in the Block panel on the ribbon's Home tab, and the Block Definition dialog box appears. Type **Chair** in the Name field. Every block must have a name.

▶

A preview image of the chair appears to the right of the Name field because you selected its constituent objects prior to opening the Block Definition dialog box.

 17. Every block has a *base point*, which should be related to its geometry. Click the Pick Point button in the Base Point section; the Block Definition dialog box disappears. Hold Shift, and right-click to open the context menu; select Midpoint. Click the midpoint of the chair's front edge. The Block Definition dialog box reappears, showing the coordinates of the point to which you snapped (see Figure 7.5).

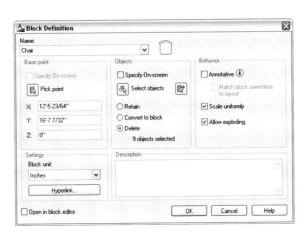

FIGURE 7.5 Defining a chair block

18. Choose the Delete radio button in the Objects section of the Block Definition dialog box. Select Scale Uniformly and Allow Exploding. Deselect Annotative and Open In Block Editor. Set the Block Unit drop-down to Inches (or Centimeters) and click OK. The chair disappears; don't worry, you will insert it later.

UNDERSTANDING THE BLOCK TABLE

When the chair disappeared from the drawing canvas, it was defined in the drawing's *block table*. Although every drawing has a block table, you can't see it. Blocks defined there can be inserted into the drawing as block references. Changes made to block definitions (stored in the block table) affect all block references in the drawing.

Drawing a Door and Defining It as a Block

In the following steps, you will draw a door and the representation of its swing (an arc) and define it as a block:

1. If the file Ch7-A.dwg (or Ch7-A-metric.dwg) is not already open, go to the book's web page, browse to Chapter 7, and open the file.

2. Pan over to the middle room. Zoom into the door opening along the bottom edge of this room.

3. Toggle on Running Object Snap mode on the status bar. Right-click this button, and turn on Endpoint snap if it's not already highlighted in the context menu.

4. Click the Rectangle tool in the Draw panel. Snap the first corner at point A, as shown in Figure 7.6. Type @1.5,2'6" (or @4,75 for metric), and press Enter to complete the door.

All door openings in the sample file measure 2'6" (75 cm) in width.

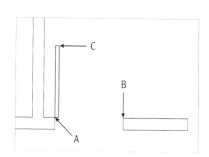

FIGURE 7.6 Drawing a door

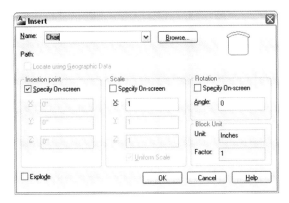

FIGURE 7.9 Selecting the Chair block definition in the Insert dialog box

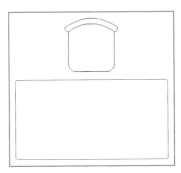

FIGURE 7.10 Chair block inserted 3″ from the desk

7. Click the Move tool in the Modify panel, select the Chair block, and press Enter. Click an arbitrary point on the drawing canvas, type **@1′3″<180** (or **@40<180** for metric), and press Enter to move the chair to the left.

8. Click the Copy tool in the Modify panel, type **L** (for Last), and press Enter twice. Click an arbitrary point on the drawing canvas, type **@2′6″<0** (or **@80<0** for metric), and press Enter to copy a chair to the right (see Figure 7.11). Press Esc to end the COPY command.

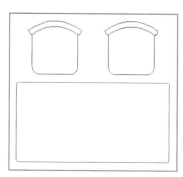

FIGURE 7.11 Copying a
block reference

9. Type **I** (for Insert), and press Enter. Type **180** in the Angle text box in the Rotation section of the Insert dialog box and click OK.

10. Hold Shift, right-click, and choose From in the context menu. Click the midpoint of the lower desk edge, and type **@0,-3"** (or **@0,-7** for metric), and press Enter. The Chair block reference appears 3" (or 7 cm) down from the center of the desk.

11. Press Enter to repeat the last command (INSERT), and select Door from the Name drop-down list in the Insert dialog box. Select Specify On-Screen in the Rotation section and click OK.

12. Click point A in the leftmost room, as shown in Figure 7.12. Verify that Ortho mode is on in the status bar; if not, toggle it on. Move the cursor to the left to rotate the door into the proper orientation (see Figure 7.12). Click on the drawing canvas to insert the door.

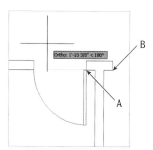

FIGURE 7.12 Inserting a
door and rotating it on screen

13. Press the spacebar to repeat the INSERT command. Select Specify On-Screen in the Scale and Rotation sections of the Insert dialog box (see Figure 7.13) and click OK.

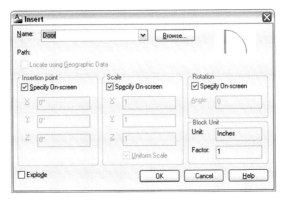

FIGURE 7.13 Specifying everything on screen when inserting a block

Specifying a negative scale factor mirrors the block about its base point.

14. Click point B, as shown in Figure 7.12. The command prompt reads:

```
Specify insertion point or [Basepoint Scale Rotate]:
Specify scale factor <1>:
```

Type **-1** and press Enter.

15. The command prompt now says:

```
Specify rotation angle <0>: 180
```

Type **180** and press Enter. The door is inserted properly in the middle room.

Copying a block has the same effect as inserting a block: a new block reference is added to the drawing.

16. Click the Copy tool in the Modify panel, select the door at the bottom of the middle room, and press Enter. Click points A and B shown in Figure 7.14 to copy a door block into the room on the right. Press Esc to end the COPY command.

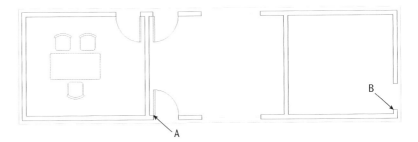

FIGURE 7.14 Copying a block

17. Select the new door in the rightmost room. Click its single blue grip to activate Grip Editing mode. Press the spacebar twice so that the command prompt reads as follows:

    ```
    ** ROTATE **
    Specify rotation angle or
    [Base point Copy Undo Reference eXit]:
    ```

    Type **90** and press Enter to rotate the door block around its base point.

18. Save your work as Ch7-C.dwg (or Ch7-C-metric.dwg).

Editing Blocks

You can edit blocks after they have been defined and inserted into the drawing as block references. In addition to editing geometry, you can assign floating properties to control property inheritance, nest blocks within blocks, or explode blocks entirely. We'll explore each of these topics in this section.

Editing Block Definition Geometry

Block definitions are not frozen in stone; you can redraw them after block references have been inserted multiple times in a drawing. In fact, this is one of the reasons to use blocks: efficient control over multiple objects from a single editable definition. In the following steps, you will alter the door block and see all its references update automatically.

1. If the file is not already open, go to the book's web page, browse to Chapter 7, get the file Ch7-C.dwg (or Ch7-C-metric.dwg), and open it.

2. Zoom in on the lower door in the middle room.

 3. Select the door, right-click, and choose Edit Block In-Place from the context menu. Click OK in the Reference Edit dialog box that appears (see Figure 7.15).

FIGURE 7.15 Editing a block reference in place

4. Click the Rotate tool on the Modify panel, select the door itself (not its swing), and press Enter. Click the hinge point and the command prompt reads:

> Specify rotation angle or [Copy Reference] <0>:

Type **-45** and press Enter.

5. Click the Trim tool in the Modify panel and press Enter. Click the portion of the wing that extends beyond the door to trim it off, and press Esc to end the TRIM command.

6. Expand the temporary Edit Reference panel on the ribbon's Home tab, and click the Save Changes button. Click OK in the AutoCAD warning dialog box that appears, which says, "All reference edits will be saved." Figure 7.16 shows the result: All door references have been automatically updated with the new door geometry.

7. Save your work as Ch7-D.dwg (or Ch7-D-metric.dwg).

FIGURE 7.16 All doors have been updated by editing the door block in place.

Assigning Floating Properties

When you set objects' color, linetype, or lineweight to specific values such as Red, Hidden, or 0.5mm, you are setting those properties explicitly. Explicit object properties assigned to objects in block definitions are retained when those blocks are inserted onto different layers in the drawing.

It is often advantageous to assign floating properties—either *ByLayer* or *ByBlock*—to the objects in block definitions. Floating properties allow block references to inherit properties from the layer on which they are inserted. Alternatively, you can override these inherited properties with explicit properties by assigning them to the block reference.

The Door layer has been current throughout this chapter, so the objects you drew to define the chair and door blocks reside on this layer. In the following steps, you will assign floating properties to the chair and door blocks.

1. If the file is not already open, go to the book's web page, browse to Chapter 7, get the file Ch7-D.dwg (or Ch7-D-metric.dwg), and open it.

2. Click on each of the three chair block references to select them. Type **qp** (for Quick Properties), and press Enter. Select Furniture from the Layer drop-down menu (see Figure 7.17). Notice that the chairs are still green, even though the Furniture layer is blue. Click the close box in the upper-right corner to close the Quick Properties palette, and press Esc to deselect.

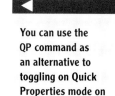

You can use the QP command as an alternative to toggling on Quick Properties mode on the status bar.

FIGURE 7.17 Assigning the Furniture layer to the chair block references

3. Select one of the chairs (it doesn't matter which one), right-click, and choose Edit Block In-Place from the context menu. Click OK in the Reference Edit dialog box that appears.

4. Create an implied window to select all nine objects making up the chair.

3. A temporary tab called Block Editor appears on the ribbon, and the selected block (desk) fills the drawing canvas. Click the Authoring Palettes tool on the Manage panel to toggle them off because they are not needed for this exercise (see Figure 7.20).

The Block Editor is an alternative to editing blocks in place.

FIGURE 7.20 The Block Editor ribbon

4. Type **I** (for Insert), and press Enter. Select Phone in the Name drop-down list. Deselect Specify On-Screen in the Scale and Rotation sections of the Insert dialog box and click OK.

5. Click an arbitrary point on the right side of the desk to insert the phone block reference there.

The phone is magenta because the objects in the phone block definition have floating properties that allow the Equipment layer's magenta color to be inherited.

6. Select the phone block, type **qp** (for Quick Properties), and press Enter. Change Layer Assignment to Equipment, click the close box to exit Quick Properties, and press Esc to deselect (see Figure 7.21).

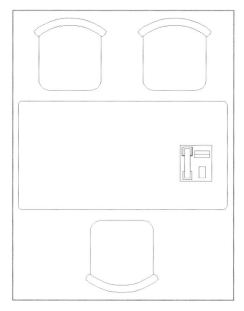

FIGURE 7.21 A phone nested within the desk block and surrounding chair blocks

7. Click the Close Block Editor button on the Close panel. Click Save Changes To Desk in the Block – Changes Not Saved dialog box that appears.

8. Save your work as Ch7-F.dwg (or Ch7-F-metric.dwg).

Exploding Blocks

There are two commands that blow away blocks, leaving you only with their defining geometry: EXPLODE and XPLODE. The former has no options whatsoever; the latter offers many options dealing with what happens to object properties after the block is disassembled. Let's explode a block using both methods:

1. If the file is not already open, go to the book's web page, browse to Chapter 7, get the file Ch7-F.dwg (or Ch7-F-metric.dwg), and open it.

2. Type **X** (for Explode), and press Enter. Select the magenta chair, and press Enter.

3. Select the parts of the chair, and observe in the Layers panel that the objects are on layer 0 and in the Properties panel that their color is set to ByBlock (see Figure 7.22). Press Esc to deselect.

Use the PURGE command to delete unused block definitions to make the drawing file smaller.

FIGURE 7.22 Investigating the layer assignment and object properties of an exploded block

 4. Click the Undo button on the Quick Access toolbar. The block is re-created.

5. Type **xp** (for Xplode), and press Enter. Select the magenta chair, and press Enter. The command prompt reads:

```
[All Color LAyer LType LWeight
Inherit from parent block Explode]
 <Explode>:
```

Type **I** (for Inherit from parent block), and press Enter.

6. Select all the parts of the chair, and observe that the objects are on the blue Furniture layer and their color is explicitly set to magenta. This time the disassembled objects received the layer assignment and object properties of the block reference.

7. Expand the Modify panel, and click the Set To ByLayer tool. The command prompt reads:

```
Change ByBlock to ByLayer? [Yes No] <Yes>:
```

Press Enter to accept the default Yes. Now the prompt says:

```
Include blocks? [Yes No] <Yes>:
```

Type **N** (for No), and press Enter. The SETBYLAYER command ends and the chair is blue now because its color has been set to ByLayer.

8. Save your work as Ch7-G.dwg (or Ch7-G-metric.dwg).

Redefining Blocks

You already know that block definitions have names and that blocks are inserted by name. So what do you suppose happens if you define a new block using a name that has already been used in the drawing?

In the following steps, you are presented with just such a situation where you will have the opportunity to redefine a block definition. Any block references in the drawing will be automatically updated with the new definition.

1. If the file is not already open, go to the book's web page, browse to Chapter 7, get the file Ch7-G.dwg (or Ch7-G-metric.dwg), and open it.

2. Zoom into the lower chair you exploded in the previous section.

3. Click the Rectangle tool on the Draw panel. The command prompt reads:

```
Specify first corner point or [Chamfer Elevation
Fillet Thickness Width]:
```

Type **F** (for Fillet), and press Enter. The prompt now says:

```
Specify fillet radius for rectangles <0'-0">:
```

Type **1″** (or **3 cm**), and press Enter. The rectangle will have rounded corners.

4. For the first corner, click point A, as shown in Figure 7.23. Then type **@3,-10** (or **@7,-25** for metric), and press Enter to complete the RECTANGLE command.

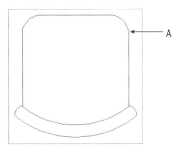

FIGURE 7.23 Drawing an armrest

5. Click the Mirror tool in the Modify panel. Type **L** (for Last), and press Enter twice. The command prompt reads:

   `Specify first point of mirror line:`

   Snap to the midpoint of the chair's front edge, toggle on Ortho on the status bar, move the cursor downward, and click on the drawing canvas to specify the second point of the mirror line. Press Enter to complete the MIRROR command (see Figure 7.24).

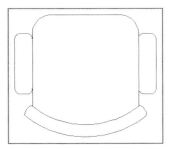

FIGURE 7.24 Mirroring an armrest

6. Select all objects in the chair and its armrests. Open the Layer drop-down menu, and select layer 0 to change the assignment of the selected objects.

7. Type **B** (for Block), and press Enter. Type **Chair** in the Name field in the Block Definition dialog box. Click the Pick Point button, and then snap to the midpoint of the chair's front edge.

8. Select the Convert To Block radio button in the Objects section of the Block Definition dialog box and click OK. Click Redefine Block in the Block – Redefine Block dialog box that appears. Figure 7.25 shows the result: All three chair block references are updated.

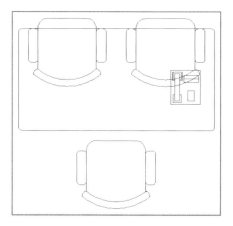

FIGURE 7.25 Redefining the chair block causes the chairs to lose their original orientation.

9. Unfortunately the redefined chair block references didn't preserve their original orientations. No matter; click the Mirror tool on the Modify panel, select the top two chairs, and press Enter. Snap to the front edge of one of the seats, move the cursor to the right, and click on the drawing canvas. The command prompt reads:

```
Erase source objects? [Yes No] <N>:
```

Type **Y** (for Yes), and press Enter. The chairs are now oriented correctly (see Figure 7.26).

10. Save your work as Ch7-H.dwg (or Ch7-G-metric.dwg).

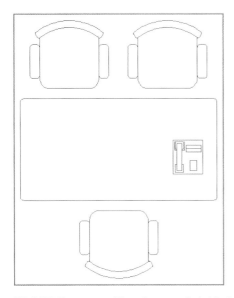

FIGURE 7.26 Mirroring two chair blocks

Working with Groups

Groups are a means of organizing objects that is less formal than blocks. Groups don't need to be named, nor do they require base points as do blocks. You can toggle group selection on and off so that you can manipulate the entire group as a unit or access individual members of the group at will. You can't redefine the many with the few as you can with blocks, however. That said, it's certainly convenient to be able to manipulate many blocks with a few groups. In the following steps, you will group the desk and chairs, copy this group into adjacent rooms, and make adjustments to various blocks within the groups.

1. If the file is not already open, go to the book's web page, browse to Chapter 7, get the file Ch7-H.dwg (or Ch7-G-metric.dwg), and open it.

2. Click the Group tool on the Groups panel on the ribbon's Home tab. Select the desk and the three chairs surrounding it, and then press Enter.

3. Click the Copy tool on the Modify panel, click the group to select it, and press Enter. Click an arbitrary point inside the desk, and then click in the middle and right rooms to copy the group twice. Press Esc to end the COPY command.

4. Click the Rotate tool on the Modify panel, select the group in the room on the right, and press Enter. Click an arbitrary point inside the desk, type **-90**, and press Enter (see Figure 7.27).

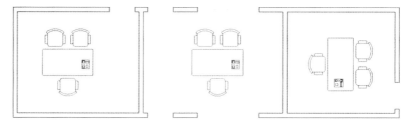

FIGURE 7.27 Copying and rotating groups in rooms

5. Click the Group Selection On/Off toggle in the Groups panel (turning it off).

6. Select the lower chair in the middle room, and press the Delete key.

7. Click the Copy tool on the Modify panel, select the chair on the right in the middle room, and press Enter. Snap to the midpoints at points A and B in Figure 7.28 and press Enter. A third chair is copied so that all three are equidistant.

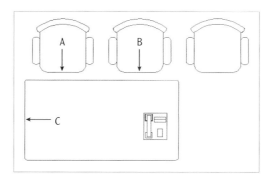

FIGURE 7.28 Copying a chair

8. Click the Mirror tool on the Modify panel, select the three chairs in the middle room, and press Enter. Click point C in Figure 7.28, move the cursor to the right, and click in the drawing canvas to complete the mirror line. Press Enter to mirror three more chairs on the opposite side of the desk.

9. Type **xp** (for Xplode), and press Enter. Select the desk, and press Enter. Type **I** (for Inherit from parent block), and press Enter.

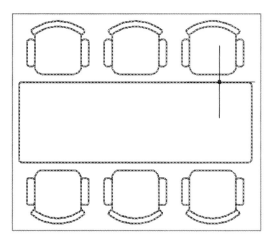

10. Click the Stretch tool on the Modify panel; select the right edge of the desk with a crossing window so that the top, bottom, and right edges are selected; and press Enter. Click an arbitrary point inside the desk, move the cursor to the right, type **2′6″** (or **80** for metric), and press Enter. The desk is enlarged.

11. Select the phone block on the desk, and press the Delete key.

12. Click the Group Edit tool on the Groups panel, select the upper-left chair in the middle room, and press Enter. The command prompt reads:

   ```
   Enter an option [Add objects Remove objects REName]:
   ```

   Type **A** (for Add objects), and press Enter. Select all six chairs and the desk, and then press Enter.

13. Click the Group Selection On/Off toggle in the Groups panel (turning it on). Hover the cursor over the desk, and observe that the entire group highlights (see Figure 7.29).

FIGURE 7.29 Reconstituted group after its constituent objects have been deleted, added, and stretched

14. Open the Layer drop-down menu, and toggle on the Door layer. Figure 7.30 shows the final result.

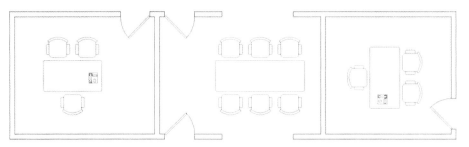

FIGURE 7.30 Final organized plan containing blocks and groups

Your drawing should now resemble Ch7-Final.dwg (or Ch7-Final-metric.dwg), which is available among the book's download files at www.sybex.com/go/ autocad2013essentials.

THE ESSENTIALS AND BEYOND

In this chapter, you learned how to organize objects into blocks and groups. More specifically, you defined, inserted, edited, nested, exploded, and redefined blocks. You saw how floating properties and layer 0 affect property inheritance when block references are inserted into a drawing. Finally, you worked with groups, manipulated them as whole units, accessed their individual members, and added objects to an existing group. In short, you now have the skills to organize objects for efficient drafting.

ADDITIONAL EXERCISE

Explore the BCONSTRUCTION command on your own. It is used to convert geometry into construction geometry that is only visible within the Block Editor for layout purposes. For example, try drawing a mirror line down the center line of the chair block and converting it to construction geometry with the BCONSTRUCTION command. The mirror line serves as a helpful visual reference while in the Block Editor, but the construction geometry will not be displayed in the block reference.

CHAPTER 8

Hatching and Gradients

The term hatching refers to filling bounded areas with solids, patterns, and/or gradients. You create hatching in the AutoCAD® program to indicate transitions between materials and to improve the readability of drawings in general. Hatching with solid fill, patterns, and/or tonal gradients can transform staid line drawings into attractive illustrations. This chapter covers the basics of hatching so that you can use it in your own drawings.

▶ **Specifying hatch areas**

▶ **Associating hatches with boundaries**

▶ **Hatching with patterns**

▶ **Hatching with gradients**

Specifying Hatch Areas

Every hatch area is defined by a boundary containing the solid fill, pattern, or gradient. The boundary can be determined either by picking a point on the drawing canvas or by selecting an object or set of objects.

Picking Points to Determine Boundaries

When a boundary is picked, AutoCAD uses a raycasting algorithm to determine the precise extents of the area bounded by the objects on screen. In the following steps, you will pick points to determine the boundaries of multiple hatch objects:

1. Go to the book's web page at www.sybex.com/go/autocad2013essentials, browse to Chapter 8, get the file Ch8-A.dwg, and open it. The drawing is based on a 100-year-old patent for fluid propulsion (CA 135174) by Nikola Tesla (see Figure 8.1). Tesla is best known for inventing the alternating electrical current that powers the modern age.

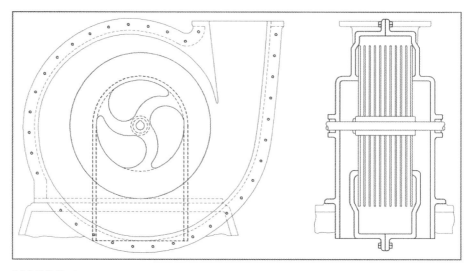

FIGURE 8.1 Initial line drawing based on Tesla's patent for fluid propulsion

2. Zoom into the center of the rotor in the drawing on the left.

Certification Objective

3. Click the Hatch tool in the Draw panel on the ribbon's Home tab. Click point A in Figure 8.2.

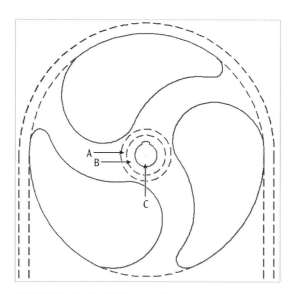

FIGURE 8.2 Picking a point to detect a boundary

4. A temporary contextual tab called Hatch Creation appears on the ribbon. This tab will remain active while you configure the hatch object that you are creating. Click Solid in the Pattern panel, and turn off Associative mode if it is on by clicking its button in the Options panel (see Figure 8.3). (You'll learn about associative hatches in the next section.)

FIGURE 8.3 Using ribbon controls when creating a hatch

5. Expand the Options panel, open the Island Detection menu, and select Outer Island Detection. The thumbnails indicate different ways of treating nested boundaries, called *islands*. In this case, you want only the outer island filled with a solid hatch.

6. Open the Hatch Color drop-down in the Properties panel, and choose Select Colors at the bottom of the list of standard colors. Choose color 255 from the Select Color dialog box and click OK (see Figure 8.4).

You can override a hatch object's default color, transparency, and layer assignment on the Hatch Creation tab's Properties panel.

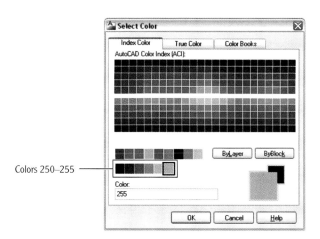

Colors 250–255

FIGURE 8.4 Selecting a color override for the hatch object

7. Expand the Properties panel, open the Hatch Layer Override drop-down, and select the Solid layer (see Figure 8.5).

FIGURE 8.5 Using
Hatch Layer Override

8. Click the Close Hatch Creation icon in the Close panel at the extreme right edge of the ribbon's Hatch Editor tab. The outer island is filled with a solid hatch object, and the HATCH command ends.

9. Type **H** (for Hatch), and press Enter. Click point B in Figure 8.2.

All the settings and overrides in the Hatch Creation tab are "sticky," meaning that they remain the same the next time you create a hatch object.

10. Open the Hatch Color drop-down in the Properties panel, and choose Select Colors at the bottom of the list of standard colors. Choose color 253 from the Select Color dialog box and click OK.

11. Click the Close Hatch Creation icon in the Close panel.

12. Press the spacebar to repeat the last command. Click point C in Figure 8.2.

13. Open the Hatch Color drop-down in the Properties panel, and choose Select Colors at the bottom of the list of standard colors. Choose color 250 from the Select Color dialog box and click OK.

Use the BOUNDARY command to create a polyline or region object from a picked point. BOUNDARY uses the same ray-casting algorithm used by the HATCH command.

14. Click the Close Hatch Creation icon in the Close panel. The Hatch Editor tab disappears.

15. Click the Isolate tool on the Layers panel of the ribbon's Home tab, drag a crossing selection over the hub, and include the selection of at least one of the dashed blue lines defining the edge of a spoke. Press Enter, and all the other layers are hidden, leaving the entire rotor.

16. Click the Hatch tool on the Draw panel, and then click point A in Figure 8.6.

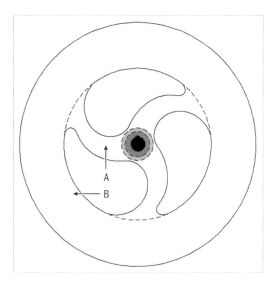

FIGURE 8.6 Picking points on the rotor

17. Open the Hatch Color drop-down in the Properties panel, and choose Select Colors at the bottom of the list of standard colors. Choose color 255 from the Select Color dialog box and click OK.

18. Drag the Hatch Transparency slider to the right until the value is approximately 50 (see Figure 8.7).

FIGURE 8.7 Overriding layer transparency within the HATCH command

19. Toggle on the Show/Hide Transparency button on the status bar. The hatch pattern you just created appears partially transparent.

20. Type **H** (for Hatch), and press Enter. Click point B in Figure 8.6. The command prompt reads:

    Analyzing the selected data...

AutoCAD can't find this particular area; press Esc before the program crashes.

21. Save your work as Ch8-B.dwg.

> The raycasting algorithm has a tendency to crash when analyzing complex areas, such as arcs, splines, and a circle forming the boundary of the outer portion of the rotor.

Selecting Objects to Define Boundaries

In complex drawings, picking points to determine boundaries sometimes doesn't work. Fortunately, you can always define boundaries successfully using closed objects. In the following steps, you will select two closed objects to define a hatch boundary.

1. If the file is not already open from performing the previous step, go to the book's web page, browse to Chapter 8, get the file Ch8-B.dwg, and open it.

Don't worry about which layer the circle you are drawing is located; you will delete the circle later.

2. In the previous section, the raycasting algorithm probably had trouble with the inner part of the rotor where the arcs and splines meet. To simplify the boundary, you will draw a circle. Click the Circle tool on the Draw panel.

3. Shift+right-click, and choose Node from the context menu. Click point A, shown in Figure 8.8, as the center point. Type **QUA** (for Quadrant), and press Enter. Click point B in Figure 8.8 to set the inner circle's radius. The CIRCLE command ends.

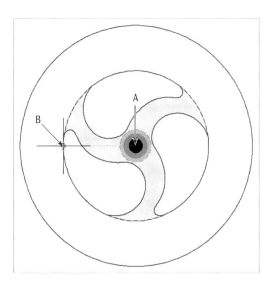

FIGURE 8.8 Drawing a circle

4. Type **H** (for Hatch), and press Enter. Click the Select Boundary Objects tool in the Boundaries panel of the ribbon's Hatch Editor tab. Select the circle making up the inner circle of the rotor, and then select the single outer circle. Select Solid in the Pattern panel and press Enter. The hatch

appears correctly (see Figure 8.9); click the Close Hatch Editor icon in the Close panel at the extreme right edge of the Hatch Editor tab.

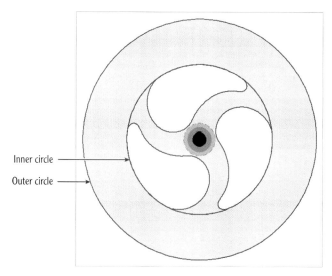

Inner circle

Outer circle

FIGURE 8.9 Hatching the outer potion of the rotor by selecting objects

 5. Click the Erase tool on the Home tab's Modify panel. Select the inner circle you drew in step 3 and press Enter. The dashed arcs are again visible after using the REGEN command to regenerate the display of objects on the screen.

6. Save your work as Ch8-C.dwg.

Associating Hatches with Boundaries

When hatches are associated with their boundary objects, the boundary objects themselves define the extents of the hatch fill, pattern, or gradient. Altering the shape of any of the boundary objects necessarily changes the extents of an associated hatch object. For example, the rotor needs to have a larger diameter and, by associating the hatch with the outer circle, you will be able to get the hatch to expand to fill the larger rotor simply by changing the diameter of the circle.

When hatches are not associated with their boundary objects, altering the boundary objects does not change the shape of the hatch.

In the following steps, you will re-create the boundary objects from the last hatch pattern created in the previous section. Then you will alter the shape of one of the boundary objects to change the extents of the solid hatch.

1. If the file is not already open from performing the previous step, go to the book's web page, browse to Chapter 8, get the file Ch8-C.dwg, and open it.

2. Click the outer portion of the rotor to select the hatch object; the Hatch Editor tab appears on the ribbon.

3. Click the Recreate Boundary tool on the Boundaries panel. The command prompt reads:

   ```
   Enter type of boundary object [Region Polyline] <Polyline>:
   ```

   Press Enter to accept Polyline as the default option. Now the prompt says:

   ```
   Associate hatch with new boundary? [Yes No] <Y>:
   ```

   Press Enter again to accept the default, Yes. Two new circles are created and associated with the hatch.

4. Click the Close Hatch Editor icon in the Close panel.

5. Toggle on Object Snap on the status bar. Right-click this toggle button, and turn on Center, Quadrant, and Endpoint running object snap modes in the context menu if they are not already on.

6. Toggle on Ortho mode on the status bar.

7. Toggle on Object Snap Tracking on the status bar.

8. Click the Scale tool on the Modify panel, select the rotor's outer circle, and press Enter. Select the center of the rotor (point A in Figure 8.10) as the base point. The command prompt reads:

   ```
   Specify scale factor or [Copy Reference]:
   ```

   Type **R** (for Reference), and press Enter. Pick the reference length by clicking points A and B in Figure 8.10.

9. Hover the cursor over point C, as shown in Figure 8.10. Then bring the cursor back toward point D. When the tracking X appears on the drawing canvas, click point D. When the SCALE command ends, the rotor matches its depiction in the drawing on the right and the solid associative hatch fills the new boundary.

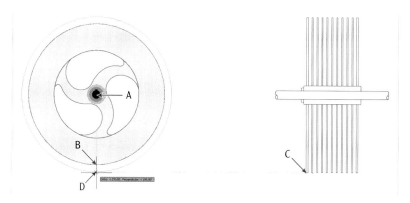

FIGURE 8.10 Scaling up the outer circle of the rotor enlarges its associative hatch.

10. Click the outer portion of the rotor to select the hatch object; the Hatch Editor tab appears on the ribbon.

11. Convert the object into a nonassociative hatch by clicking to toggle off the Associative button in the Options panel, and then click the Close Hatch Editor icon.

12. Click the Erase tool on the Modify panel, select the two re-created boundaries as shown in Figure 8.11, and press Enter.

13. Click the Unisolate tool on the Layers panel.

14. Save your work as Ch8-D.dwg.

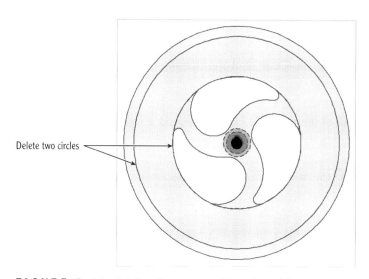

Delete two circles

FIGURE 8.11 Deleting the re-created boundary objects

ACCESSING THE HATCH EDIT DIALOG BOX

You can access all the hatching tools that you see on the ribbon in a dialog box interface by selecting a hatch object using the HATCHEDIT command. You'll see this dialog box when using the HATCH command if you are using a workspace that doesn't have the ribbon (such as AutoCAD Classic).

Hatching with Patterns

Hatch patterns are repeating arrangements of lines and/or dots used to identify a material or a cutting plane, or to highlight an area visually. You'll learn how to specify pattern properties, separate hatch areas, and set the origin point of the pattern.

Specifying Properties

Hatch patterns have a few additional properties as compared to solid hatch objects. In the following steps, you will select a pattern, set its scale, and adjust the pattern angle.

1. If the file is not already open from performing the previous step, go to the book's web page, browse to Chapter 8, get the file Ch8-D.dwg, and open it.

2. Pan over to the drawing on the right.

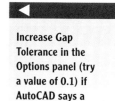

3. Click the Hatch tool on the Draw panel.

4. Click points A through F inside the red housing, as shown in Figure 8.12. A solid hatch appears within the red boundaries.

Increase Gap Tolerance in the Options panel (try a value of 0.1) if AutoCAD says a boundary is not closed.

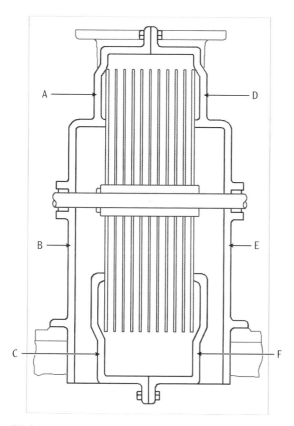

FIGURE 8.12 Picking points inside the metal housing to determine hatch boundaries

5. Select the pattern called ANSI31 in the Pattern panel if it is not already selected. Select Red in the Color drop-down in the Properties panel. Select Color 255 in the Background Color drop-down. Repeatedly click Scale's up arrow to increase the value to 2.000. Expand the Properties panel, and select Pattern from the Hatch Layer Override drop-down (see Figure 8.13).

6. Click Close Hatch Editor in the Close panel.

7. Save your work as Ch8-E.dwg.

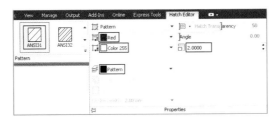

FIGURE 8.13 Configuring hatch properties

Separating Hatch Areas

When you picked points within multiple boundaries in the previous section, it formed a single hatch object. The properties you specified were assigned to this object. However, at this point we want to rotate the cross-sectional pattern 90° on the right side to illustrate better the separate pieces of metal that are bolted together. In the following steps, you will separate the multiple bounded areas of a single object into individual hatch objects and then rotate patterns on half of them:

1. If the file is not already open from performing the previous step, go to the book's web page, browse to Chapter 8, get the file Ch8-E.dwg, and open it.

2. Select the hatch object you created in the previous section.

3. Expand the Options panel, and click Separate Hatches (see Figure 8.14).

FIGURE 8.14 Separating multiple bounded areas into multiple hatch objects

4. Click Close Hatch Editor in the Close panel.

5. Select the upper-right hatch pattern, type **90** in the Angle text box, and press the Tab key. Click the Set Origin button, and then click point A shown in Figure 8.15. Press Esc to exit the ribbon's Hatch Editor tab.

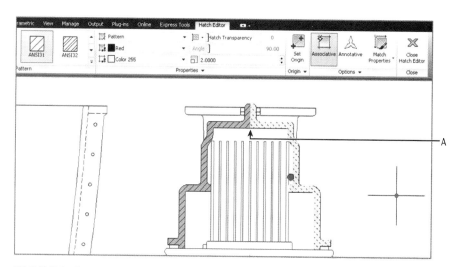

Exploding hatch patterns removes their associativity (if any). Exploding them again converts the hatch pattern into its constituent lines; background color fill is lost in the process.

FIGURE 8.15 Changing the angle and setting the origin of an individual hatch pattern object

6. Select the hatch pattern on the left side, click the Set Origin button, click point A as shown in Figure 8.15, and press Esc. The outer patterns on left and right both meet symmetrically at point A.

7. Select the pattern on the lower right, click the Match Properties tool in the Options panel, and select the upper-right pattern. Press Esc to deselect; the lower pattern matches the upper pattern's angle.

8. Select the inner pattern on the right. Click the Match Properties tool in the Options panel, and select the lower-right pattern.

9. Click the Set Origin button, and click point B in Figure 8.16. Press Esc to deselect.

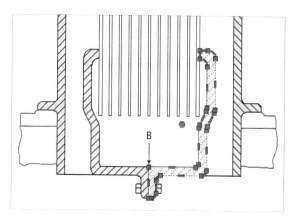

FIGURE 8.16 Setting the origin of the inner-right pattern

10. Select the inner pattern on the left. Click the Set Origin button, and click point B in Figure 8.16. Press Esc to deselect. The inner patterns on the left and right both meet symmetrically at point B. Figure 8.17 shows the result.

11. Save your work as Ch8-F.dwg.

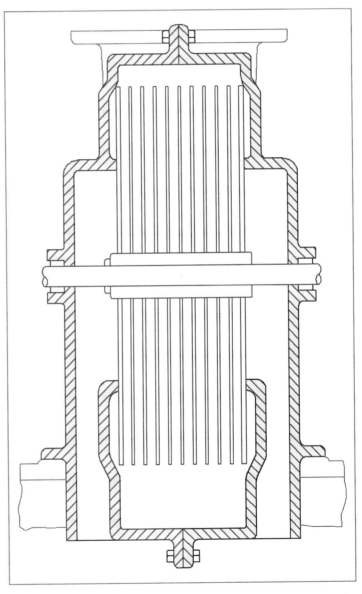

FIGURE 8.17 Symmetrical crosshatching highlights separate metal castings.

Hatching with Gradients

In addition to hatching with solid fill and line patterns, you can hatch with one- and two-color *gradients* to vary tonality in a smooth fashion. Gradients can subtly hint at an extra dimension that helps make drawings more readable. In the following steps, you will create gradient hatches that give depth to metal parts in the drawings.

1. If the file is not already open from performing the previous step, go to the book's web page, browse to Chapter 8, get the file Ch8-F.dwg, and open it.

Certification Objective

2. Open the flyout next to the Hatch tool on the Draw panel, and select Gradient from the menu. Click points A through F shown in Figure 8.18.

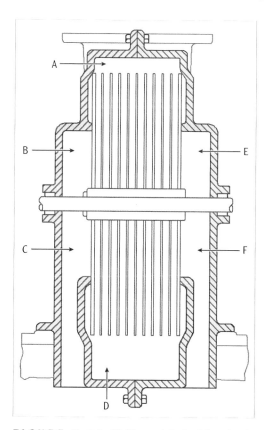

FIGURE 8.18 Picking points to determine boundaries for gradient hatch

Click the Gradient Tint And Shade button to toggle one- or two-color gradients. You can select both colors in two-color gradients whereas one-color gradients fade to white.

3. Scroll down in the Pattern panel, and select the GR_CURVED gradient. Select Color 253 in the Gradient Color 1 drop-down. Click the Gradient Tint And Shade button (if it is not already highlighted in blue) to create a one-color gradient. Drag the Hatch Transparency slider all the way to the left until its value reads 0. Expand the Properties panel and select Gradient in the Hatch Layer Override drop-down (see Figure 8.19). Click the Close Hatch Creation icon at the right edge of the ribbon.

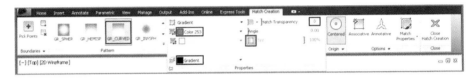

FIGURE 8.19 Configuring a gradient hatch

4. Zoom in on the rotor shaft.

5. Type **GRADIENT**, and press Enter. Click a point in the center of the shaft to determine the boundary for a new gradient hatch. Select the GR_CYLIN pattern, set Angle to 90, and select Color 250 in the Gradient Color 1 drop-down. Click the Close Hatch Creation icon. Figure 8.20 shows the result.

Use the DRAWORDER command to change the display behavior of individual overlapping objects.

6. Objects typically overlap other objects that were drawn earlier. Type **HATCHTOBACK**, and press Enter. All hatch objects (solid fills, patterns, and/or gradients) are sent to the back of the *draw order* stack so that they don't overlap any of the other objects in the drawing.

7. Your drawing should now resemble Ch8-G.dwg, which is available for download at the book's web page.

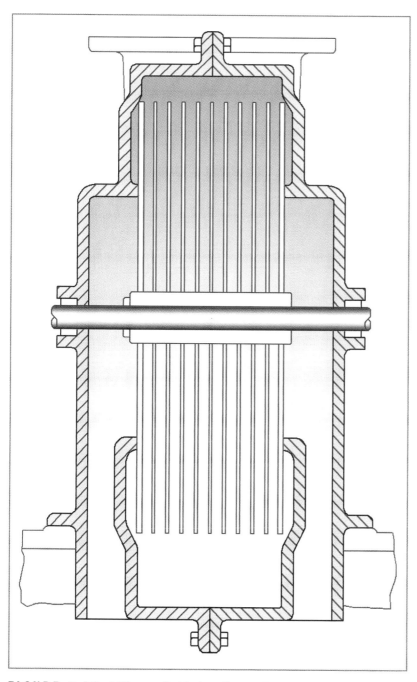

FIGURE 8.20 Adding a cylindrical gradient to the shaft

THE ESSENTIALS AND BEYOND

In this chapter, you have learned how to create hatch objects that are filled with solid color, line patterns, and/or gradients. You now have the tools to improve the readability of your drawings by graphically indicating transitions between materials and section cutting planes, and by adding depth to parts with variable shading.

ADDITIONAL EXERCISE

Explore the WIPEOUT command on your own. Think of wipeouts as solid hatches that completely obscure what they cover with the current canvas background color. They can be useful in complex drawings when you want to wipe out areas to make room for notes. Try creating a wipeout object that obscures a portion of the upper rotor blades in the cross-sectional drawing on the right of Ch8-G.dwg.

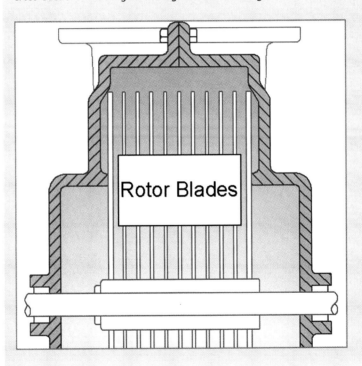

CHAPTER 9

Working with Blocks and Xrefs

In Chapter 7, "Organizing Objects," you learned how to define and reference blocks within a single drawing in the AutoCAD® program. In this chapter, you will create and insert *global blocks* from outside the current drawing. Harnessing the power of a search engine, you'll cast a net across multiple drawings to locate specific blocks and a variety of other content. Once key content is found, you will place it on tool palettes for quick access in the future. In addition, you will make external references (*Xrefs*) to drawings outside the current file.

► **Working with global blocks**

► **Accessing content globally**

► **Storing content on tool palettes**

► **Referencing external drawings and images**

Working with Global Blocks

Global blocks are drawing files that you will later insert as blocks into another drawing. In this section, you will learn how to write local blocks to files, insert a drawing file as a local block, and redefine local blocks with global blocks.

Writing a Local Block Definition to a File

Certification
Objective

In the following steps, you will export one of the current drawing's block definitions to an individual drawing file. In addition, you will open the newly created file and alter its contents.

1. Go to the book's web page at www.sybex.com/go /autocad2013essentials, browse to Chapter 9, get the file Ch9-A.dwg, and open it.

The Sofa block that was written to Sofa.dwg does not itself have a Sofa block definition; only the geometry was transferred to the new file.

2. Type **W** (for Write block), and press Enter. Select the Block radio button in the Source area of the Write Block dialog box. Select Sofa from the Block drop-down. Select Inches from the Insert Units drop-down in the Destination area (see Figure 9.1). Click OK, and the geometry within the Sofa block definition is written to Sofa.dwg.

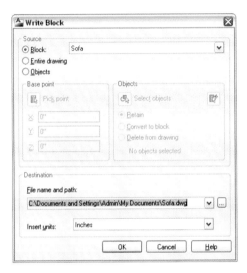

FIGURE 9.1 Writing a block to a file

3. Click the Open tool on the Quick Access toolbar. Browse to the following folder:

C:\Documents and Settings\<your user name>\My Documents

Open Sofa.dwg (see Figure 9.2).

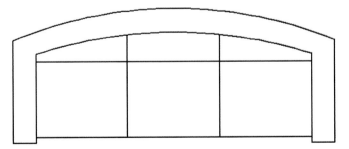

FIGURE 9.2 Open the Sofa.dwg file.

4. Click Zoom Extents on the Navigation bar.

5. Click the Erase tool on the Modify panel, select the two arcs in the sofa's backrest, and press Enter.

6. Toggle on Ortho mode on the status bar.

7. Toggle on Object Snap on the status bar. Right-click the Object Snap toggle, and select Endpoint if it is not already selected.

8. Click the Line tool on the Draw panel. Snap the first point of the line to the endpoint shown in Figure 9.3. Move the cursor to the right, and click an arbitrary second point. Press Esc to end the LINE command.

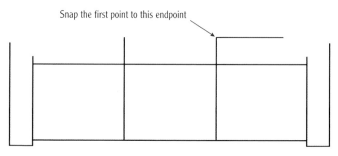

Snap the first point to this endpoint

FIGURE 9.3 Drawing a straight-backed sofa

9. Click the Fillet tool on the Modify panel. Press F2 to open the Command window, and verify that the command prompt says the following:

```
Current settings: Mode = TRIM, Radius = 0'-0"
```

If the radius is not 0, type **R** (for Radius), press Enter, type **0**, and press Enter again. Select the line you just drew, and then click the inner line on the right arm of the sofa.

10. Press the spacebar to repeat the FILLET command. Click the inner line on the left arm of the sofa, and then click the back line. Figure 9.4 shows the result.

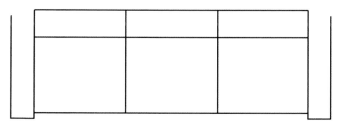

FIGURE 9.4 Filleting lines to meet at sharp corners

11. Click the Offset tool on the Modify panel. Click points A and B in Figure 9.5 to set the offset distance. Select the back line of the sofa, and then click above it to offset another line.

5. Select the receptionist's chair. Drag this chair (not using a grip) onto the Furniture palette. TaskChair appears with a preview icon (see Figure 9.21).

▶

Blocks dragged to tool palettes are global blocks that can be inserted into any drawing.

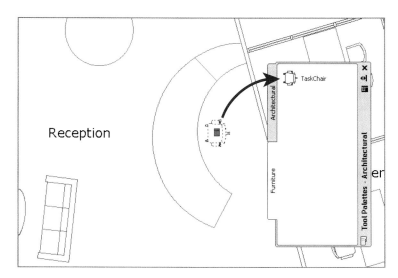

FIGURE 9.21 Creating a tool on a new palette by dragging a chair block onto it

6. Right-click the TaskChair tool in the Furniture palette, and choose Properties from the context menu. Change Prompt For Rotation to Yes in the Tool Properties dialog box that appears (see Figure 9.22). Click OK.

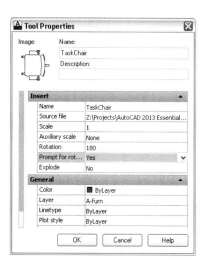

FIGURE 9.22 Adjusting tool properties to prompt for rotation

7. Select the Manager's offices on the other side of the wall behind the receptionist's chair. Type **UNGROUP**, and press Enter. Erase the manager's chair immediately behind the receptionist's chair.

8. Click the TaskChair tool on the Furniture tool palette. Click the place where the manager's chair used to be, and then specify the rotation by clicking a second time. Click OK or Cancel to close the Edit Attributes dialog box that appears. Figure 9.23 shows the result.

9. Close the Tool Palettes, and save your work as Ch9-E.dwg.

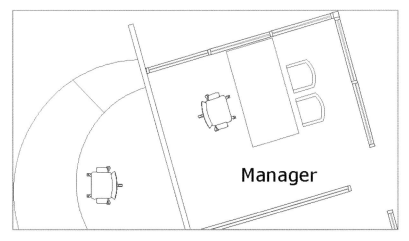

FIGURE 9.23 Inserting a chair from the tool palette

Referencing External Drawings and Images

External references (called *Xrefs*) are a more dynamic alternative to blocks. Xrefs linked to the current drawing are automatically updated every time the current drawing is opened. Blocks, on the other hand, must be edited in place or redefined when they are changed. The real efficiency with Xrefs comes when you link one file into multiple drawing files because changes made to the linked file are automatically reloaded in all the files that have the Xref attached.

In the following steps, you will externally reference a *core* (elevators, stairs, shafts) and *shell* (exterior envelope) drawing into the drawing containing items owned by the building tenant (walls, doors, furniture, and so on). The advantage of working this way is that the core and shell generally do not change from floor to floor, whereas the tenant improvement drawings are typically unique to each

This is just one example of using Xrefs in the case of a high-rise building. Xrefs can be used in every discipline whenever you want the advantages they provide.

floor. Changes made to the core and/or shell can be made in separate drawings that are linked to all the individual tenant drawings.

1. Go to the book's web page, browse to Chapter 9, get the file Ch9-CoreShell.dwg, and open it. Figure 9.24 shows the building core and shell.

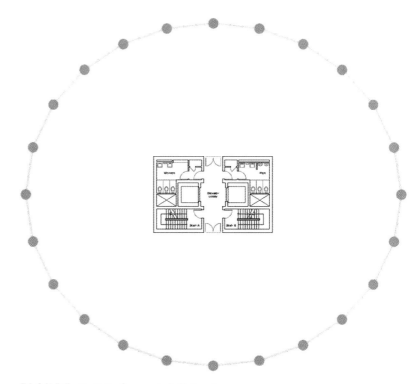

FIGURE 9.24 Core and shell drawing

2. Return to the book's web page, browse to Chapter 9, get the file Ch9-F .dwg, and open it. Figure 9.25 shows the objects owned by the tenant.

3. Select the ribbon's View tab, and click the External References Palette button in the Palettes panel. Open the Attach menu, as shown in Figure 9.26.

4. Select Attach DWG from the menu. Select the file Ch9-CoreShell.dwg, and click Open in the Select Reference dialog box.

5. In the Attach External Reference dialog box that appears, deselect Specify On-Screen in the Insertion Point area. Relative Path is now the default in AutoCAD 2013 (see Figure 9.27). Click OK.

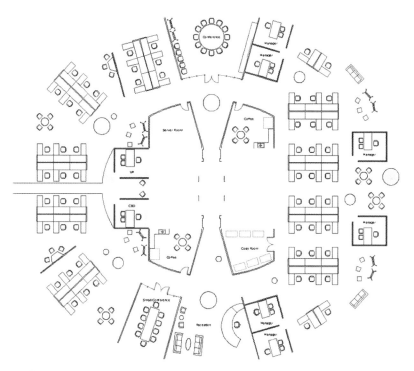

FIGURE 9.25 Tenant improvement floor plan

Attach menu

FIGURE 9.26 Attaching a
DWG file in the External References
palette

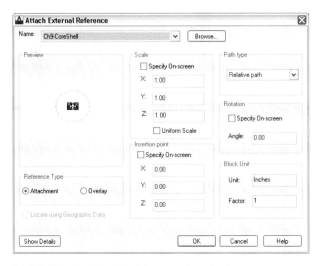

FIGURE 9.27 Attaching an external reference

You can adjust the amount of fading the Xref displays in the OPTIONS command on the Display tab within the Options dialog box.

6. The core and shell appear faded with respect to the tenant drawing (see Figure 9.28).

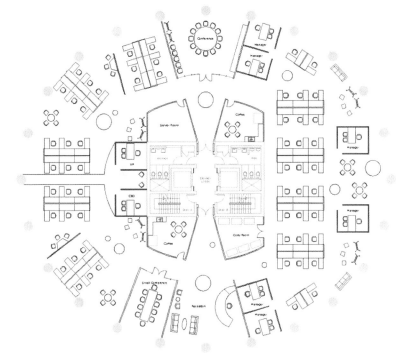

FIGURE 9.28 Core and shell drawing is externally referenced into the tenant drawing.

7. Select the core or shell to select the single Xref object. Click the Open Reference tool on the Edit panel of the External Reference tab that appears on the ribbon.

8. Redesign the Women's washroom so that it has three sinks, as shown in Figure 9.29.

9. Type **CLOSE**, and press Enter twice to close and save Ch9-CoreShell.dwg.

10. A balloon appears in the drawing status bar informing you that an external reference has changed (see Figure 9.30). If no notification balloon appears, right-click the Xref that needs to be reloaded in the External References palette and choose Reload. Click the hyperlinked blue text to reload the Ch9-CoreShell Xref. The changes made to the Women's washroom are now visible in the tenant drawing.

11. Save your work as Ch9-G.dwg.

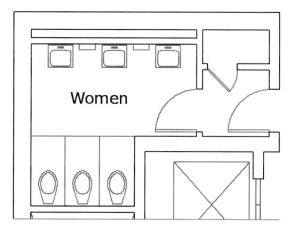

FIGURE 9.29 Redesigning the Women's washroom for three sinks

FIGURE 9.30 Balloon notification that an Xref has changed

THE ESSENTIALS AND BEYOND

In this chapter, you learned how to work with global blocks, the Content Explorer, Tool Palettes, and Xrefs. You learned how to increase drawing and editing efficiency by using blocks and Xrefs. You can now access and work with content beyond the current drawing. This is the key to working in a team because team members regularly need to share content with one another. Global blocks and Xrefs are the means for exchanging design data within a team. The Content Explorer and the Tool Palettes feature make finding and using design data much easier.

ADDITIONAL EXERCISE

Explore the Autodesk Design Center using the ADC command. The Design Center is similar to the Content Explorer but without the search engine functionality. Reopen Ch9-G.dwg if it's not still open. Expand the folder list in the DesignCenter palette, and navigate to the Chapter 06 folder on your hard drive; then expand Ch6-Final.dwg. Select Blocks, and then drag the Phone-Desk block into the drawing canvas of Ch9-G.dwg. Move this phone to the President's desk.

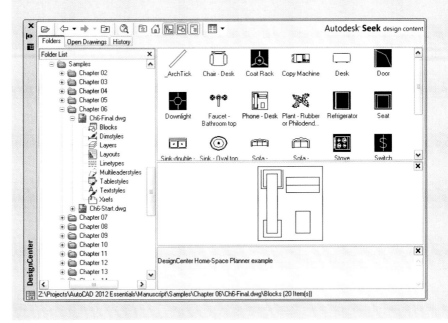

CHAPTER 10

Creating and Editing Text

Text is an essential part of every drawing. You use the written word to clarify graphical depictions and delineate your design intent with specific language. It's good to remember that drawings can be used as part of legal construction documents, and you typically need to clarify your design intent with text that appears on the drawings themselves. In this chapter, you'll learn how to style text, how to write both lines and paragraphs of text using specialized commands, and how to edit existing text.

▶ **Creating text styles**

▶ **Writing lines of text**

▶ **Writing and formatting paragraphs of text using MTEXT**

▶ **Editing text**

Creating Text Styles

The AutoCAD® software can't help you with your grammar or linguistic style, but it can style the appearance of text. Text styles associate specific fonts, optional text heights, and special effects with text objects. In the following steps, you will create the text styles that you will use in the next section when creating text objects.

1. Go to the book's web page at www.sybex.com/go /autocad2013essentials, browse to Chapter 10, get the file Ch10-A.dwg or Ch10-A-metric.dwg, and open it.

Certification Objective

2. On the ribbon's Home tab, expand the Annotation panel and open the first drop-down menu (for text styles). Every drawing has both an Annotative and Standard style by default. Select Manage Text Styles at the bottom of the panel (see Figure 10.1).

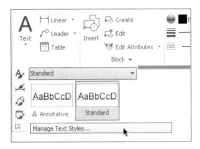

FIGURE 10.1 Managing text styles

3. Click the New button in the Text Style dialog box that appears. Type **Title** in the New Style dialog box and click OK.

4. Open the Font Name drop-down and select Garamond. The symbol next to the font name indicates this is a TrueType font. Set Font Style to Bold, and deselect Annotative (see Figure 10.2). Click the Apply button.

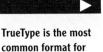

TrueType is the most common format for fonts on both Mac OS and Windows. The names that appear in the Font Name drop-down reflect the fonts installed on your operating system.

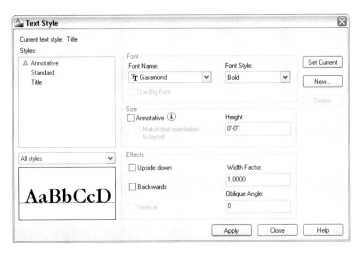

FIGURE 10.2 Configuring the Title style

AutoCAD SHX fonts were designed to optimize motion in pen plotters (now obsolete) but are still commonly used today as simple fonts suitable for architectural and engineering lettering.

5. Select Standard in the Styles list on the left side of the Text Style dialog box. Open the Font Name drop-down and select simplex.shx. The symbol next to the font name indicates this is a shape-based font that is specific to AutoCAD. Type **1'-0"** (or **30** cm) in the Height text box. Type **0.8000** as the Width Factor value in the Effects area so that this style will be 20 percent narrower than the default. Click the Apply, Set Current, and Close buttons (in that order).

6. Save your work as Ch10-B.dwg or Ch10-B-metric.dwg. The styles you created are saved within the drawing even though you can't see them on the drawing canvas.

Writing Lines of Text

You will use the TEXT command when you want to create a single line of text. TEXT creates independent objects on every line so that these objects are suitable for use in symbols or labels on drawings. You will learn how to create text that fits within a specified linear distance so that the text fits within a rectangle or circle, for example. In addition, you will justify text so that it can be easily reused and its content changed without having to reposition the text every time to maintain alignment with surrounding geometry. You will also discover that text objects can be manipulated and duplicated using many of the commands you already know.

Creating Text to Fit

There are many situations where you will want to fit text within geometric objects. For example, you might employ a rectangular symbol in which a number of room names might be displayed in each case where the symbol is to be used. If a text object were always to fit perfectly within the given rectangle, it would simplify having to create rectangles of different widths for each room in which the symbol is to be used. In the following steps, you will create single-line text, justified to fit within just such a rectangular symbol:

1. If the file is not already open from performing the previous step, go to the book's web page, browse to Chapter 10, get the file Ch10-B.dwg or Ch10-B-metric.dwg, and open it.

2. Zoom in on the small rectangle in the upper-left corner of the drawing canvas.

3. Click the Offset tool in the Modify panel, type **4″** (or **10** cm) to set the offset distance, and press Enter. Select the small rectangle, and then click a point inside the rectangle to offset another smaller rectangle inside.

4. Toggle on Object Snap on the status bar. Right-click the same button, and select both Endpoint and Center running object snap modes if they are not already selected.

5. Open the menu under the Text tool on the Annotation panel, and select Single Line from the menu. The command prompt reads:

```
Current text style: "Standard"
Text height: 1'-0" Annotative: No
Specify start point of text or [Justify Style]:
```

Type **J** (for Justify), and press Enter.

6. The command prompt now reads as follows:

```
Enter an option [Align Fit Center Middle
Right TL TC TR ML MC MR BL BC BR]:
```

Type **F** (for Fit), and press Enter. Click points A and B in Figure 10.3. A blinking cursor appears.

FIGURE 10.3 Specifying ends of fit baseline

7. Type **OFFICE**, and press Enter twice. The TEXT command ends and the single line of text appears on the drawing canvas (see Figure 10.4).

FIGURE 10.4 Making single-line text fit within a predefined space

8. Select the inner rectangle, and press the Delete key.

9. Toggle on Ortho mode on the status bar.

10. Click the Move tool on the Modify panel, type **L** (for Last), and press Enter twice. Click an arbitrary point on the drawing canvas, move the cursor upward from that point, type **2"** (or **5** cm), and press Enter. The text moves up so that the word OFFICE is centered within the rectangle (see Figure 10.5).

FIGURE 10.5 Centering the text within the rectangle by moving it upward

11. Save your work as Ch10-C.dwg or Ch10-C-metric.dwg.

Justifying Text

AutoCAD has numerous options that let you justify text to suit almost any conceivable geometric situation. In the following steps, you will align text so that it appears centered within a *callout symbol* indicating the drawing and sheet number:

1. If the file is not already open from performing the previous step, go to the book's web page, browse to Chapter 10, get the file Ch10-C.dwg or Ch10-C-metric.dwg, and open it.

2. Click the Pan tool in the Navigation bar, and drag from right to left to reveal the circle with a line running through it. Press Esc to exit the Pan tool.

3. Type **TEXT**, and press Enter. The command prompt reads:

```
Specify start point of text or [Justify Style]:
```

Type **J** (for Justify), and press Enter.

4. The command prompt now reads:

```
Enter an option [Align Fit Center Middle Right
TL TC TR ML MC MR BL BC BR]:
```

Type **MC** (for Middle Center), and press Enter. Type **CEN** (for Center), and click the circle to make the center of the circle the middle point of the text. Press Enter to accept zero as the default rotation angle. Type **3**, and press Enter twice.

5. Click the Move tool on the Modify panel, type **L** (for Last), and press Enter twice. Click an arbitrary point on the drawing canvas, move the cursor upward from that point, type **18″** (or **40** cm), and press Enter. The text is centered within the upper semicircle.

6. Save your work as Ch10-D.dwg or Ch10-D-metric.dwg.

If you press **Enter** when the command prompt says **Specify start point of text or [Justify Style]:**, the new text object will appear directly below the previous text object on the next line. Be aware that each text line is a separate object, however.

Transforming and Creating Text

Text objects can be transformed with the same commands you might use on other types of objects, commands such as MOVE, COPY, ROTATE, SCALE, and MIRROR. In the following steps, you will mirror and copy existing text to create new text objects whose content you will alter later in the "Editing Text" section. In addition, you will create new text in a different style.

1. If the file is not already open, go to the book's web page, browse to Chapter 10, get the file Ch10-D.dwg or Ch10-D-metric.dwg, and open it.

2. Click the Mirror tool on the Modify panel, select the text object (3), and press Enter. Click the Endpoint at point A and the Center point at B, as shown in Figure 10.6, to define the mirror. The command line reads:

   ```
   Erase source objects? [Yes No] <N>:
   ```

3. Press Enter to accept the default, No, and the MIRROR command is done.

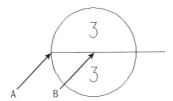

FIGURE 10.6 Mirroring text to create a duplicate text object

Transforming and editing existing text is an alternative to creating new text objects from scratch.

4. Click the Copy tool on the Modify panel, type **L** (for Last), and press Enter twice. Click an arbitrary point on the drawing canvas, move the cursor to the right from this point, type **4′** (or **140** cm), and press Enter twice. A new text object is created to the right of the text you mirrored in the previous step.

5. Click the Single line text tool on the Annotation panel. The command prompt reads:

   ```
   Specify start point of text or [Justify Style]:
   ```

6. Type **S** (for Style), and press Enter. Type **Title** (the name of one of the styles you created in the "Creating Text Styles" section), and press Enter. Title is now the current style.

7. Click point A in Figure 10.7 as the start point of text. The command prompt now reads:

   ```
   Specify height <6">:
   ```

MIRRORING TEXT

Set the MIRRTEXT system variable to 1 to mirror text as well as objects with the MIRROR command. Text mirrored with MIRRTEXT set to 1 appears backward or upside down.

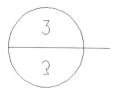

8. Type **1′-6″** (or **45** cm) to specify the text height and press Enter. Press Enter again to accept a default rotation of zero degrees (horizontal). Type **Drawing Title**, and press Enter twice to end the TEXT command.

9. Save your work as Ch10-E.dwg or Ch10-E-metric.dwg.

> You are only prompted to enter a text height in text objects whose style's text height is set to zero.

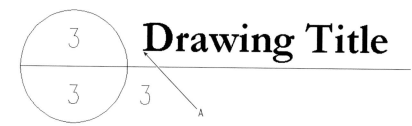

FIGURE 10.7 Creating Title text

Writing and Formatting Paragraphs of Text Using MTEXT

The MTEXT command is a word processing program within AutoCAD that treats all the lines and paragraphs you write as a single object. The powerful MTEXT command gives you word wrap, per-letter style overrides, tabs, inline spell checking, control over line spacing, bulleted and numbered lists, column formatting, and many other features.

MTEXT is ideally suited to writing general notes on drawings and other lengthy blocks of text. In the following steps, you will create and format some unusual general notes. Instead of typing multiple paragraphs, you'll import one of the most famous monologues in the English language and turn it into a series of hypothetical steps.

1. If the file is not already open, go to the book's web page, browse to Chapter 10, get the file Ch10-E.dwg or Ch10-E-metric.dwg, and open it. In addition, get the file Hamlet.txt and double-click the file to open it in Notepad on the PC or TextEdit on the Mac. Select Format ➤ Word Wrap in Notepad to see the text wrap onto multiple lines if necessary.

2. Press Alt+Tab to switch back to AutoCAD. Pan over to the large rectangle in Ch10-E.dwg or Ch10-E-metric.dwg.

Text objects are created in the current style.

3. Type **ST** (for Style), and press Enter. Double-click Standard in the Styles list on the left side of the Text Style dialog box. Standard is now the current style. Click the Close button.

Certification Objective

4. Open the menu under the Text tool on the Annotation panel, and select Multiline Text from the menu. Click points A and B, as shown in Figure 10.8.

FIGURE 10.8 Specifying the opposite corners of a block of multiline text

5. The Text Editor context tab appears on the ribbon. Expand its Tools panel, and click the Import Text button, as shown in Figure 10.9.

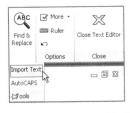

FIGURE 10.9 The Text Editor context tab appears when you're creating or editing MTEXT objects.

CONTEXT TAB OR IN-PLACE EDITOR

If you are in a workspace that doesn't support the ribbon (such as AutoCAD Classic), then the Text Editor context tab cannot appear. Instead, you will see the In-Place Editor, which has most of the same functionality.

6. Click Hamlet.txt in the Select File dialog box that appears. Click Open, and text appears within the large rectangle (see Figure 10.10). The built-in spell checker identifies misspelled words by underlining them in red. Perhaps this is not surprising for English written 400 years ago, but in your own projects, right-click any underlined word that seems incorrect (which wouldn't include company or product names, or technical jargon most likely) for correctly spelled suggestions.

To be, or not to be — that is the question: whether 'tis nobler in the mind to suffer the slings and arrows of outrageous fortune or to take arms against a sea of troubles, and by opposing end them. To die to sleep no more; and by a sleep to say we end the heartache, and the thousand natural shocks that flesh is heir to. 'Tis a consummation devoutly to be wish'd. To die to sleep. To sleep perchance to dream: ay, there's the rub! For in that sleep of death what dreams may come when we have shuffled off this mortal coil, must give us pause. There's the respect that makes calamity of so long life. For who would bear the whips and scorns of time, th' oppressor's wrong, the proud man's contumely, the pangs of despis'd love, the law's delay, the insolence of office, and the spurns that patient merit of th' unworthy takes, when he himself might his quietus make with a bare bodkin? Who would these fardels bear, to grunt and sweat under a weary life, but that the dread of something after death the undiscover'd country, from whose bourn no traveller returns puzzles the will, and makes us rather bear those ills we have than fly to others that we know not of? Thus conscience does make cowards of us all, and thus the native hue of resolution is sicklied o'er with the pale cast of thought, and enterprises of great pith and moment with this regard their currents turn awry and lose the name of action. Soft you now! The fair Ophelia! Nymph, in thy orisons be all my sins rememb'red.

FIGURE 10.10 Importing text with the MTEXT command

7. Drag the cursor from the end to the beginning of the block of text, and highlight all the text. Open the Bullets And Numbering menu, and choose Numbered from the list. The number 1 appears at the start of the text. Click strategic points in the text, and press Enter to separate the paragraph into the numbered notes shown in Figure 10.11. Don't worry if the text extends below the lower edge of the rectangle (it should).

If you exit the text editor, reactivate it by double-clicking the text block. Click within a block of text you are creating or editing to place the cursor at that location. Double-click to select an entire word. Triple-click to select an entire paragraph.

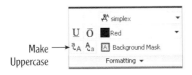

1. To be, or not to be — that is the question: whether 'tis nobler in the mind to suffer the slings and arrows of outrageous fortune or to take arms against a sea of troubles, and by opposing end them.
2. To die to sleep no more; and by a sleep to say we end the heartache, and the thousand natural shocks that flesh is heir to. 'Tis a consummation devoutly to be wish'd. To die to sleep.
3. To sleep perchance to dream: ay, there's the rub! For in that sleep of death what dreams may come when we have shuffled off this mortal coil, must give us pause. There's the respect that makes calamity of so long life.
4. For who would bear the whips and scorns of time, th' oppressor's wrong, the proud man's contumely, the pangs of despis'd love, the law's delay, the insolence of office, and the spurns that patient merit of th' unworthy takes, when he himself might his quietus make with a bare bodkin?
5. Who would these fardels bear, to grunt and sweat under a weary life, but that the dread of something after death the undiscover'd country, from whose bourn no traveller returns puzzles the will, and makes us rather bear those ills we have than fly to others that we know not of?
6. Thus conscience does make cowards of us all, and thus the native hue of resolution is sicklied o'er with the pale cast of thought, and enterprises of great pith and moment with this regard their currents turn awry and lose the name of action.
7. Soft you now! The fair Ophelia! Nymph, in thy orisons be all my sins rememb'red.

FIGURE 10.11 Turning a block of text into a series of numbered notes

AutoCAD 2013 now includes a Strikethrough text toggle so that you can show errata.

8. Click within the block of text to deselect all text. Drag out a selection that includes the phrase "To be or not to be – that is the question." Open the Text Editor Color Gallery drop-down in the Formatting panel and select Red. Click the Make Uppercase button in the same panel (see Figure 10.12).

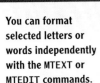

FIGURE 10.12 Formatting selected text

9. Click anywhere outside the block of text on the drawing canvas to end the MTEXT command.

You can format selected letters or words independently with the MTEXT or MTEDIT commands.

10. Save your work as Ch10-F.dwg or Ch10-F-metric.dwg.

Editing Text

Editing text can mean many different things, from changing content (the words) and text object properties, to creating multiple columns of text. You would be very frustrated indeed if you couldn't correct typographical errors because everyone seems to make them. Fortunately, editing text is as simple as double-clicking, highlighting the text in question, and retyping. It is also easy to create multiple columns in AutoCAD by dragging a grip. Creating columns of text can help you fit the required words into the space available on your drawings.

Editing Content and Properties

Editing text content is as simple as double-clicking existing text and typing something new. Editing text properties requires you to use the Quick Properties palette or the Properties panel. In the following steps, you will edit both content and properties:

1. If the file is not already open, go to the book's web page, browse to Chapter 10, get the file Ch10-F.dwg or Ch10-F-metric.dwg, and open it.

2. Double-click the text in the lower semicircle of the drawing title symbol to invoke the DDEDIT command. The number 3 is highlighted. Type **A-4**, click outside the editing window on the drawing canvas, and press Esc to stop editing. The bubble now references the hypothetical drawing 3 on sheet A-4 (see Figure 10.13).

Certification Objective

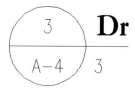

FIGURE 10.13 Edited text

3. Toggle on Quick Properties on the status bar, and select the 3 under the text Drawing Title. In the Quick Properties window that appears, change Justify to Middle Left and type **Scale: 1/8″ = 1′-0″** (or **Scale: 1:20**) in the Contents text box (see Figure 10.14).

Use the Properties palette to access more property values than Quick Properties shows.

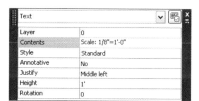

FIGURE 10.14 Editing text content and justification using Quick Properties

4. Press Enter to update the selected object. Press Esc to deselect. Toggle off Quick Properties. Figure 10.15 shows the result.

5. Save your work as Ch10-G.dwg or Ch10-G-metric.dwg.

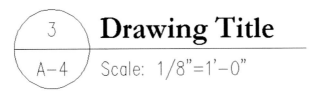

FIGURE 10.15 Edited text content and properties

Working with Columns

You can create multiple columns easily with any multiline text object. This feature is perfect if the text you have written doesn't fit into the space between the drawing and its title block on a typical drawing. Creating multiple columns gives you more layout options, allowing you to find the best fit for paragraphs of text within the space available. In the following steps, you will move object grips to create and size two columns:

1. If the file is not already open, go to the book's web page, browse to Chapter 10, get the file Ch10-G.dwg or Ch10-G-metric.dwg, and open it.

2. Click once on the numbered Hamlet text to select it and reveal its grips. Click the Column Height (bottom) grip, move it upward, and click again, automatically creating two columns, as shown in Figure 10.16.

FIGURE 10.16 Moving the bottom grip up to create two columns

3. Click the Column Width (middle) grip, and move it to the left to reduce the size of both columns simultaneously. Click to set its new position. Click and move the right grip until it reaches the right edge of the rectangle, and then click to set its new position (see Figure 10.17).

4. The first column is too short compared to the right column. Move the Column Height (bottom) grip down until the text in both columns is roughly equalized. Press Esc to deselect the text. Select the rectangle, and press the Delete key. Figure 10.18 shows the result.

5. Save your work as Ch10-H.dwg or Ch10-H-metric.dwg.

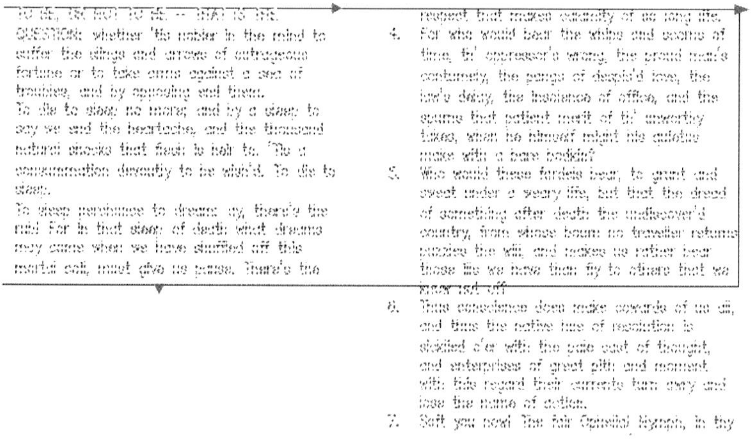

FIGURE 10.17 Moving the middle grip to the left to resize columns

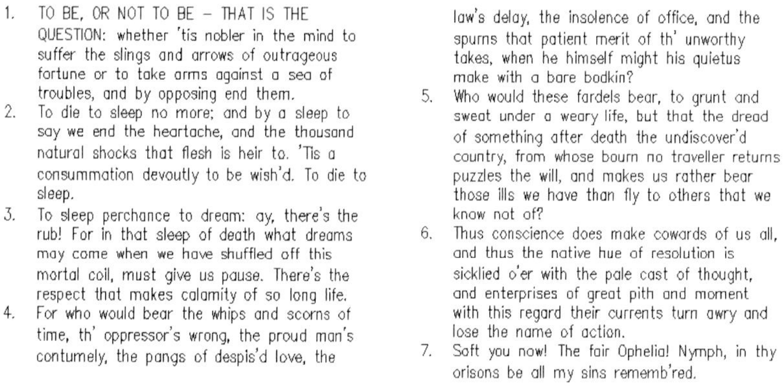

1. TO BE, OR NOT TO BE – THAT IS THE QUESTION: whether 'tis nobler in the mind to suffer the slings and arrows of outrageous fortune or to take arms against a sea of troubles, and by opposing end them.
2. To die to sleep no more; and by a sleep to say we end the heartache, and the thousand natural shocks that flesh is heir to. 'Tis a consummation devoutly to be wish'd. To die to sleep.
3. To sleep perchance to dream: ay, there's the rub! For in that sleep of death what dreams may come when we have shuffled off this mortal coil, must give us pause. There's the respect that makes calamity of so long life.
4. For who would bear the whips and scorns of time, th' oppressor's wrong, the proud man's contumely, the pangs of despis'd love, the law's delay, the insolence of office, and the spurns that patient merit of th' unworthy takes, when he himself might his quietus make with a bare bodkin?
5. Who would these fardels bear, to grunt and sweat under a weary life, but that the dread of something after death the undiscover'd country, from whose bourn no traveller returns puzzles the will, and makes us rather bear those ills we have than fly to others that we know not of?
6. Thus conscience does make cowards of us all, and thus the native hue of resolution is sicklied o'er with the pale cast of thought, and enterprises of great pith and moment with this regard their currents turn awry and lose the name of action.
7. Soft you now! The fair Ophelia! Nymph, in thy orisons be all my sins rememb'red.

FIGURE 10.18 The result after resizing the column length and deleting the rectangle

THE ESSENTIALS AND BEYOND

In this chapter, you learned how to work with text. You created text styles, wrote and justified single lines of text, and imported multiple paragraphs of text. In addition, you edited and styled multiline text and learned to control its appearance. You should now be able to express yourself in written form within AutoCAD, and thus convey your design intent both graphically and literally.

(Continues)

8. The area within the circle turns green to give you a visual indication of which area and circumference are measured. Figure 11.12 shows the circle's area of π and circumference of 2 π. Press Esc and the MEASUREGEOM command ends.

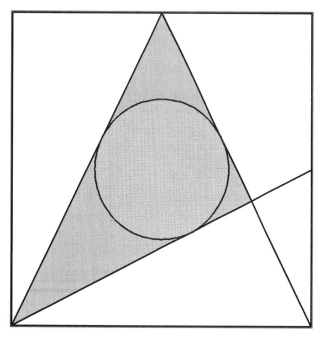

FIGURE 11.12 Measured area shown in green

Adding Dimension Objects

In the following steps, you'll add dimension objects one at a time using a variety of specialized tools to produce dimensions that are linear, aligned, angular, radial, and so on.

1. If the file is not already open from performing the previous step, go to the book's web page, browse to Chapter 11, get the file Ch11-B.dwg, and open it.

2. Toggle on Object Snap mode on the status bar if it is not already on. Right-click this button, and turn on Endpoint and Intersection running object snap modes if necessary.

Certification Objective **3.** Click the Linear dimension tool on the Annotation panel. Click points A and B to specify the first and second extension line origin points, as shown in Figure 11.13. Click point C to specify the dimension line location.

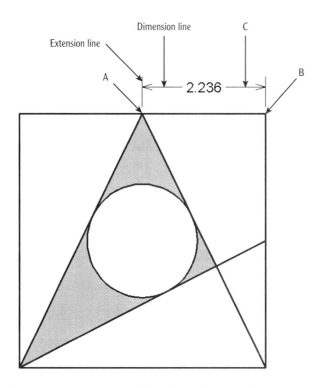

Extension line

Dimension line   C

A   B

2.236

FIGURE 11.13 Creating a linear dimension by clicking three points

4. Press the spacebar to repeat the last command. The command prompt reads:

    Specify first extension line origin or <select object>:

Press Enter to accept the default option (Select Object). Click the top red line, and then click point A, as shown in Figure 11.14.

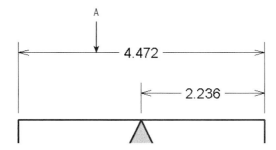

A

4.472

2.236

FIGURE 11.14 Creating a linear dimension by selecting an object and its dimension line location

5. Type **DIMCENTER** (for Dimension Center Mark), and press Enter. Select the circle, and a small crosshair symbol appears at the center of the circle.

6. Type **DIMLIN** (the alias for the DIMLINEAR command), and press Enter. Click points A, B, and C, as shown in Figure 11.15.

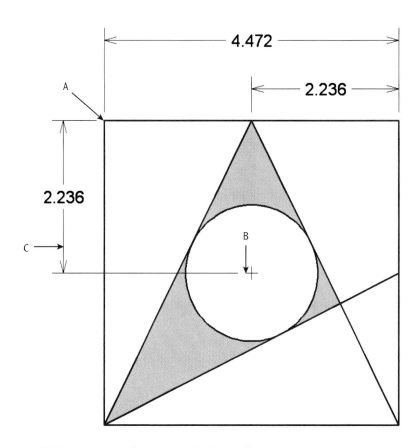

FIGURE 11.15 Creating another linear dimension

Using DIMCONTINUE to add adjacent linear dimensions is more efficient than using DIMLINEAR.

7. Type **DIMCONTINUE** (for Dimension Continue), and press Enter. Click point A, as shown in Figure 11.10, to add another linear dimension below the previous one. Press Esc to end the command.

8. Open the dimension menu in the Annotation panel, and select the Aligned tool. Click points A, B, and C, as shown in Figure 11.16.

9. Add the four additional aligned dimensions shown in Figure 11.17 measuring 1, 2, 3, and 4 units.

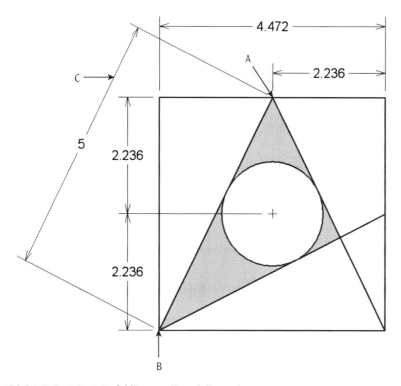

FIGURE 11.16 Adding an aligned dimension

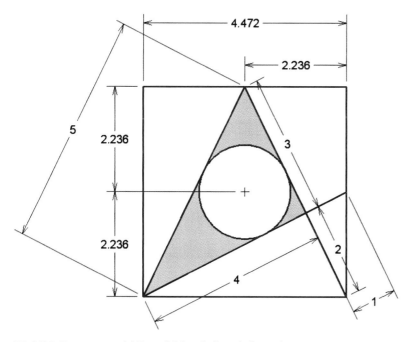

FIGURE 11.17 Adding additional aligned dimensions

10. Open the dimension menu in the Annotation panel, and select the Angular tool. Select lines 1 and 2, as shown in Figure 11.18, and then click point A. Press the spacebar to repeat the DIMANGULAR command, select lines 2 and 3, and then click point B.

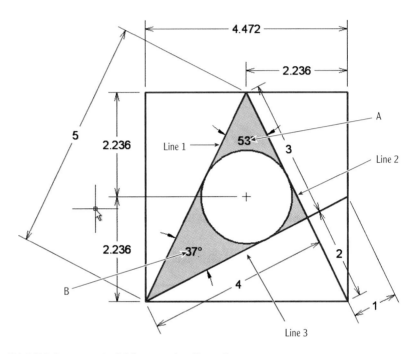

FIGURE 11.18 Adding angular dimensions

11. Open the dimension menu in the Annotation panel, and select the Radius tool. Select the circle, and then click a point inside the circle to locate the radius value (see Figure 11.19).

12. Save your work as Ch11-C.dwg.

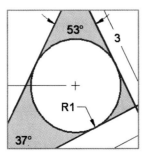

FIGURE 11.19 Adding a radius dimension

Adding and Styling Multileaders

A *multileader* is text with a line tipped by an arrowhead that leads the eye to specific geometric features. Multileader styles control the appearance of leader objects in much the same way that dimension styles control the appearance of dimensions. In the following steps, you will add a leader object and then configure the multileader style.

1. If the file is not already open, browse to Chapter 11, get the file Ch11-C.dwg, and open it.

 2. Select the Leader tool in the Annotation panel. Click points A and B, type **Area of circle** = **3.142** (as shown in Figure 11.20), and then press Ctrl+Enter. You have to use Ctrl in addition to Enter to end the command because Enter by itself advances to the next line.

Certification
Objective

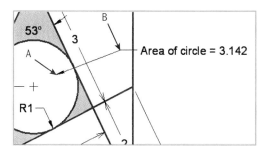

FIGURE 11.20 Adding a leader object

 3. Expand the Annotation panel, and select the Multileader Style button. Click the Modify button in the Multileader Style Manager dialog box that appears.

4. Choose Dot from the Symbol drop-down in the Arrowhead section on the Leader Format tab of the Modify Multileader Style: Standard dialog box (see Figure 11.21). Click OK and Close, and the leader object automatically has a dot on its end.

5. Save your work as Ch11-D.dwg.

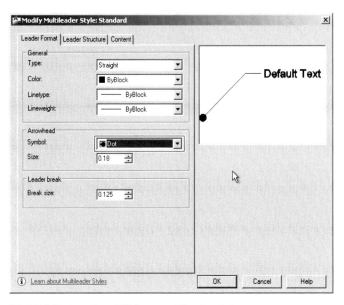

FIGURE 11.21 Editing a multileader style

Editing Dimensions

Dimensions have grips that allow you to reposition extension lines, the dimension line, and dimension text independently of one another. In the following steps, you will edit the length and location of extension and dimension lines directly with grips, adjust a dimension style to affect the appearance of dimension objects, and use a few specialized dimension-editing commands:

1. If the file is not already open, browse to Chapter 11, get the file Ch11-D.dwg, and open it.

2. Toggle on Object Snap mode on the status bar if it is not already on. Right-click the Object Snap button, and turn on Endpoint and Intersection running object snap modes.

Certification Objective

3. Click the horizontal linear dimension with a value of 2.236 to select it. Click the lower-left grip to adjust the length of this extension line. Snap the grip to point A, as shown in Figure 11.22. Press Esc to deselect.

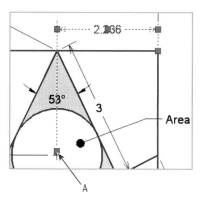

FIGURE 11.22 Grip-editing a dimension object

4. Type **D** (alias for the DIMSTYLE command), and press Enter. Select the Angular substyle in the Dimension Style Manager that appears, and click the Modify button.

5. Select the Fit tab in the Modify Dimension Style: Standard: Angular dialog box. Select the Text radio button in the Fit Options section (see Figure 11.23). Click OK and Close to close all open dialog boxes. The angular values appear outside the lines being measured.

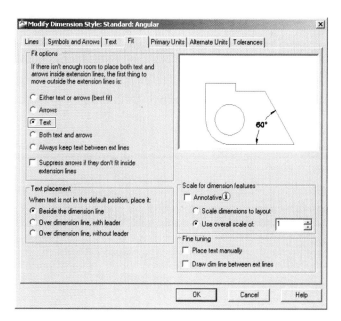

FIGURE 11.23 Changing a fit option in the dimension style

6. Type **DIMEDIT** (for Dimension Edit), and press Enter. The command prompt reads:

```
Enter type of dimension editing
[Home New Rotate Oblique] <Home>:
```

7. Type **N** (for New), and press Enter. A text-editing window appears below the last text you entered. Delete the zero.

8. Type **EQ** (for Equal), and then press Ctrl+Enter to end text entry mode. Select both vertical linear dimensions having values of 2.236, and press Enter. Figure 11.24 shows the result.

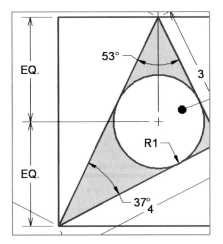

FIGURE 11.24 Editing dimension text content with DIMEDIT

9. Type **DIMTEDIT** (for Dimension Text Edit), and press Enter. Select the aligned dimension with a value of 2 and press Enter. The command prompt reads:

```
Specify new location for dimension text or
[Left Right Center Home Angle]:
```

10. Type **L** (for Left), and press Enter. The dimension text is now left-justified in relation to the dimension line, so the 2 is more easily read within the whitespace left within the red lines (see Figure 11.25).

11. Select the ribbon's Annotate tab, and click the Break tool on the Dimensions panel. The command prompt reads:

```
Select dimension to add/remove break or [Multiple]:
```

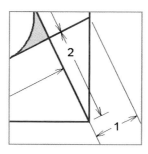

FIGURE 11.25
Changing dimension text
justification with DIMTEDIT

12. Type **M** (for Multiple), and press Enter. Select the dimensions with values of 2.236, 3, and 5 and press Enter. The command prompt reads:

```
Select object to break dimensions or [Auto Remove] <Auto>:
```

13. Press Enter to accept the default Auto option, and the DIMBREAK command ends. Breaks are made in the selected dimensions where they cross other objects (see Figure 11.26).

14. Your drawing should now resemble Ch11-E.dwg, which is available at this book's web page.

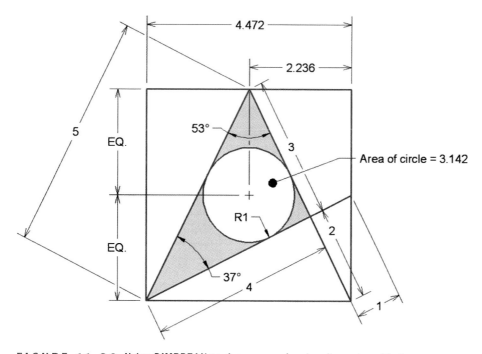

FIGURE 11.26 Using DIMBREAK to clean up overlapping dimension objects

THE ESSENTIALS AND BEYOND

In this chapter, you took your first steps in the art of dimensioning. You learned how to adjust dimension styles and create new substyles; how to add linear, aligned, angular, and radial dimension objects; and how to edit dimensions using a variety of techniques.

ADDITIONAL EXERCISE

Explore the DIMBASELINE command on your own. Baseline dimensions all reference the same base point to eliminate cumulative errors that can crop up due to rounding errors between consecutive adjacent dimensions. Try creating two sets of baseline dimensions that reference the left and bottom edges of the diagram shown here:

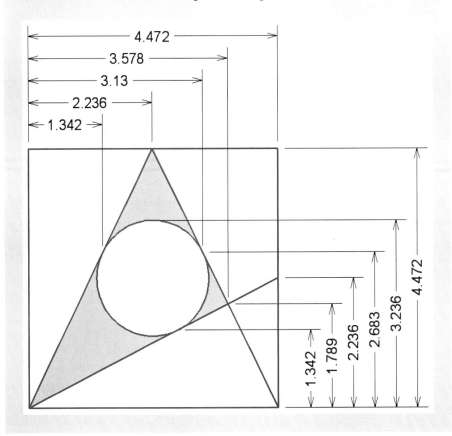

Keeping In Control with Constraints

Constraints are specific restrictions applied to objects that allow for design exploration while maintaining object shape and/or size within predefined limits. In this chapter, you will create three types of constraints in the AutoCAD® program: geometric, dimensional, and user-created. Once the design has been sufficiently constrained, you will make a host of geometric and dimensional changes simply by changing a single parameter.

▶ **Working with geometric constraints**

▶ **Applying dimensional constraints and creating user parameters**

▶ **Constraining objects simultaneously with geometry and dimensions**

▶ **Making parametric changes to constrained objects**

Working with Geometric Constraints

Geometric constraints allow you to force specific 2D objects to be coincident, collinear, concentric, parallel, perpendicular, horizontal, vertical, tangent, smooth, and symmetric; to have equal lengths; or to be fixed in world space. In the following steps, you will assign sufficient geometric constraints to ensure that a rectangle will always remain square even when it is stretched:

1. Go to the book's web page at www.sybex.com/go /autocad2013essentials, browse to Chapter 12, get the file Ch12-A.dwg, and open it.

2. Select the Rectangle tool on the Draw panel. Click two points on the drawing canvas to create an arbitrarily sized rectangle.

3. Toggle Infer Constraints mode on in the status bar.

4. Press the spacebar to repeat the RECTANG (for Rectangle) command, and then click two more points to draw another arbitrarily

sized rectangle adjacent and to the right of the first one (see Figure 12.1). AutoCAD automatically infers perpendicular and parallel constraints from the geometry of the second rectangle.

Parallel, collinear, concentric, and equal constraints always appear in pairs.

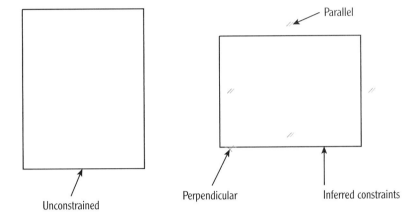

FIGURE 12.1 Drawing two rectangles, one unconstrained

5. Toggle off Infer Constraints mode by pressing Ctrl+Shift+I.

6. Select both rectangles with a crossing selection window. Hover the cursor over the upper-right grip of the left rectangle, select Stretch Vertex from the grip menu that appears, and stretch it up and to the right so that the rectangle deforms. Hover the cursor over the upper-right grip of the right rectangle, select Stretch Vertex from the grip menu, stretch it up and to the right, and click to set its new location. The rectangle remains a rectangle because of the constraints (see Figure 12.2). Press Esc to deselect.

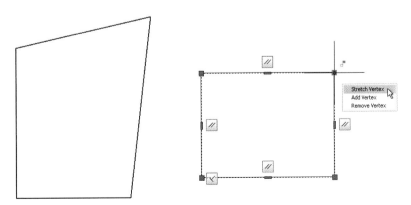

FIGURE 12.2 Stretching constrained geometry limits the types of transformation that can occur.

7. Select the Parametric tab on the ribbon, and select the Auto Constrain tool in the Geometric panel. Select the unconstrained rectangle on the left and press Enter. Two constraints are applied: perpendicular and horizontal (see Figure 12.3).

> **Objects are never repositioned when inferring constraints or when using the Auto Constrain tool. Objects can be repositioned when applying constraints manually.**

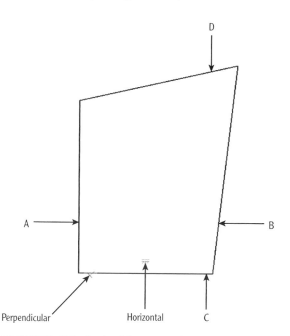

FIGURE 12.3 Applying constraints with the Auto Constrain tool

8. Select the Parallel constraint tool in the Geometric panel. Click lines A and B, as shown in Figure 12.3. Line B is automatically repositioned to conform to the parallel constraint applied to line A.

9. Press the spacebar to repeat the GCPARALLEL (for Geometric Constraint Parallel) command. Click lines C and D, as shown in Figure 12.3.

10. The left rectangle not only has parallel and perpendicular constraints like the right rectangle, but also has a horizontal constraint that was applied by the Auto Constrain tool. Select the right rectangle, and press the Delete key.

11. Select the Equal constraint tool in the Geometric panel. Click lines A and C, as shown in Figure 12.3. The rectangle becomes a square (see Figure 12.4).

> **The order in which you select objects can be significant when you apply constraints. The second object will be repositioned in some cases, depending on the constraint that is applied and the shape and position of the objects.**

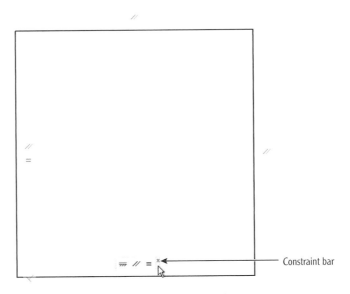

FIGURE 12.4 Applying Equal constraints to adjacent sides turns the rectangle into a square.

Hiding constraints does not remove them; it merely reduces visual clutter.

12. Multiple constraints are grouped together in what is called a *constraint bar*. Position the cursor over the constraint bar, and you'll see a tiny close box. Click it to hide the constraint bar.

 13. Click the Show All button in the Geometric panel. The hidden constraint bar reappears.

14. Right-click the horizontal constraint, and choose Delete from the context menu. The rectangle is no longer constrained horizontally (so you could rotate it if desired).

 15. Click the Hide All button in the Geometric panel. The constraints are hidden but still active.

16. Save your work as Ch12-B.dwg.

Applying Dimensional Constraints and Creating User Parameters

Dimensional constraints allow you to control object sizes with specific numerical values and to set up dynamic dimensional relationships with mathematical equations and formulas. User constraints are not tied to specific geometry but hold values calculated from dimensional constraints. In the following steps, you will create dimensional and user constraints:

1. If the file is not already open from performing the previous step, go to the book's web page, browse to Chapter 12, get the file Ch12-B.dwg, and open it.

2. Select the ribbon's Home tab, open the Layer drop-down in the Layers panel, and select Layer 2 to make it the current layer.

3. Select the Parametric tab on the ribbon. Select the Linear constraint tool in the Dimensional panel, and click *constraint points* A and B, as shown in Figure 12.5. Constraint points highlight in red on screen when you are choosing them. Click point C to locate the dimension line. Press Enter to accept the default dimension text. This dimensional constraint is automatically given the variable name d1.

Constraint points behave similarly to object snaps but are limited to endpoints, midpoints, center points, and insertion points.

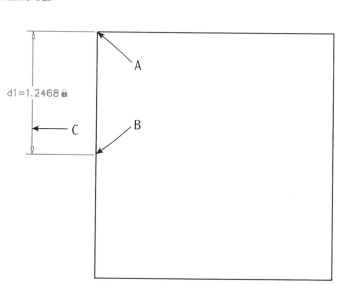

FIGURE 12.5 Creating a vertical linear dimensional constraint

4. Type C (for Circle), and press Enter. Draw an arbitrarily sized circle anywhere within the square.

5. Click the Linear constraint tool in the Dimensional panel, and click the first constraint point in the upper-left corner of the rectangle. Click the circle to accept its center as the second constraint point. Move the cursor upward (see Figure 12.6), and click to place the

3. Click the New Layer button in the Layer Properties Manager that appears. Type **Z-Viewport**, and press Enter. With the Z-Viewport line still highlighted, press Alt+C to make the new layer current. Click the printer icon in the Z-Viewport layer's Plot column to make this layer nonplotting (see Figure 13.9). Close the Layer Properties Manager.

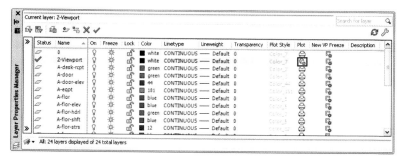

FIGURE 13.9 Creating a nonplotting viewport layer and setting it current

LAYOUT AND MODEL TABS

Layout and model tabs are a legacy interface that longtime AutoCAD users may prefer to keep using. If you see tabs at the bottom of the drawing canvas labeled Model and Layout1, then you are looking at the older interface. Right-click either of these tabs, and choose Hide Layout And Model Tabs to use the more streamlined, modern interface.

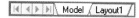

Certification Objective

Paperspace is a 2D space representing a sheet of virtual paper. Modelspace is a 3D space containing both 2D drawings and 3D models.

4. If layout tabs are displayed, click the Layout1 button. If the layout tabs are hidden, click the Quick View Layouts button and then click Layout1 on the status bar or the Layout1 tab on the lower edge of the drawing window. The image in the drawing canvas changes as you enter paperspace: a white representation of paper appears having an automatically created viewport through which you can see the drawing in modelspace. The viewport object is on the Z-Viewport layer. The viewport frame will not appear in the output because it is on a nonplotting layer. The contents of the viewport will be output, however. The dashed lines indicate the limits of the plotting device's printable area (see Figure 13.10).

Edge of paper   Limits of plot device   Viewport

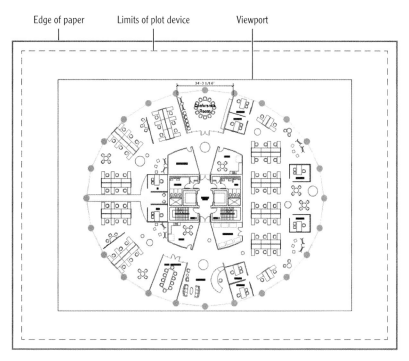

FIGURE 13.10 Viewing a layout in paperspace

5. Select the ribbon's Output tab. Click the Page Setup Manager tool in the Plot panel, and click the Modify button in the Page Setup Manager dialog box that appears. When the Page Setup: Layout1 dialog box opens, select the DWG To PDF.pc3 plotter from the Name drop-down, choose monochrome.ctb from the Plot Style Table drop-down, check Display Plot Styles, and select ANSI Expand A (8.50 × 11.00 Inches)—or ISO Full Bleed A4 (297.00 × 210.00 MM) in metric—as the paper size (see Figure 13.11). Imperial users leave the plot scale at 1 inch = 1 unit, and metric users set the plot scale to 10 mm = 1 unit. Click OK, and then click Close.

Certification
Objective

Available paper sizes are dependent on the plotter selection.

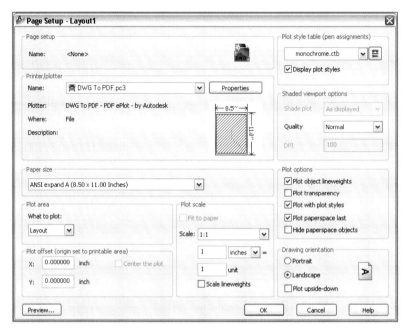

FIGURE 13.11   Configuring a page setup

6. Click Quick View Layouts in the status bar. Click the New Layout icon at the bottom of the Quick View Layouts interface that appears at the bottom of the drawing canvas. Click Layout2 to open it (see Figure 13.12). Click the Close Quick View Layouts icon.

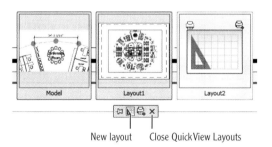

New layout   Close QuickView Layouts

FIGURE 13.12   Creating a new layout through the Quick View Layouts interface

7. Click the Page Setup Manager in the Plot panel. Click the Modify button in the Page Setup Manager dialog box that appears to modify

Layout2. Select the DWG To PDF.pc3 plotter, select monochrome.ctb from the Plot Style Table drop-down, and check Display Plot Styles. Imperial users select ARCH E1 (30.00 × 42.00 Inches) as the paper size; metric users select ISO A0 (841.00 × 1189.00 MM) as the paper size. Imperial users leave the plot scale at 1 inch = 1 unit; metric users set the plot scale to 10 mm = 1 unit. Click OK, and then click Close.

8. A single tiny viewport was automatically created on the current layer in the corner of the layout. You will configure this viewport in the next section and create an additional viewport. Save your work as Ch13-D.dwg or Ch13-D-metric.dwg.

Adjusting Floating Viewports

Think of floating viewports as windows that exist in paperspace through which one sees into modelspace. Viewports are termed *floating* because you can position and size their frames however you like in relation to the paper represented in a layout. You will configure a single floating viewport on Layout1 and two separate viewports on Layout2 to gain experience with viewports.

Working on Layout1

In the following steps, you will set the scale of the building floor plan on Layout 1 and then adjust its viewport to fit the floor plan:

1. If the file is not already open, go to the book's web page, browse to Chapter 13, get the file Ch13-D.dwg or Ch13-D-metric.dwg, and open it.

 2. Click the Quick View Layouts icon on the status bar. Select Layout1, and then press Esc to exit Quick View Layouts mode.

PAPER **3.** Click the PAPER icon on the status bar. This icon toggles between paperspace and modelspace, and the word displays which space you are currently in (now modelspace). The viewport's frame highlights with a thicker representation when displaying modelspace (see Figure 13.13). Move the cursor inside the viewport, and observe that the crosshair cursor is available only within the viewport.

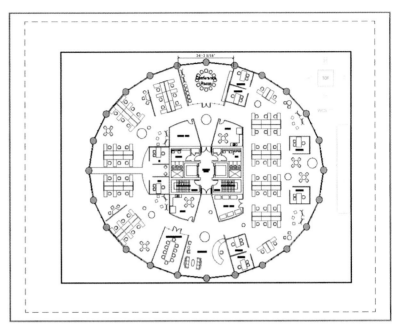

FIGURE 13.13 Modelspace active inside a floating viewport

4. Choose ¹⁄₁₆″ = 1′-0″ (or 1:200 in metric) from the Viewport Scale menu button on the status bar, as shown in Figure 13.14. The viewport zooms into the building core, which is in the center of the plan. At this exact zoom magnification, the plan appears in ¹⁄₁₆″ scale (or 1:200) in the layout.

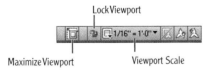

FIGURE 13.14 The status bar's appearance when a floating viewport is active

5. Click the MODEL icon on the status bar to switch back to paperspace. Move the crosshair cursor across the drawing canvas, and observe that it appears across the entire paper.

6. Viewport frames exist in paperspace only. Click the single viewport frame to select it. Select the upper-right grip and move it upward and to the right until it is close to the upper-right corner of the paper but inside the plot device limits. Click the lower-left grip, and move it to the lower-left corner inside the device limits (see Figure 13.15). Press Esc to deselect the viewport.

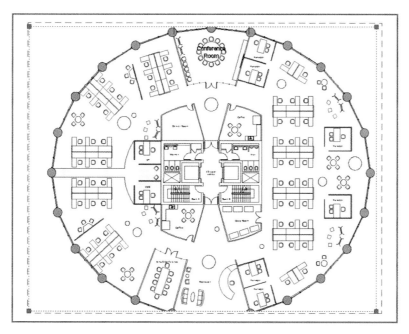

FIGURE 13.15 Adjusting the viewport in an attempt to display the entire floor plan at ⅟₁₆″ scale (or 1:200 in metric)

7. Unfortunately the plan doesn't fit on the page in ⅟₁₆″ scale. Click the PAPER icon on the status bar to switch back into modelspace. Toggle on the Automatically Add Scales to Annotative Objects button in the status bar. Select ⅟₃₂″ = 1′-0″ (or 1:300 in metric) from the Viewport Scale menu button on the status bar. The drawing fits on the page, and new annotative objects are created in this scale.

8. Zoom in and select the single dimension object, and move its dimension line upward for clarity. Note, however, that by zooming, you have changed the viewport scale. Again select ⅟₃₂″ = 1′-0″ (or 1:300 in metric) from the Viewport Scale menu button on the status bar, and pan the drawing to the center of the page (see Figure 13.16).

9. Click the MODEL icon on the status bar to switch back to paperspace.

10. Save your work as Ch13-E.dwg or Ch13-E-metric.dwg.

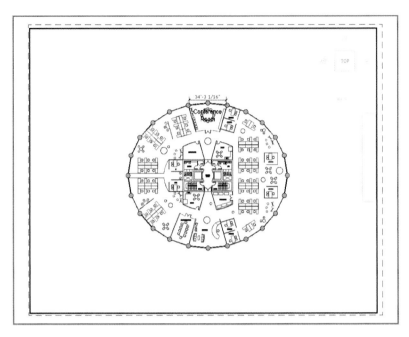

FIGURE 13.16 Finding the largest scale that will fit on the page

Working on Layout2

In the following steps, you will adjust the viewport on Layout2 and, in the process, discover that certain combinations of building geometry, viewport scales, and paper sizes do not always mesh. You will fix the problem by selecting a different viewport scale, and then adjust the viewport to fit the floor plan. In addition, you'll create a viewport from scratch and adjust it.

1. If the file is not already open, go to the book's web page, browse to Chapter 13, get the file Ch13-E.dwg or Ch13-E-metric.dwg, and open it.

Changing the viewport scale automatically triggers a corresponding change in the annotation scale.

2. Click the Quick View Layouts icon on the status bar. Select Layout2, and then press Esc to exit Quick View Layouts mode.

3. As an alternative to clicking PAPER on in the status bar, double-click inside the viewport to activate it. The Paper/Model toggle now indicates that you are in the modelspace of the viewport.

4. Choose ¼″ = 1′-0″ (or 1:40 in metric) from the Viewport Scale menu on the status bar.

5. Double-click the layout outside of the viewport to switch back into paperspace. Move the cursor across the drawing canvas, and observe that you can move it now that it is active across the entire paper.

6. Viewport frames exist in paperspace only. Click the viewport frame to select it. Select the upper-right grip, and move it upward until it is close to the upper-right corner of the paper but inside the plot device limits. Click the lower-left grip, and move it to the lower-left corner inside the device limits. Press Esc to deselect.

7. Double-click inside the viewport to switch back into modelspace. Drag the mouse wheel (but do not turn the wheel) to pan the drawing over within the viewport to center it on the paper. The ¼″ (or 1:50 in metric) scale drawing almost fits, but it's too tight to fit comfortably on ARCH E1 or ISO A0 paper. You couldn't have known this without first creating the layout and trying to fit the drawing to the paper at this specific scale.

8. Verify that the option Automatically Add Scales To Annotative Objects When The Annotation Scale Changes is toggled on in the status bar, and then select ³⁄₁₆″ = 1′-0″ scale (or 1:60 in metric) in the Viewport Scale menu. The floor plan now fits the layout.

9. Double-click the paper outside the viewport to switch back into paperspace. Select the viewport, and grip-edit it so that it closely surrounds the plan geometry. Move the plan to the left on the paper to make room for another drawing on this layout. Figure 13.17 shows the result.

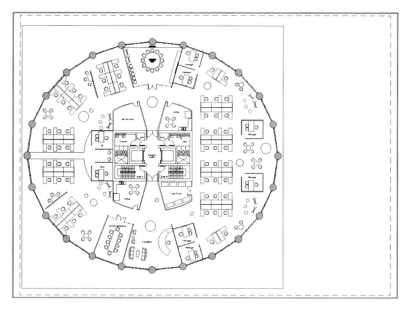

FIGURE 13.17 The drawing fits the paper at ³⁄₁₆″ scale (or 1:50 in metric)

Certification
Objective

10. Type **MV** (for Make Viewport), and press Enter. Click two arbitrary corner points to the right of the existing viewport to create a new viewport. The MVIEW command ends.

11. Double-click within the new viewport to enter its modelspace. Select ½″ = 1′-0″ (or 1:20 in metric) in the Viewport Scale menu on the status bar; the viewports zoom into the Elevator Lobby again. Pan downward until you center the view on the Conference Room. Double-click outside the viewport to return to paperspace. Figure 13.18 shows the result.

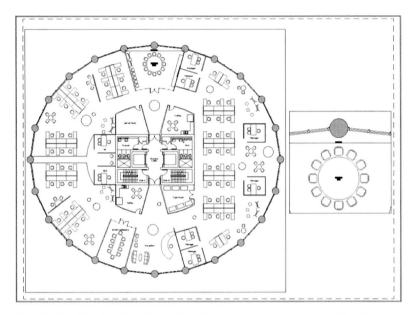

FIGURE 13.18 Creating and configuring a new viewport detailing the Conference Room

12. Select both viewport objects, and then click the Lock Viewport icon on the status bar. Press Esc to deselect. Double-click inside the new viewport, and roll the mouse wheel forward to zoom in. Whereas before when you locked the viewport, only the space within the viewport zoomed in, now the entire layout zooms in.

13. Save your work as Ch13-F.dwg or Ch13-F-metric.dwg.

I recommend that you lock viewports immediately after configuring them so that you don't inadvertently change the drawing scale by zooming.

Overriding Layer Properties in Layout Viewports

Each viewport maintains its own set of layer properties that can override the drawing's basic layer properties. In the following steps, you will use this feature to turn off a selection of layers in a particular viewport, while continuing to display these same layers in another viewport.

1. If the file is not already open, go to the book's web page, browse to Chapter 13, get the file Ch13-F.dwg or Ch13-F-metric.dwg, and open it.

2. Double-click within the larger viewport on Layout2 that shows the entire floor plan to activate it and switch into floating modelspace.

3. Click the Layer Properties tool on the Layers panel on the ribbon's Home tab.

4. Expand the palette to the right by dragging its edge. Observe a set of properties in columns preceded with the letters VP (viewport). Freeze layers A-furn, A-flor-fill, and A-flor-patn in the VP Freeze column (see Figure 13.19).

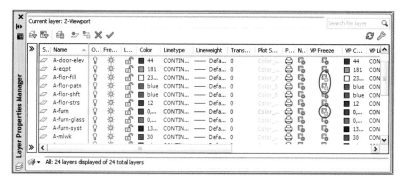

You can override the color, linetype, lineweight, transparency, and/or plot style layer properties independently in each viewport if so desired.

FIGURE 13.19 Freezing selected layers in the current viewport only

5. Double-click on the paper outside the viewport to switch back into paperspace. The furniture and furniture systems disappear from the current viewport, but the Conference Room round table is still visible in the viewport on the right of Layout2 (see Figure 13.20). Close the Layer Properties Manager.

6. Save your work as Ch13-G.dwg or Ch13-G-metric.dwg.

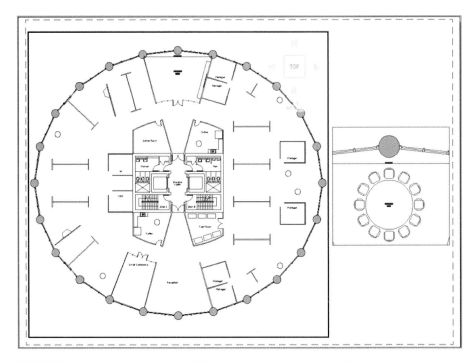

FIGURE 13.20 Furniture is visible in the viewport on the right but not in the left viewport, whose layer properties have been overridden.

Drawing on Layouts

You can draw on layouts just as you can draw in modelspace. However, the types of content drawn on layouts will necessarily be of a different character, such as a title block, viewports and, optionally, dimensions. Layouts have the measurements of physical sheets of paper and are not meant to hold real-world geometry directly (that is what modelspace is used for).

One way to draw directly on layouts is to use *title blocks*, which are borders surrounding the drawing that also have rectangles wherein text identifying the sheet is placed. You can also draw dimensions directly on layouts. Dimensions added in paperspace are associated with geometry in modelspace. Thus if the real-world geometry changes, the dimensions will automatically update.

In the following steps, you will draw a title block and add a dimension to the paperspace of the layout:

1. If the file is not already open, go to the book's web page, browse to Chapter 13, get the file Ch13-G.dwg or Ch13-G-metric.dwg, and open it.

2. Type **LA** (for Layer Properties Manager), and press Enter. Click the New Layer icon, type **Z-Title**, and press Enter. Double-click the new layer to make it current. Select a Lineweight value of 0.039″ (or 1.00 mm) for a thick border. Toggle the Plot icon on. Close the Layer Properties Manager.

3. Click the Rectangle tool in the Draw panel. Click the corner points as closely as possible (you cannot snap to the paper) to the edges of the paper in Layout2.

TITLE BLOCKS

Drawings are legal documents and, as such, typically indicate the drawing scale, sheet name, and sheet number. This information is traditionally shown with text or attributes in a title block, which is drawn directly on the layout.

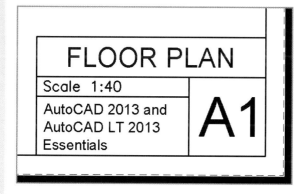

4. Set layer Text current by selecting it in the Layer drop-down in the Layers panel.

5. Verify that the PAPER/MODEL toggle on the status bar reads PAPER. Zoom into the smaller viewport on the right of Layout2.

6. Right-click the Object Snap icon in the status bar, and toggle on quadrant snap. Click the Linear tool in the Annotation panel, and click points A, B, and C as shown in Figure 13.21. Points A and B are on the quadrants of the circle. A dimension measuring 9′-0″ (274 for metric) appears on the layout in paperspace that looks similar to the dimension you drew earlier in this chapter in modelspace.

> Dimensions added in paperspace are necessarily specific to each drawing and cannot be shown simultaneously in multiple viewports as annotative, modelspace dimensions can.

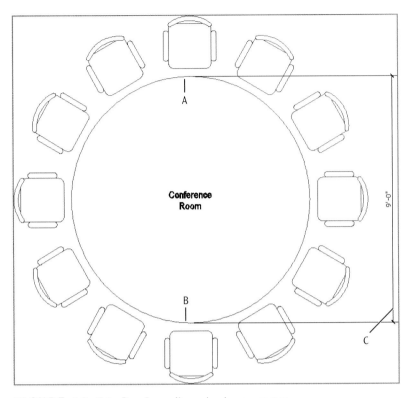

A

Conference
Room

B

9'-0"

C

FIGURE 13.21 Drawing a dimension in paperspace

7. Click Maximize Viewport on the status bar. A red border indicates that you are working in the modelspace of a viewport in maximized mode.

WORKING IN MULTIPLE MAXIMIZED VIEWPORTS

When you work in a maximized viewport on a layout that has more than one viewport, the Next and Previous arrows appear surrounding the status bar toggle. Click these arrow icons to cycle through each and every viewport on a layout while staying in maximized mode.

8. Select the circle representing the table, and select its top quadrant grip. Type **4'8"** (**140** cm in metric), and press Enter to input the new radius. The circle grows slightly larger.

9. Click Minimize Viewport in the status bar. The drawing canvas returns to Layout2. The dimension in paperspace is automatically updated with the value of 9′-4″ (280 cm in metric).

10. Select the Output tab on the ribbon, and click the Preview tool in the Plot panel. What you now see is what you would get if you published this drawing (see Figure 13.22). Press Esc to exit the preview.

11. Save your work as Ch13-H.dwg or Ch13-H-metric.dwg. Your drawing should now resemble the files available on the book's web page.

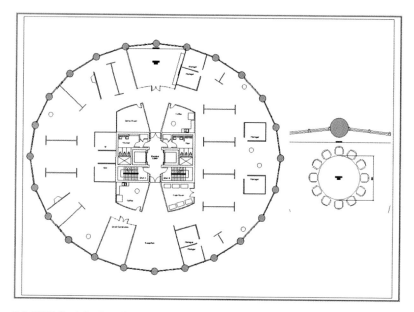

FIGURE 13.22 Plot preview of Layout2

THE ESSENTIALS AND BEYOND

In this chapter, you learned the differences between modelspace and paperspace. You created layouts and viewports, set viewport scales, and adjusted viewports to fit the real-world geometry. In addition, you overrode layer properties in viewports, worked in maximized viewports, drew a title block, and dimensioned in paperspace. In short, you are now fully prepared to create physical and electronic output in the next chapter.

(Continues)

THE ESSENTIALS AND BEYOND   *(Continued)*

ADDITIONAL EXERCISES

TILEMODE is the system variable that switches between modelspace where tiled viewports are possible (TILEMODE=1) and paperspace where floating viewports are possible (TILEMODE=0). Create tiled modelspace viewports with the VPORTS command on your own. You can alternatively create tiled viewports using the leftmost menu in the upperleft corner of the drawing canvas.

Tiled viewports are most useful when working on 3D models to get multiple simultaneous views of complex geometry, but they can also be used to get a simultaneous overview and detailed view of a 2D drawing. Try working at a few different magnifications in Ch13-H .dwg or Ch13-H-metric.dwg with three viewports so that you can see the overall plan and two detailed views simultaneously.

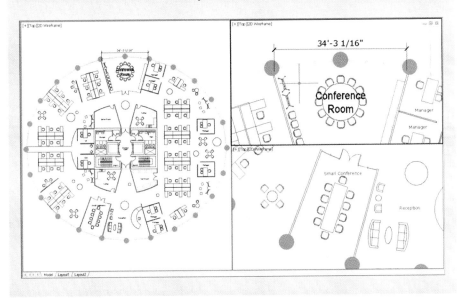

CHAPTER 14

Printing and Plotting

Plotting is the term for producing physical prints using a large-format printer, which is either networked or directly connected to an AutoCAD® workstation. There is much more to plotting a drawing or publishing an entire sheet set than hitting the Print icon, however. Before you can successfully print, you must first learn to configure a plotter and a plot style table; you'll then learn how to create professional output from modelspace and/or paperspace. As you'll see in this chapter, you'll also have the option to keep everything in digital format and export DWF or PDF files that can be shared on the Internet with your partners and clients.

- ▶ **Configuring output devices**

- ▶ **Creating plot style tables**

- ▶ **Using plot style tables**

- ▶ **Plotting in modelspace**

- ▶ **Plotting layouts in paperspace**

- ▶ **Exporting to an electronic format**

Configuring Output Devices

In the most general sense, everything you do on a computer is a form of *input*. Creating physical or even electronic drawings, on the other hand, are forms of *output*. Output devices are more commonly known as printers.

Large-format (24″ wide or larger) printers are marketed as "plotters" because of the history of technology. When I started my career more than 20 years ago, plotters had technical pens in them that you had to refill individually with ink. The paper (actually Mylar film) was rolled back and forth, and the pens literally *plotted* one line at a time. Thankfully, modern inkjet technology is much faster, so you no longer wind up with clogged pens and ink on your hands.

In the following sections, you will configure an output device by setting up a system printer and also an AutoCAD plotter. Once these steps are completed, you won't have to perform them again on the same computer.

Setting Up a System Printer

The first thing you'll need to do is set up a system printer, which contains *drivers* that your operating system uses to control the output device. System printers are not specific to AutoCAD; device manufacturers supply drivers, which you then install to become printers on your system.

If you are reading this book at work, you undoubtedly already have a system printer or your CAD manager has installed one for you. For the purposes of this book however, you will install a driver for the HP DesignJet 800 plotter (an industry workhorse), whether you own this device or not. You will be using the HP DesignJet 800 system printer in this chapter. The following steps guide you in installing this typical system printer:

1. Open your browser, and type **HP DesignJet 800 42 driver** as a Google search. Select the first search result, or go to www.hp.com and search for Download Drivers and Software.

2. Select your operating system from the list, and download the appropriate driver.

3. Install the driver following the manufacturer's instructions. Select File:Port in the installation options because you don't have access to the actual device. If you did have the physical device, you would select the relevant connection port, such as Parallel, Ethernet, USB, or Wireless.

Setting Up an AutoCAD Plotter

AutoCAD for Mac doesn't use AutoCAD plotters but instead outputs directly to the system printers listed under System Preferences.

Most programs send output directly to system printers, but AutoCAD is an exception. AutoCAD has another layer of software between the program and the operating system known as an AutoCAD plotter. In this section, you will set up an AutoCAD plotter that sends its output to the system printer, which in turn hands off the print job to the output device itself.

1. In AutoCAD, type **PLOTTERMANAGER** and press Enter. The Windows Explorer dialog box appears displaying the Add-A-Plotter Wizard and various AutoCAD plotters that have the .pc3 file extension (see Figure 14.1).

2. Double-click the Add-A-Plotter Wizard. Read the Introduction page and click Next.

3. Select the System Printer radio button (see Figure 14.2) and click Next.

FIGURE 14.1 Explorer window showing two folders, the Add-A-Plotter Wizard and various AutoCAD plotters

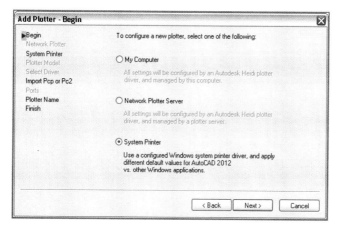

FIGURE 14.2 Selecting the System Printer option in the Add Plotter wizard

PLOTTING RASTER IMAGES TO SCALE

For more information on setting up and plotting to a raster plotter driver in AutoCAD, see my book *Enhancing Architectural Drawings and Models with Photoshop* (Sybex, 2010). Raster images of drawing layers can be output to scale from AutoCAD and enhanced in Photoshop for presentation.

4. Select the HP DesignJet 800 system printer from the list in the Add Plotter – System Printer dialog box (see Figure 14.3). The listed printers will differ on your computer depending on which drivers you (or your CAD manager) have already installed on your system. Click Next.

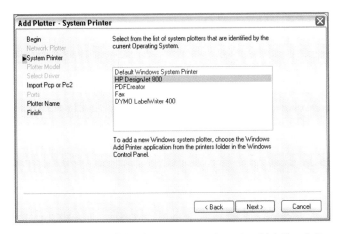

FIGURE 14.3 Selecting a system printer to which the plotter will send data

5. The next page allows you to import a legacy PCP or PC2 file from older versions of AutoCAD. Since you are creating a PC3 file from scratch, click Next to open the Add Plotter – Plotter Name page.

6. AutoCAD now suggests a name for the plotter that is identical to the name of the system printer. Type the name **HP DesignJet 800 Plotter** to differentiate the new printer name from the system printer (see Figure 14.4). Click Next.

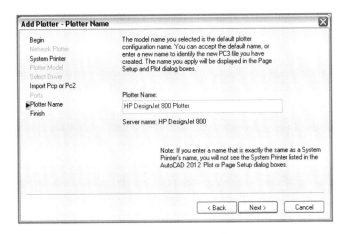

FIGURE 14.4 Giving the plotter a unique name

7. The final page of the Add Plotter wizard allows you to edit the newly created plotter driver itself. Click the Edit Plotter Configuration button to do this.

8. Select the Device And Document Settings tab, and then select the Filter Paper Sizes node in the Plotter Configuration Editor dialog box that appears. Click the Uncheck All button. You should filter the list of paper sizes to display only the sizes you use. Scroll down the list, and select the following paper sizes: Arch C (landscape) and Arch D (landscape). Figure 14.5 shows the result.

Edit the Custom Properties in the Plotter Configuration Editor to access settings specific to the system printer driver.

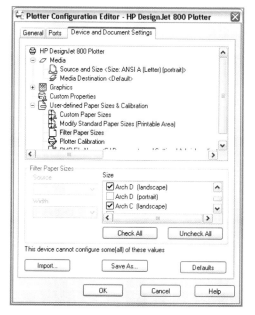

FIGURE 14.5 Filtering out all unused paper sizes

9. Click OK to close the Plotter Configuration Editor. Click Finish to close the Add-A-Plotter Wizard.

10. The new AutoCAD plotter driver you just created, HP DesignJet 800 Plotter.pc3, appears in the Windows Explorer window that was opened in step 1 (see Figure 14.6). Close Windows Explorer.

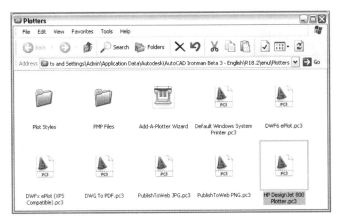

FIGURE 14.6 The new AutoCAD plotter driver appears in Windows Explorer.

Creating Plot Style Tables

Plot style tables determine the final appearance of objects in terms of their color, linetype, lineweight, end cap, line fill, and screening percentage. Plot style tables take precedence over layer properties when the drawing is printed.

In addition to creating a system printer and AutoCAD plotter, you will need to create a plot style table or use an existing one. AutoCAD has two types of plot style tables: color-dependent and named.

Color-Dependent Plot Style Tables (CTB Files) These have been used since the days of pen plotters when you assigned a number of colors in AutoCAD to a specific physical pen. For example, red objects might plot using the 0.5 mm pen and green and yellow objects might use the 0.7 mm pen. Many firms still use color-dependent plot style tables today.

Named Plot Styles (STB Files) These were a new feature in AutoCAD 2000. Named plot style tables offer greater flexibility as compared with color-dependent plot styles because plot criteria can be assigned by layer or by object rather than by color only. In the following exercise, you will create a named plot style. Named plot styles use the .stb file extension.

You cannot create or modify plot styles on the Mac version of AutoCAD—you can use only the default plot styles.

1. Type **STYLESMANAGER**, and press Enter. Windows Explorer appears and displays a number of preset plot style table files (see Figure 14.7).

2. Double-click the Add-A-Plot Style Table Wizard. Click Next after reading the introductory page.

3. Select Start From Scratch on the next page (see Figure 14.8). Click Next.

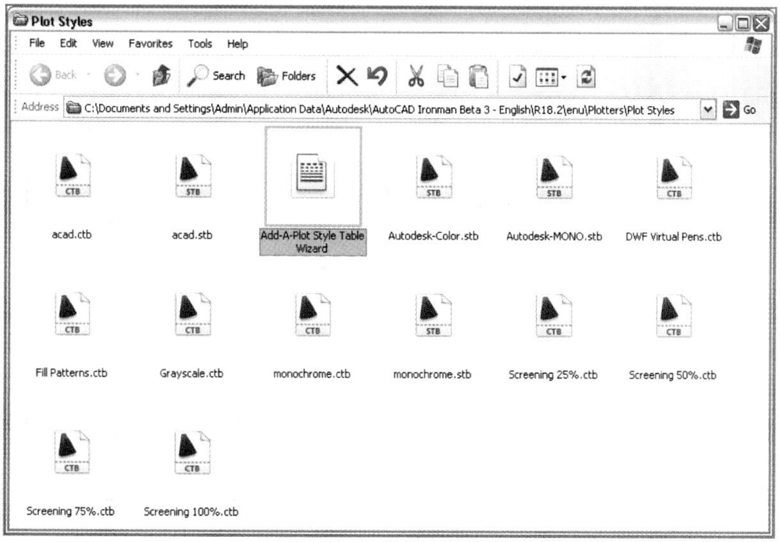

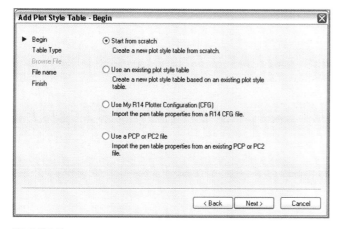

FIGURE 14.7 Windows Explorer showing the plot styles folder

FIGURE 14.8 Starting a plot style table from scratch

4. Select the Named Plot Style radio button on the next page. This will create a named plot style having one default style called Normal. Click Next.

5. For lack of a more descriptive name, type **My plot style** on the File Name page (see Figure 14.9). Click Next.

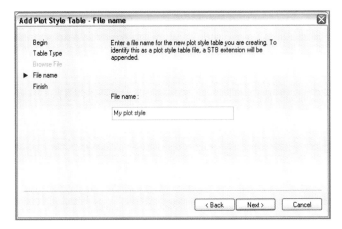

FIGURE 14.9 Typing a name for the plot style

6. The final page of the wizard allows you to edit the newly created STB file itself. Click the Plot Style Table Editor button.

7. Select the Form View tab in the Plot Style Table Editor that appears. Click the Add Style button. Type **Black**, and press Enter.

8. Open the Color drop-down, and select Black (see Figure 14.10).

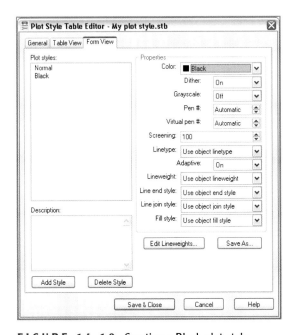

FIGURE 14.10 Creating a Black plot style

9. Click the Add Style button again, type **20% Screen**, and press Enter. Highlight the value next to the word Screening, type **20**, and press Tab. Click Save & Close to close the Plot Style Table Editor.

10. Click Finish to close the Add Plot Style Table wizard. The named plot style table you just created, My plot style.stb, appears in the Windows Explorer window that was opened in step 1 (see Figure 14.11). Click the close box in Windows Explorer.

Screening refers to the intensity of ink sprayed on the paper while plotting. Selecting 100 sprays at full intensity whereas 0 sprays no ink. Intermediate values produce varying levels of grayscale.

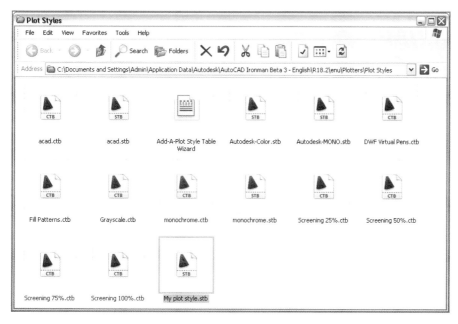

FIGURE 14.11 The newly named plot style table appears in Windows Explorer.

Using Plot Style Tables

New drawings are created using either color-dependent or named plot style tables. A setting in the Options dialog box controls this behavior. Existing drawings must go through a conversion process to switch from utilizing one plot style table type to the other.

In the following exercise, you will configure new drawings to utilize named plot style tables and learn how to use plot styles by layer or by object.

After you or your CAD manager decides which type of plot style table to use consistently, you will want to save a template that records this preference so that you don't have to revisit this issue every time you create a new drawing.

Configuring New Drawings for Named Plot Style Tables

In the following steps, you will configure new drawings to use named plot styles and you will save a template having a named plot style table assigned:

1. Type **OP** (for Options), and press Enter. Select the Plot And Publish tab in the Options dialog box that appears.

2. Click the Plot Style Table Settings button in the lower right of the Options dialog box. Select the Use Named Plot Styles radio button in the Plot Style Table Settings dialog box that appears. Select My plot style .stb from the Default Plot Style Table drop-down menu. Select Black from the Default Plot Style for Layer 0 drop-down menu. Select ByLayer as the Default Plot Style For Objects drop-down menu if it is not already selected (see Figure 14.12). Click OK, and then click OK again to close both of the open dialog boxes.

FIGURE 14.12 Configuring the default plot style behavior and settings for new drawings

3. Click the New button in the Quick Access toolbar. Click the arrow button adjacent to the Open button in the Select Template dialog box that appears. Choose Open With No Template – Imperial from the drop-down menu (see Figure 14.13).

4. Type **UN** (for Units), and press Enter. Choose Architectural units (or Decimal units in metric) with a precision of ¼″ (metric users

choose a precision of 0.0). Set Units To Scale Inserted Content under the Insertion Scale area to Inches (or Centimeters in metric) (see Figure 14.14). Click OK.

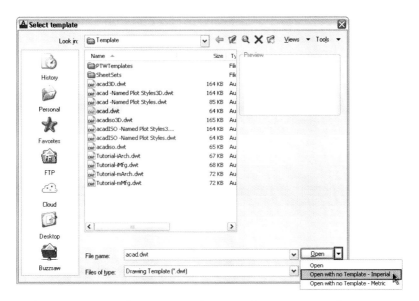

FIGURE 14.13 Creating a new drawing without using a template

FIGURE 14.14 Setting architectural drawing units

5. Click the Save As button in the Quick Access toolbar. Change the Files Of Type drop-down in the Save Drawing As dialog box that

appears to AutoCAD Drawing Template (*.dwt). Type **My template** in the File Name text box (see Figure 14.15). Click Save.

AutoCAD 2013 allows you to save a copy of any template or drawing file automatically in the cloud in the Save As dialog box.

FIGURE 14.15 Saving a new drawing template

6. Type **Named plot styles and architectural units** in the Template Options dialog box that appears (see Figure 14.16). Click OK.

FIGURE 14.16 Describing the template

7. Type **CLOSE**, and press Enter.

You can now create new drawings having named plot styles (and architectural or decimal units) simply by selecting My Template—no other configuration is required.

SWITCHING PLOT STYLE TABLE TYPES IN EXISTING DRAWINGS

If you are switching from named plot styles to color-dependent plot styles in an existing drawing, use the CONVERTPSTYLES command to make the conversion. If you are going in the other direction and converting an existing drawing from color-dependent plot styles to named plot styles, you must first use the CONVERTCTB command and then use CONVERTPSTYLES.

Assigning Plot Styles by Layer or by Object

If you are working in a drawing that uses a color-dependent plot style table, then the plot styles are automatically configured by color. When working on a drawing that uses a named plot style table, you will need to assign named plot styles by layer and/or by object, as shown in the following exercise:

1. Go to the book's web page at www.sybex.com/go/autocad2013essentials, browse to Chapter 14, click on the file Ch14-A.dwg, and open it.

2. Type **LA** (for Layer), and press Enter. Right-click any one of the layer names in the Layer Properties Manager that appears, and choose Select All from the context menu. Click the word Normal in the Plot Style column. The plot style table you created earlier (My plot style .stb) is selected. Choose Black in the Select Plot Style dialog box (see Figure 14.17). Click OK. Now all the layers will plot in black.

FIGURE 14.17 Selecting a plot style to assign to a layer

6. Click the Plot Stamp Settings button, as shown in Figure 14.23. Select Drawing Name, Device Name, and Plot Scale in the Plot Stamp dialog box that appears (see Figure 14.24). Click OK.

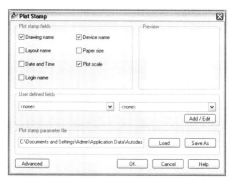

FIGURE 14.24 Configuring the Plot Stamp feature

7. Click the Preview button in the Plot – Model dialog box. Click Continue in the Plot – Plot Scale Confirm dialog box that appears. A preview window temporarily replaces the user interface (see Figure 14.25).

FIGURE 14.25 What you see is what you get in the plot preview window.

8. Click the Plot icon, as shown in Figure 14.25. The plot is immediately sent to the hypothetical HP DesignJet 800 output device. If this device were really attached to your computer, it would start plotting within a few seconds. Once the plot has been sent, a notification window appears in the lower-right corner of the user interface (see Figure 14.26). The plot is complete; click the close box in the notification window.

9. Save your work as Ch14-C.dwg.

FIGURE 14.26 Plot notification window

Plotting Layouts in Paperspace

Layouts are the preferred plotting environment where you can display multiple scaled drawings within viewports, surrounded by title blocks containing text, and/or having dimensions in paperspace. In the following steps, you will create and plot two layouts from paperspace:

1. Open the Ch14-C.dwg file. If this file is not open, find it on the book's web page.

 2. Click the Layout1 icon on the status bar. A single viewport is automatically generated on the layout.

 3. Click the ribbon's Output tab, and click the Page Setup Manager icon in the Plot panel. Click the New button in the Page Setup Manager dialog box that appears. Click OK in the New Page Setup dialog box to accept the default name of Setup1. Click OK to return to the Page Setup Manager.

4. In the Page Setup dialog box that appears, click the Modify button and open the Name drop-down menu and select HP DesignJet 800 Plotter.pc3, select Arch C (landscape) in the Paper Size drop-down menu, and select My plot style.stb in the Plot Style Table drop-down menu (see Figure 14.27). Click OK.

Layouts are always plotted at 1:1 scale in Imperial units. Metric layouts are also plotted at 1:1 scale if one millimeter equals one drawing unit, or at 10:1 scale if you decide one centimeter equals one drawing unit.

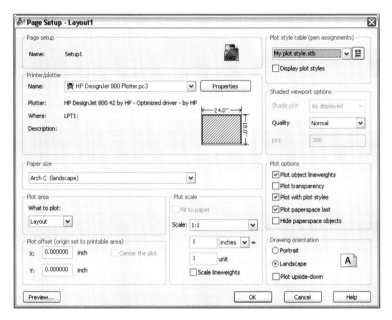

FIGURE 14.27 Configuring a new layout in the Page Setup dialog box

5. The Page Setup Manager dialog box now lists Setup1 as a saved page setup. Select Display When Creating A New Layout (see Figure 14.28). Click the Set Current button, and then click Close.

FIGURE 14.28 Saving a page setup for use in the next layout

6. Double-click within the viewport to activate floating modelspace. Select ⅜″ = 1′-0″ from the Viewport Scale menu on the status bar. Double-click outside the viewport on the drawing canvas to return to paperspace.

7. Select the viewport, and stretch its grips to reveal and center the entire building as shown in Figure 14.29. You might need to move the viewport to center the building on the page, depending on how you stretch the grips.

FIGURE 14.29 Configuring Layout1 to display the drawing in 3/8 scale

8. Press Ctrl+P to execute the PLOT command. Deselect Plot Stamp On in the Plot dialog box that appears. Click OK, and the plot is processed. Close the plot notification window when it appears.

Certification
Objective

 9. Click the Quick View Layouts icon in the status bar. Click New Layout in the toolbar that appears, and then click the Layout2 icon to initialize it.

10. Select Setup1 in the Page Setup Manager that appears, and click the Set Current and Close buttons. Layout2 is configured the same way as Layout1.

11. Double click inside the viewport to activate floating modelspace. Select ⅜″ = 1′-0″ from the Viewport Scale menu on the status bar.

12. Type **LAYERSTATE**, and press Enter. Select the Reflected Ceiling Plan layer state, and then click the Restore button (see Figure 14.30).

FIGURE 14.30 Restoring a layer state in floating modelspace

13. Double-click outside the viewport on the drawing canvas to return to paperspace. Open the Application menu, choose the Print category, and then click Plot. Click the Preview button to open a preview window (see Figure 14.31).

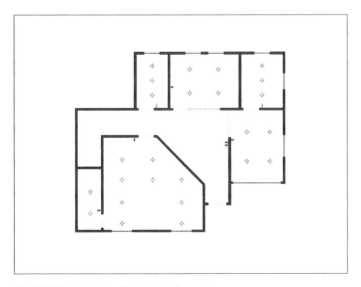

FIGURE 14.31 Previewing Layout2

14. Click the Plot icon in the upper-left corner of the preview window, and the plot is processed. Close the plot notification window.

15. Your drawing should now resemble Ch14-D.dwg, which is available among the book's download files.

Exporting to an Electronic Format

If you'd like to reduce the amount of paper you use and eliminate reprographics and drawing shipment costs, Windows users can consider exporting their drawings to electronic formats such as DWF (Design Web Format) and/or PDF (Portable Document Format). Mac for AutoCAD users can't export to DWF (they can, however, save as PDF in the Plot dialog box). You can email, FTP, or use an online service to transfer electronic files to your subcontractors and clients for collaboration or approval purposes. In the following steps, you will export a DWF file:

1. Open the Ch14-D.dwg file on the book's web page.

 2. Click the ribbon's Output tab and, in the Export To DWF/PDF panel, click on the drop-down arrow under the Export icon. Select DWFx from the menu that appears.

3. Click the Save button in the Save As DWFx dialog box.

4. Right-click the Ch14-D.dwfx file on your hard drive; select Open With, and select Microsoft Internet Explorer. After a few moments, the vector drawing appears in the browser. Click the Fit To Width button at the bottom of the interface (see Figure 14.32).

You may remove the HP DesignJet 800 plotter from your system or use it for practicing plotting.

DWFx files are written in XML (Extensible Markup Language) as opposed to Autodesk's proprietary DWF format. DWFx files can be viewed in the Internet Explorer browser without installing a plug-in.

Use Autodesk Design Review if you want to view and mark up DWF or DWFx files.

Fit to width

FIGURE 14.32 DWFx drawing displayed in Internet Explorer

THE ESSENTIALS AND BEYOND

In this chapter, you learned how to configure a typical output device by creating both a system printer and an AutoCAD plotter. You configured a plot style table and created a template that uses it. In addition, you plotted from both modelspace and layouts in paperspace, saved a page setup, and learned the entire plotting process. Finally, you learned how to keep everything in a digital format and export a DWFx file that can be shared over the Internet.

ADDITIONAL EXERCISE

Explore the PUBLISH command on your own. Experiment with publishing multiple layouts from one drawing or any combination of modelspace views and layouts from multiple sheets all at once. The Publish feature is a great time-saver when you are ready to plot a stack of sheets. You can even try saving a sheet list for printing an identical set of the same drawings at another time.

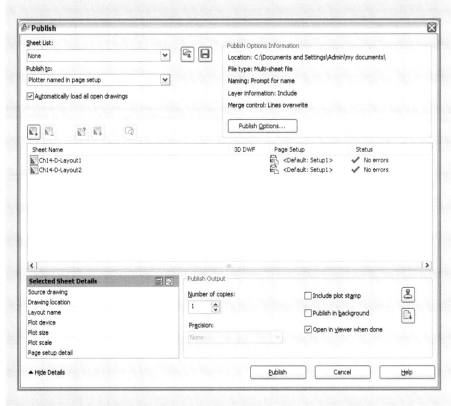

CHAPTER 15

Storing, Presenting, and Extracting Data

The AutoCAD® 2013 program has several features that allow you to manipulate nongraphical data within your drawings. (Please note that AutoCAD® LT doesn't support these features.) In this chapter, you'll begin by defining *attributes* within a block definition in order to store data. You'll proceed to enter values in several block references, and then you'll create a *table* to organize and display this data on a drawing layout. The data shown in the table will be a mixture of static text and dynamically linked *fields* that display textual information in modelspace. After creating this complex data-management system, you'll change one of the attribute's values and watch as the fields displaying data in the table automatically update.

▶ **Defining attributes and blocks**

▶ **Inserting attributed blocks**

▶ **Editing table styles and creating tables**

▶ **Using fields in table cells**

▶ **Editing table data**

Defining Attributes and Blocks

Blocks can be defined with *attributes* that contain any manner of textual information relevant to the object in question. Let's explore this topic in an exercise. First you'll alter the Annotative text style that will be used by the attributes you create. Then you'll create attribute definitions to store employees' names and ID numbers. Finally, you'll define a simple block composed of two rectangles containing the attribute definitions.

1. Go to the book's web page at www.sybex.com/go /autocad2013essentials, browse to Chapter 15, get the file Ch15-A .dwg or Ch15-A-metric.dwg, and open it. The drawing is an elaboration on the diagram you dimensioned in Chapter 11, "Dimensioning" (see Figure 15.1).

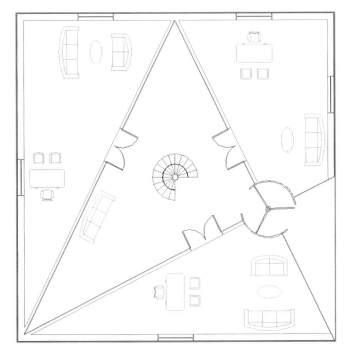

FIGURE 15.1 Diagram shown in Figure 11.1 converted into a floor plan for use in this chapter

2. Type **ST** (for Style), and press Enter. Select the Annotative style in the Styles list on the left side of the Text Style dialog box. Select romans.shx in the Font Name drop-down menu. Type **1/8"** (or **0.30** cm) in the Paper Text Height box (see Figure 15.2). Click Apply, select Set Current, and then click Close.

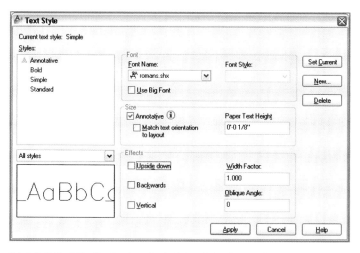

FIGURE 15.2 Setting the height of the Annotative text style

3. Click the Rectangle tool on the Draw panel of the ribbon's Home tab. Click a point at some arbitrary distance from the building as the start point, type **@3',1'** (or **@90,25** in metric), and press Enter.

4. Click the Copy tool in the Modify panel, select the rectangle you just drew, and press Enter. Press F3 to toggle on Endpoint object snap if it is not already on, click the upper-left corner of the rectangle, and then click its lower-left corner to create two vertically stacked rectangles. Press Enter to end the COPY command.

5. Click the Line tool in the Draw panel, and click points A, B, and C in Figure 15.3. Press Enter to end the LINE command.

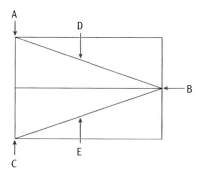

FIGURE 15.3 Drawing simple geometry to form the basis of an attributed block

6. Select ¼″ = 1′-0″ scale (or 1:40 scale in metric) from the Annotation Scale menu on the status bar.

7. Right-click the Object Snap toggle on the status bar, and turn on Midpoint running object snap mode if it is not already on.

8. Expand the Block panel, and click the Define Attributes tool to open the Attribute Definition dialog box. Type **NAME** as the tag, **Employee Name?** as the prompt, and **Smith** as the default. Set Justification to Middle Center and Text Style to Annotative (see Figure 15.4).

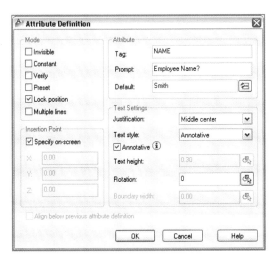

FIGURE 15.4 Specifying the properties of an attribute definition

UNDERSTANDING THE PARTS OF AN ATTRIBUTE

Tag, Prompt, and Value, along with a number of additional settings and optional modes, define every attribute. Tag is the programming name (typically capitalized without any spaces in the tag). Prompt is the question you'll be asking the person who inserts the attributed block, prompting them to enter the attribute value. The value is entered only when the attributed block is inserted, and not when the attribute is defined (see the next section). The optional Default setting displays a default value when the attributed block is eventually inserted into a drawing.

9. Click OK to close the Attribute Definition dialog box. Click the midpoint at point D in Figure 15.3. Figure 15.5 shows the result.

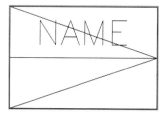

FIGURE 15.5 Placing an attribute definition in relation to the block definition geometry

10. Press the spacebar to repeat the ATTDEF command. Type **IDNO** as the tag, **Identification Number?** as the prompt, and **1234** as the default (see Figure 15.6). Set Justification to Middle Center and click OK. Click the midpoint of the lower diagonal line at point E in Figure 15.3.

FIGURE 15.6 Creating another attribute definition

11. Click the Erase tool on the Modify panel, select the two diagonal lines, and press Enter.

12. Click the Create tool on the Block panel, and type **Employee Data** in the Name text box.

13. Click the Pick Insertion Base Point icon, and then click point C in Figure 15.3.

14. Click the Select Objects icon, click the NAME attribute definition, and then click IDNO. Select both rectangles, and press Enter. Click the Delete radio button in the Objects area of the Block Definition dialog box, and select Inches (or Centimeters) in the Block Unit dropdown menu (see Figure 15.7). Click OK and the attribute definitions and geometry disappear as expected.

The order in which you select attribute definitions when defining them as a block determines the order their prompts will appear in block references.

15. Save your work as Ch15-B.dwg or Ch15-B-metric.dwg.

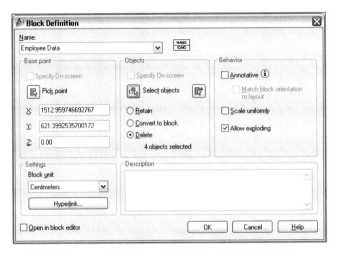

FIGURE 15.7 Defining a block with attribute definitions

Inserting Attributed Blocks

After you (or your CAD manager) has gone to the trouble of defining blocks with attributes, inserting them and entering values is easy. In the following steps, you'll insert three Employee Name blocks and enter appropriate values in each block reference:

1. If the file is not already open, go to the book's web page, browse to Chapter 15, get the file Ch15-B.dwg or Ch15-B-metric.dwg, and open it.

2. Set the Symbol layer as current in the Layer drop-down menu in the Layers panel.

3. Click the Insert tool in the Block panel. Open the Name drop-down menu, and select Employee Data. Verify that Specify On-Screen is selected in the Insertion Point area (see Figure 15.8).

4. Click OK in the Insert dialog box, and then click a point in the center of the room on the right. The command prompt reads:

   Employee name? <Smith>:

   Type **Bruno**, and press Enter. The prompt now reads:

   Identification number? <1234>:

   Type **108**, and press Enter. The block reference appears in the room with the values you typed in (see Figure 15.9).

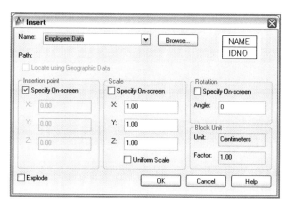

FIGURE 15.8 Inserting the Employee Data block you defined in the previous section

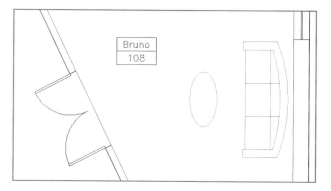

FIGURE 15.9 Inserting a block and entering its attribute values at the command prompt

5. Type **ATTDIA**, and press Enter. Type **1**, and press Enter.

6. Type **I** (for Insert), and press Enter twice. Click a point in the center of the room on the left. Type **Andreae** as the employee name, press Tab, and type **864** as the identification number in the Edit Attributes dialog box (see Figure 15.10). Click OK.

7. Press the spacebar to repeat the INSERT command and press Enter. Click a point in the center of the room on the bottom. Type **Dee** as the employee name, press Tab, and type **273** as the identification number in the Edit Attributes dialog box. Click OK. Figure 15.11 shows the result.

8. Save your work as Ch15-C.dwg or Ch15-C-metric.dwg.

ATTDIA is a system variable that controls whether attribute values are input at the command prompt or entered in a dialog box.

FIGURE 15.10 Entering values in the Edit Attributes dialog box

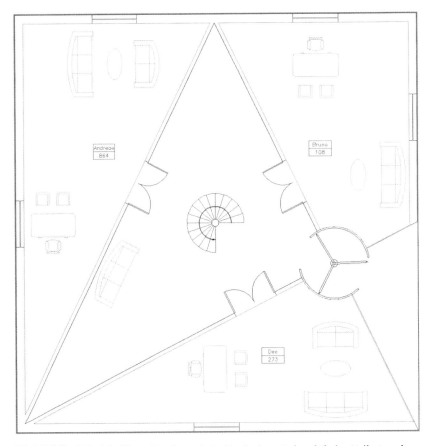

FIGURE 15.11 Three Employee Data blocks inserted and their attribute values entered

Editing Table Styles and Creating Tables

Tables are like having Microsoft Excel or another spreadsheet program within AutoCAD. The overall appearance of tables is controlled by table styles. Cell spacing, borders, and background coloring is controlled by individual table cells. In the following steps, you'll adjust a table style, create a new table, and begin adding content to its cells.

1. If the file is not already open, go to the book's web page, browse to Chapter 15, get the file Ch15-C.dwg or Ch15-C-metric.dwg, and open it.

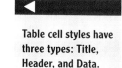

2. Expand the Annotation panel, and click the Table Style icon. Click the Modify button in the Table Style dialog box that appears.

3. In the Modify Table Style: Standard dialog box that appears, open the Cell Styles drop-down menu and select Title. Select the General tab if it is not already selected. Double-click in the Horizontal text box in the Margins area. Type **1/16″** (or **0.20** cm), press Tab, and type **1/16″** (or **0.20** cm) to specify an equal vertical margin (see Figure 15.12).

Table cell styles have three types: Title, Header, and Data.

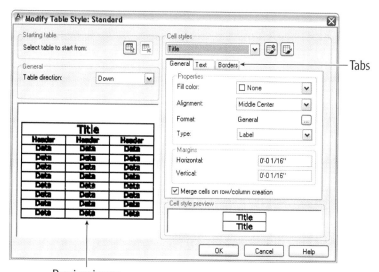

Preview image

FIGURE 15.12 Modifying the margins around the Title cell style

4. Select the Text tab within the Modify Table Style: Standard dialog box. Open the Text Style drop-down menu, and select Bold. Double-click the Text Height text box, and type **3/8″** (or **0.80** cm) (see Figure 15.13).

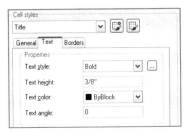

FIGURE 15.13 Editing the Title
cell style text properties

5. Open the Cell Styles drop-down menu and select Header. Open the
Text Style drop-down menu and select Bold. Double-click the Text
Height text box, type **1/4″** (or **0.50** cm), press Tab, and observe the
preview image update.

6. Open the Cell Styles drop-down menu and select Data. Open the
Text Style drop-down menu and select Simple. Double-click the Text
Height text box, and type **1/4″** (or **0.50** cm). Press Tab to update.
The updates to the table style are complete. Click OK, and then click
Close to end the TABLESTYLE command.

7. Click the Quick View Layouts tool on the status bar. Select Layout1,
and press Esc to exit Quick View Layouts mode.

8. Open the Layer drop-down menu in the Layers panel, and set the
Table layer as current.

9. Click the Table tool in the Annotation panel. Set the number of
Columns to 4 and Data Rows to 3 in the Insert Table dialog box.
Set Column Width to 1″ (or 2.5 cm) (see Figure 15.14). The Title,
Header, and Data cell styles you customized within the Standard
table style will be used by default. Click OK.

LINKING TO TABLES IN EXTERNAL SPREADSHEETS

Select the From A Data Link radio button in the Insert Table dialog box,
and click the Launch The Data Link Manager icon to link dynamically to a
spreadsheet in Microsoft Excel, for example.

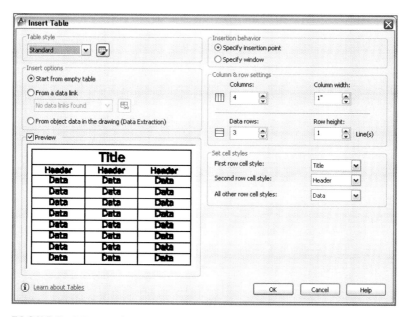

FIGURE 15.14 Specifying the number of columns and rows in the Insert Table dialog box

10. Click approximately at point A in Figure 15.15 to place the empty table on the layout.

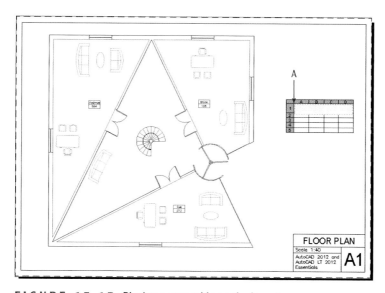

FIGURE 15.15 Placing a new table on the layout

11. The cursor is highlighted within the table's top cell. Zoom into the table by turning the mouse wheel. Type **Room Schedule**, and press the Tab key. Type **Employee**, press Tab, and type **ID No**. Press Tab again. The Tab key advances to the next cell from left to right, and then from top to bottom at the end of each row.

12. Type **Area (ft** in Imperial units or **Area (m** in metric units.

13. Right-click to open the context menu. Select Symbol ➤ Squared as shown in Figure 15.16. Type **)** and press Tab. Now the column header indicates an area in square feet (or square meters). Click outside the table on the layout to deactivate it.

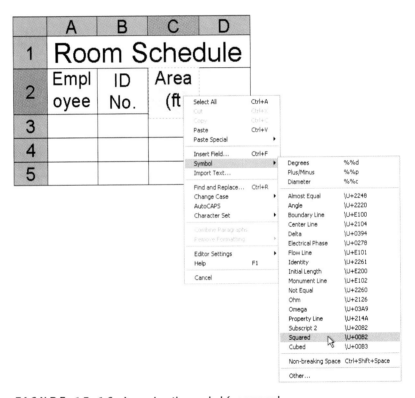

FIGURE 15.16 Accessing the symbol for squared

You can insert or delete any number of rows and columns using tools on the Table Cell tab's Rows and Columns panels.

14. Click in the table to highlight it, and then select cell D2 to highlight it for editing. Click the Delete Column tool in the Columns panel within the ribbon's contextual Table Cell tab.

15. Use the arrow keys to move between cells in the table. Press the left arrow key twice to move to cell A2. Each cell has four grips. Click cell A2's right grip, and move it to the right to stretch column A wider. Click a point a short distance to the right to set the column width approximately as shown in Figure 15.17.

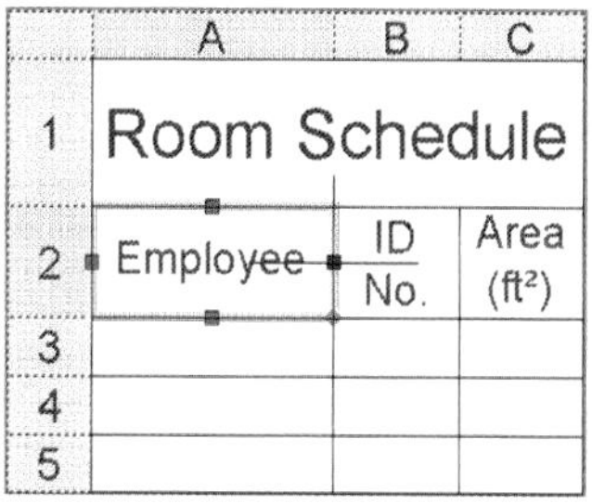

FIGURE 15.17 Resizing a column with cell grips

16. Press the right arrow key twice to move to cell B2. Click B2's right grip, and stretch it to the right so that its entire header fits on one line. Repeat for cell C2. Press Esc to deselect (see Figure 15.18).

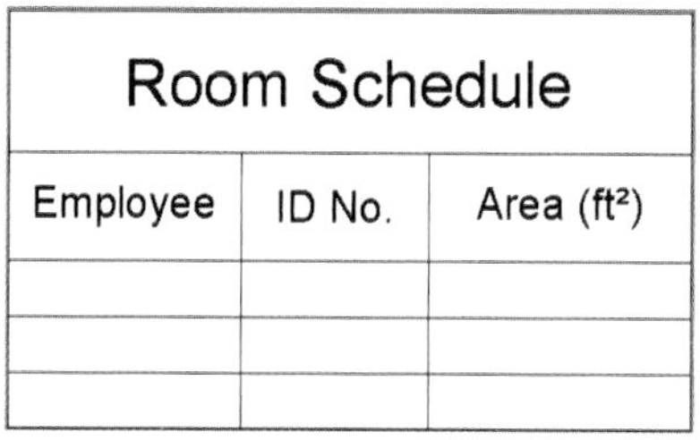

FIGURE 15.18 Formatted table

17. Save your work as Ch15-D.dwg or Ch15-D-metric.dwg.

Using Fields in Table Cells

Fields are variables that are inserted into blocks of text that can change what they display over time. For example, you can insert a date field onto a title block that will update to show the current date every time the drawing is plotted. You can also link fields to objects in the drawing so that the field will display any one of the object properties. In the following steps, you'll insert fields into cells within the table you designed in the previous section:

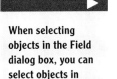

1. If the file is not already open, go to the book's web page, browse to Chapter 15, get the file Ch15-D.dwg or Ch15-D-metric.dwg, and open it.

2. Select cell A3, which is the first data cell in the Employee column. Double-click within this cell to activate the Text Editor contextual tab on the ribbon. Click the Field tool on the Insert panel.

3. In the Field dialog box that appears, open the Field Category drop-down menu and select Objects. Select Object in the Field Names list. Click the Select Objects button, and select the attribute Bruno in the room on the right.

4. Select Value in the Property list that appeared after selecting the attribute in the previous step (see Figure 15.19). Click OK. The word Bruno appears in table cell A3.

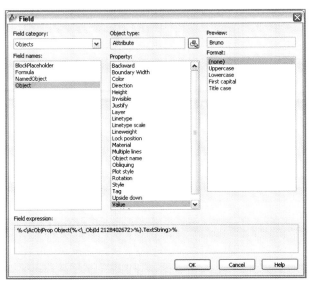

FIGURE 15.19 Accessing the attribute value in the Field dialog box

5. Press the down arrow, and move to cell A4. Right-click and choose Insert Field from the context menu. Click the Select Objects button, and select the attribute Andreae in the room on the left. Choose Value from the Property list and click OK.

6. Repeat the previous step, selecting the attribute Dee in the room at the bottom.

When selecting objects in the Field dialog box, you can select objects in floating viewports even when you are in paperspace.

Fields are displayed against a gray background to identify them as fields on screen. The gray field background does not appear in plotted output.

7. Continue adding fields in the ID No column, selecting each attribute value as shown in Figure 15.20.

	A	B	C
1	Room Schedule		
2	Employee	ID No.	Area (ft²)
3	Bruno	108	
4	Andreae	864	
5	Dee	273	

FIGURE 15.20 Inserting fields that link to attribute values in modelspace

8. Double-click in cell C3 to activate the Text Editor. Press Ctrl+F to open the Field dialog box. Click the Select Objects button, and select the magenta line in the doorway of Bruno's office. Choose Area from the Property list. The preview shows the area value as 347.014 SQ. FT. or 322388.23 (in units of square centimeters).

9. Click the Additional Format button. In Imperial units, remove the SQ. FT. text from the Suffix text box and type **1/144** in the Conversion Factor text box to convert from square inches to square feet. (This is converted to its decimal equivalent.) In metric type **1/10000** in the Conversion Factor text box in order to convert square centimeters to square meters manually (see Figure 15.21). Click OK twice.

AutoCAD automatically inserts a factor that converts from square inches to square feet in the Additional Format dialog box.

FIGURE 15.21 Converting units in the Additional Format dialog box

10. Press the down arrow to move to cell C4. Repeat the previous two steps, selecting the magenta line in Andreae's office and displaying its area value in square feet (or square meters).

11. Press the down arrow to move to cell C5. Repeat steps 8 and 9, selecting the magenta line in Dee's office and displaying its area value in square feet (or square meters). Click outside the table on the layout to deselect the table. Figure 15.22 shows the result.

Room Schedule		
Employee	ID No.	Area (ft²)
Bruno	108	347.014
Andreae	864	439.451
Dee	273	346.052

FIGURE 15.22   Adding all the relevant fields to the table

12. Save your work as Ch15-E.dwg or Ch15-E-metric.dwg.

Editing Table Data

Beyond filling in a table with all the relevant information, you can also format it to display the data in an aesthetically pleasing fashion. You can change justification, alter border color and/or lineweight, and even change the background color of chosen cells to highlight them. In the following steps, you'll format cells, add an additional row and a formula, and finally change an attribute and regenerate the drawing to see the table update:

1. If the file is not already open, go to the book's web page, browse to Chapter 15, get the file Ch15-E.dwg or Ch15-E-metric.dwg, and open it.

2. Click the word Dee (cell A5 in the table) to activate the ribbon's Table Cell contextual tab. Click the Insert Below button in the Row panel.

3. Press the down arrow, and move to cell A6. Hold down Shift, and click cell B6. Open the Merge Cells menu in the Merge panel, and select Merge By Row. Cells A6 and B6 are merged. Type **Total**, and click outside the table on the layout to deactivate Text Editing mode (see Figure 15.23).

FIGURE 15.23 Merging two cells, and typing the word Total

fx

4. Click the cell to the right of the word Total to activate cell C6. Click the Formula button in the Insert panel and select Sum. Click points A and B, as shown in Figure 15.24. Press Enter to accept the formula =Sum(C3:C5).

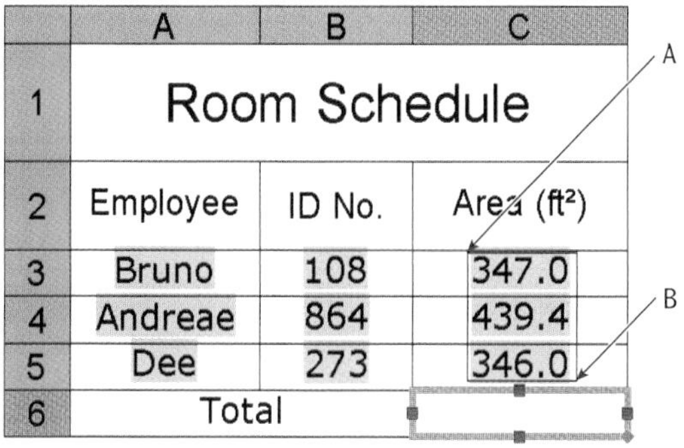

FIGURE 15.24 Selecting a range of cells for a formula

5. Select the number 163082.582 (or 1052147.80 in metric) that appears in cell C6 (total area in square inches or square centimeters). Hold down Shift, and select cell C3. Open the Data Format menu on the Cell Format panel, and select Custom Table Cell Format from the context menu.

%..

6. Click the Additional Format button in the Table Cell Format dialog box that appears. Type **0.006944** (or **1/10000** in metric) in the Conversion Factor text box, and click OK to close the Additional Format dialog box.

7. Select Decimal in the Format list in the Table Cell Format dialog box. Open the Precision drop-down menu, and select 0.0 (see Figure 15.25). Click OK.

Formatting applied to a range of cells affects all selected cells.

FIGURE 15.25 Formatting a range of cells

 8. Open the text justification menu (currently set at Top Center) in the Cell Styles panel, and select Top Right. Cells C3 through C6 are right-justified.

9. Select cell B3, hold down Shift, and select cell B5. Change the justification to Top Right in the Cell Styles panel. Select cell A3, hold down Shift, and select cell A5. Change its justification to Top Left. Select merged cell AB6. Change its justification to Top Right. Click outside the table to deselect. Figure 15.26 shows the result.

Room Schedule		
Employee	ID No.	Area (ft²)
Bruno	108	347.0
Andreae	864	439.4
Dee	273	346.0
	Total	1132.4

FIGURE 15.26 Table after adding a total row and justifying its data cells

10. Type **TABLESTYLE**, press Enter, and click the Modify button in the Table Style dialog box. In the Modify Table Style: Standard dialog box that appears, select Data from the Cell Styles drop-down menu if it is not

already selected. Select the General tab if it is not already selected, double-click the Horizontal text box in the Margins area, type **1/8″** (or **0.15** cm), and press Tab. Type **1/8″** (or **0.15** cm), and click OK and then Close. There is a bit more space around the data cells.

 11. Click the words Room Schedule to select merged cell ABC1. Open the Table Cell Background Color menu in the Cell Styles panel, and choose Select Colors. Select the True Color tab in the Select Color dialog box that appears. Type **36,36,36** in the Color text box and press Tab (see Figure 15.27). Click OK.

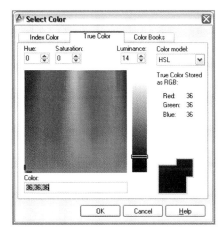

FIGURE 15.27 Selecting a very dark table cell background color

12. Double-click in cell ABC1 to activate the Text Editor contextual tab on the ribbon. Drag a selection encompassing the entire phrase Room Schedule. Open the Text Editor Color Gallery in the Formatting panel, and choose Select Colors. Select the True Color tab in the Select Color dialog box that appears. Type **255,255,255** in the Color text box, press Tab, and click OK. White text now appears on a black background. Click outside the table to exit Text Editor mode.

 13. Toggle on Show/Hide Lineweight on the status bar if it is not already on.

14. Select cell ABC1, hold Shift, and select cell C6 to activate all the table's cells. Click the Edit Borders icon in the Cell Styles panel. Open the Lineweight drop-down menu, and select 0.70 mm. Click the Outside Borders button to apply the properties and click OK (Figure 15.28). A thicker line appears around the outside borders of the table.

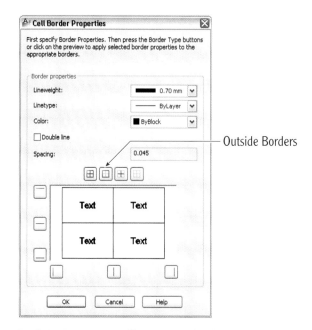

FIGURE 15.28 Changing cell border properties

15. Click the border of the table to select the table itself. Click the Uniformly Stretch Table Height grip in the lower-left corner, and move it upward until the table reaches its maximum compactness (see Figure 15.29). Press Esc to deselect the table.

	A	B	C
1	Room Schedule		
2	Employee	ID No.	Area (ft²)
3	Bruno	108	347.0
4	Andreae	864	439.4
5	Newton	33	346.0
6		Total	1132.4

FIGURE 15.29 Stretching the table's height uniformly upward to compact its cells

 16. Now you'll change an attribute value and observe that this change appears automatically in the table through the fields linked to the attribute values. Click the Maximize Viewport icon in the status bar. Double-click the Employee Data block in Dee's office to open the Enhanced Attribute Editor. Type **Newton**, press Enter, type **33**, and press Enter again (see Figure 15.30). Click OK to end the EATTEDIT command.

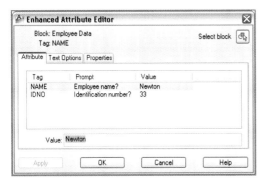

FIGURE 15.30 Editing attribute values in a maximized viewport

17. Click Minimize Viewport in the status bar. The table in Layout1 has automatically been updated, and it lists Newton and his newly entered identification number.

18. Select the Output tab, and click the Preview icon on the Plot panel. The gray background in the fields disappears and you see the table exactly as it would plot (see Figure 15.31). Press Esc to exit preview mode.

19. Your drawing should now resemble Ch15-F.dwg or Ch15-E-metric.dwg, which are available for download at the book's web page.

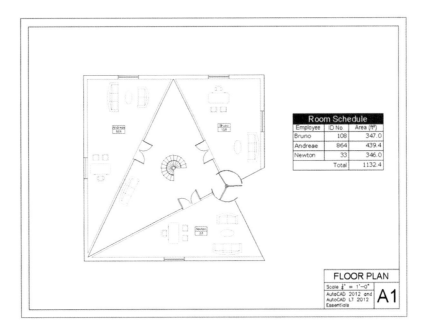

FIGURE 15.31 The final appearance of the drawing

real-time views of your model compared to wireframe representations. In the following steps, you will sample the visual styles available in AutoCAD 2013.

The model in this chapter is a conceptual model of the O_2 Arena in London that you will build in Chapter 17, "Modeling in 3D." The O_2 Arena (designed by architect Richard Rogers) was originally known as the Millennium Dome because it opened on January 1, 2000. This distinctive, mast-supported, dome-shaped cable network structure will be one of the venues for the London 2012 Olympics (see Figure 16.1).

Symbolizing the number of days, weeks, and months in a year, the O_2 Arena is 365 m in diameter and 52 m high, and is supported by 12 masts. It is also on the Prime Meridian that runs through Greenwich.

FIGURE 16.1 You will navigate a 3D conceptual model of the O_2 Arena in this chapter.

1. Go to the book's web page at www.sybex.com/go /autocad2013essentials, browse to Chapter 16, get the file Ch16-A.dwg, and open it. The sample file is displayed in 2D Wireframe visual style by default.

2. Select the 3D Modeling workspace from the Quick Access toolbar.

3. Select the ribbon's View tab, and open the Visual Styles drop-down menu at the top of the Visual Styles panel (see Figure 16.2).

FIGURE 16.2 Selecting a visual style

4. Select the Wireframe icon. The UCS icon displays a colorful axis tripod in this visual style (see Figure 16.3).

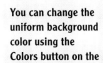

You can change the uniform background color using the Colors button on the Display tab of the Options dialog box, invoked with the OPTIONS command.

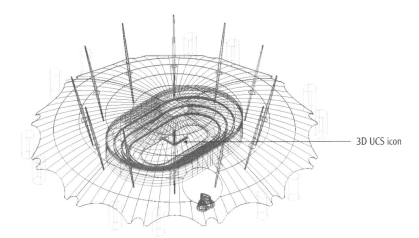

3D UCS icon

FIGURE 16.3 Wireframe visual style

5. Select the Visual Styles Manager icon in the Palettes panel to alter visual style settings. Scroll down the list of Available Visual Styles In Drawing, and select Shaded With Edges. Change Color to Tint in the Face Settings group (see Figure 16.4).

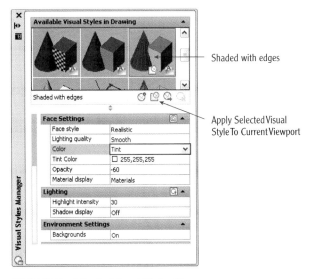

FIGURE 16.4 Visual Styles Manager

6. Select the Apply Selected Visual Style To Current Viewport button, as shown in Figure 16.4. Close the Visual Styles Manager. Figure 16.5 shows the result in the drawing canvas.

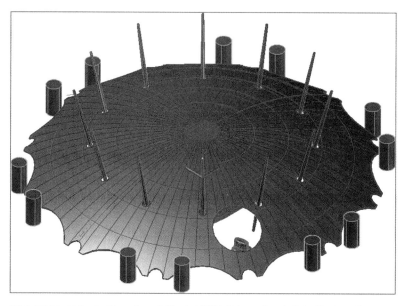

FIGURE 16.5 The altered Shaded With Edges visual style displays the model tinted with white.

By saving a visual style, you can recall it later after switching to another visual style.

7. Open the Visual Styles drop-down menu in the Visual Styles panel, and select Save As A New Visual Style. The command prompt reads:

   ```
   Save current visual style as or [?]:
   ```

   Type **Tinted with edges**, and press Enter. These words appear on the Visual Styles drop-down menu, showing that this is now the current visual style.

8. You can also change visual styles using the in-canvas controls located in the upper-left corner of the viewport. Select the Visual Style Controls to open a menu (see Figure 16.6).

9. Choose X-ray from the in-canvas menu that appears. Figure 16.7 shows the result: a transparent, shaded view with edges.

10. Save your work as Ch16-B.dwg.

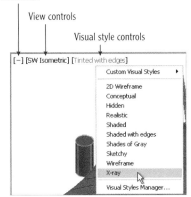

FIGURE 16.6 In-canvas controls

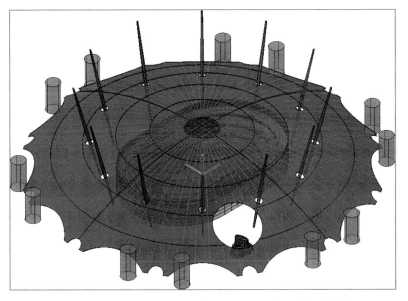

FIGURE 16.7 The X-ray visual style lets you see through solid objects.

Working with Tiled Viewports

Tiled viewports allow you to visualize a 3D model from different simultaneous vantage points. By starting a command in one viewport and finishing it in another, you can more easily transform objects in 3D. To help you get a better grasp of how

Tiled viewports can only exist in modelspace with the system variable TILEMODE equal to 1. Floating viewports exist only on layouts.

this works, the following steps show you how to divide the single default viewport into three tiled viewports:

1. If the file is not already open, go to the book's web page, browse to Chapter 16, get the file Ch16-B.dwg, and open it.

2. Type **VPORTS**, and press Enter. In the Viewports dialog box that appears, select Three: Right in the Standard Viewports list. Open the Setup drop-down menu, and select 3D (see Figure 16.8). Click OK.

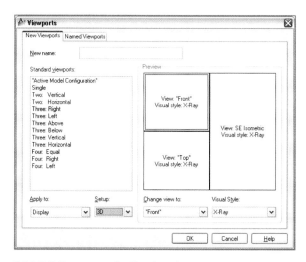

FIGURE 16.8 Configuring viewports

3. Click anywhere inside the viewport showing the front view to activate it. Open the in-canvas Visual Style Controls menu in this viewport and select Shaded. Click anywhere inside the viewport showing the top view to activate it. Open the in-canvas Visual Style Controls menu in this viewport and select Wireframe. Click OK. Figure 16.9 shows the result.

4. Select the plus (+) symbol in the upper-left viewport displaying the front view to open the in-canvas Viewport menu. Select Maximize Viewport. The front view fills the drawing canvas.

You can maximize or minimize viewports as needed at any time to get a better view of a 3D object.

5. Observe that what was formerly a plus (+) symbol in the in-canvas Viewport menu is now a minus (–) symbol. Double-click the minus symbol to minimize this viewport, displaying the front view.

6. Click anywhere inside the right viewport showing the SE Isometric view to activate it. Double-click this viewport's plus symbol to maximize it. The SE Isometric view once again fills the drawing canvas.

7. Save your work as Ch16-C.dwg.

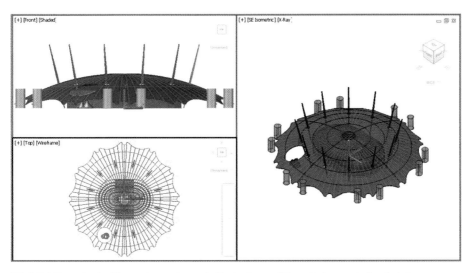

FIGURE 16.9 Three viewports each displaying a different view and visual style

Navigating with the ViewCube

The ViewCube is a 3D navigation interface that lets you easily rotate through numerous preset orthogonal and isometric views. The ViewCube's instant visual feedback keeps you from getting lost in 3D space, even when you orbit into a custom view.

The ViewCube helps you visualize the relationship between the current user coordinate system (UCS) and the world coordinate system (WCS).

In the following steps, you will experiment with the ViewCube and learn how to view a 3D model from almost any angle.

1. If the file is not already open, go to the book's web page, browse to Chapter 16, get the file Ch16-C.dwg, and open it.

2. Open the ViewCube menu (see Figure 16.10), and select Set Current View As Home.

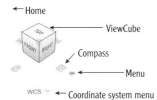

FIGURE 16.10 ViewCube navigation interface

Autodesk uses the ViewCube and SteeringWheel navigation controls in many 3D applications, including AutoCAD, Autodesk® Revit®, Autodesk® Inventor®, and Autodesk® 3ds Max®.

Ventilation towers

FIGURE 16.13 Using the ViewCube to view the ventilation towers

 4. Click the Orbit tool in the Navigation bar. Drag down in the drawing canvas to orbit your point-of-view upward until you can see the ventilation towers unobstructed by the dome membrane (see Figure 16.14). Press Esc to end the 3DORBIT command.

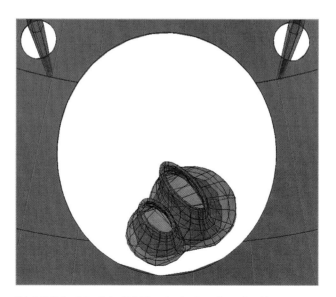

FIGURE 16.14 Orbiting for better view of subject

The Orbit tool is constrained so that it doesn't roll by default. Use 3DFORBIT to orbit with roll.

5. Hold down Shift and drag the mouse wheel to orbit (without roll) about the ventilation towers once more. You will find that it is not possible to gain an eye-level view of the towers without other objects

obstructing the view. You will learn how to set up this type of view using a camera in the next section.

6. Save your work as Ch16-E.dwg.

Using Cameras

AutoCAD uses virtual cameras to set up views similar to those achieved in the real world with physical cameras. The CAMERA command creates a camera object that you can manipulate in an isometric view to position the viewpoint in relation to the camera target. In the following steps, you will create a virtual camera and position it in an isometric view:

1. If the file is not already open, go to the book's web page, browse to Chapter 16, get the file Ch16-E.dwg, and open it.

2. Open the in-canvas View Controls menu, and select SW Isometric.

3. Zoom out by rolling the mouse wheel backward.

4. Toggle off Object Snap in the status bar.

5. Type **CAMERA**, and press Enter. Click points A and B, as shown in Figure 16.15, and press Enter.

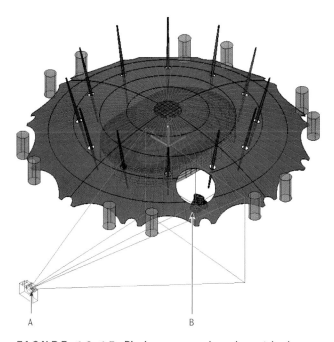

FIGURE 16.15 Placing a camera in an isometric view

6. Select the camera object. Select the Shaded visual style in the Camera Preview window that appears. Drag the Lens Length/FOV grip to the right, and click approximately at point A to expand the field of view (see Figure 16.16).

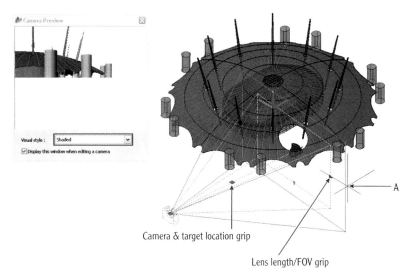

Camera & target location grip

Lens length/FOV grip

FIGURE 16.16 Placing a camera in an isometric view

Camera views are in perspective so that objects diminish in size according to their distances from the camera.

7. Drag the Camera & Target Location grip forward until the camera is under the outer edge of the dome. Figure 16.17 shows the Camera Preview window. You will correct the fact that the camera is "on the ground" in the next step.

FIGURE 16.17 Camera Preview window showing the new position of the camera "on the ground"

8. Right-click in the drawing window, and choose Set Camera View. Drag the mouse wheel downward to move the camera and its target upward, as shown in Figure 16.18.

9. Save your work as Ch16-F.dwg.

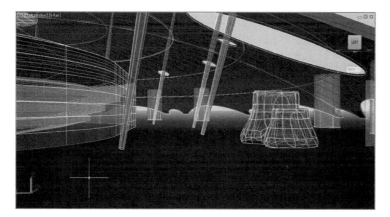

FIGURE 16.18 Looking through the camera

Navigating with SteeringWheels

The SteeringWheel is an interactive navigation control that Autodesk uses in many 3D applications, including AutoCAD. In the following steps, you will use the SteeringWheel's full navigation wheel feature (displaying all eight navigation tools) to compose a view under the dome.

1. If the file is not already open, go to the book's web page, browse to Chapter 16, get the file Ch16-F.dwg, and open it.

2. Select the SteeringWheel tool in the Navigation bar. The full navigation wheel appears in the drawing canvas in close proximity to the cursor (see Figure 16.19).

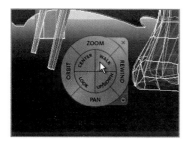

FIGURE 16.19 Full navigation SteeringWheel interface

ADDITIONAL STEERINGWHEELS

There are eight commands appearing on variations of the SteeringWheels: Zoom, Pan, Orbit, Rewind, Center, Walk, Up/Down, and Look.

There are three basic SteeringWheels: Full Navigation, View Object, and Tour Building. The latter two wheels have four commands—each suitable to their purposes of navigating around an object or touring through a building.

Each one of the basic wheels has a corresponding mini-wheel with the same commands as the larger interface. I suggest starting with the basic wheels and then graduating to mini-wheels as you gain experience. Mini-wheels are more efficient because the mouse has less distance to travel to select navigation commands.

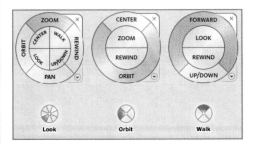

3. Position the cursor over the Walk tool within the inner ring of the SteeringWheel. Click and hold the mouse button, and observe a walk circle appear in the lower portion of the drawing canvas. Drag the cursor relative to the walk circle to move in that direction (see Figure 16.20). The further from the walk circle you drag, the faster you walk in that direction. Release the mouse button.

4. Position the cursor over the Look tool in the SteeringWheel's inner ring. Click and hold the mouse button, and drag upward to rotate the camera to look up at the hole in the dome above the ventilation towers. Release the mouse button.

5. Position the cursor over the Rewind tool in the SteeringWheel's outer ring. Drag to the left to go backward in the history of movements made using the steering wheel. Drag back to the point before you looked up (see Figure 16.21). Press Esc to exit the SteeringWheel.

6. Save your work as Ch16-G.dwg.

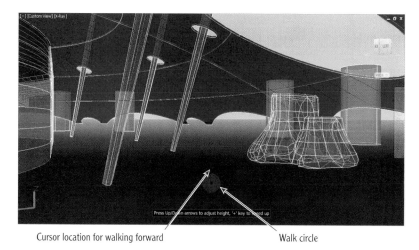

Cursor location for walking forward   Walk circle

FIGURE 16.20 Walking under the dome

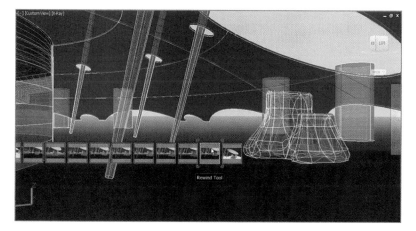

FIGURE 16.21 Interactively rewinding through navigation history

Saving Views

Named views allow you to save where you are in space so that you can recall
these positions in the future. In the following steps, you will save the current
position in the viewport, change the view, switch out of perspective, and then
return to the saved view.

1. If the file is not already open, go to the book's web page, browse to
   Chapter 16, get the file Ch16-G.dwg, and open it.

2. Type **V** (for view), and press Enter. Click the New button in the View
   Manager dialog box that appears.

Many different properties can be saved with views, including **Camera Position, Layer Snapshot, UCS, Live Section, Visual Style,** and **Background.**

3. In the New View / Shot Properties dialog box that appears, type **Camera2** as the view name (see Figure 16.22). Click OK twice to close both open dialog boxes.

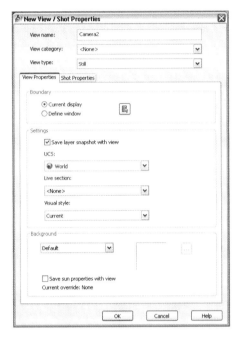

FIGURE 16.22 Saving a new view

4. Click the upper-left corner of the left face of the ViewCube to switch to the NW Isometric view. The model is still in perspective even after switching out of the Camera2 view (see Figure 16.23).

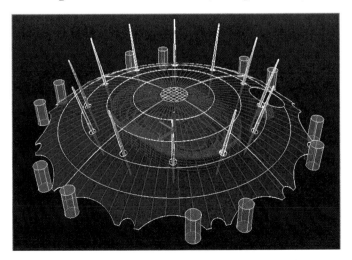

FIGURE 16.23 Perspective overview of the 3D model

5. You can toggle in and out of perspective view at any time. Open the in-canvas View Controls menu, and select Parallel to switch out of perspective.

6. Type **V** (for view), and press Enter. Select Camera2 in the list of Model Views in the View Manager dialog box (see Figure 16.24). Click Set Current, Apply, and then OK. The initial perspective view is restored.

7. Save your work as Ch16-H.dwg. Figure 16.25 shows the result.

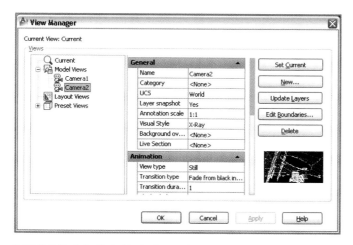

FIGURE 16.24 Restoring a view

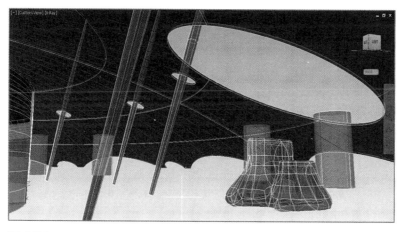

FIGURE 16.25 The X-ray view from Camera 2

THE ESSENTIALS AND BEYOND

In this chapter, you learned how to view a 3D model in a variety of ways, including changing its visual styles and working with tiled viewports. You also picked up important 3D navigation skills using the ViewCube, SteeringWheel, and 3DORBIT command. In addition, you placed a camera, adjusted its position and field of view in Isometric mode, looked through its virtual lens, and walked around an interior building space. Finally, you learned how to save and restore views so that you can get back to the places the virtual camera has been.

ADDITIONAL EXERCISE

Did you know AutoCAD can create walkthrough and/or flyby animations? First draw a spline to act as a camera motion path. Edit the spline (see Chapter 5, "Shaping Curves," if necessary) so that the spline has a smooth 3D shape. Use the ANIPATH command to create a motion path animation, linking the camera's path to the spline you just drew. Export the animation to your hard drive and watch the video. You can share video files with people who don't have AutoCAD.

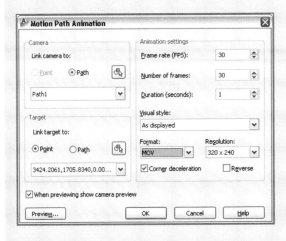

CHAPTER 17

Modeling in 3D

The AutoCAD® program has three different 3D modeling toolsets comprising surfaces, solids, and meshes reflecting the historical evolution of computer graphics. Each toolset was initially developed to suit specific industries: surfaces for industrial design, solids for engineering, and meshes for games and movies. Each toolset has its particular strengths and limitations that become evident the more you use it. Yet AutoCAD allows you to pick the best tool for the job no matter what type of work you do, so that you can find the best solutions for your drawings. We will explore these tools throughout this chapter, where you will learn how to create and edit surfaces and solid models, and how to smooth out geometry with mesh tools.

▶ **Creating surface models**

▶ **Editing surface models**

▶ **Creating solid models**

▶ **Editing solid models**

▶ **Smoothing meshes**

Creating Surface Models

In this chapter, you will create a conceptual model of the O_2 Arena in London, the same model used in Chapter 16, "Navigating 3D Models."

In AutoCAD, *surfaces* are defined as infinitely thin shells that do not contain any mass or volume. Two-dimensional profile shapes have been provided in this chapter's sample file that you will use to create 3D surfaces. You will begin the following exercise by creating a planar surface and then revolving, sweeping, and extruding 2D profiles into 3D surfaces.

Making Planar Surfaces

Planar surfaces differ from flat bounded areas like circles and closed polylines in that they display surfaces rather than edges only, in shaded visual styles. In the following steps, you will create this simplest of all surfaces from a circle:

1. Go to the book's web page at www.sybex.com/go/autocad2013essentials, browse to Chapter 17, get the file Ch17-A.dwg, and open it. The sample file is displayed in the Shaded With Edges visual style so that surfaces will be visible when you create them.

 2. Select the 3D Modeling workspace from the Quick Access toolbar.

 3. Select the ribbon's Home tab, and click the Make Object's Layer Current tool in the Layers panel. Select the circle at the center of the drawing to set the Dome Membrane layer as current.

 4. Select the ribbon's Surface tab, and click the Surface Associativity toggle in the Create panel if it is not already highlighted in blue.

 5. Select the Planar tool in the Create panel. The command prompt reads:

       Specify first corner or [Object] <Object>:

   Press Enter to accept the default Object option. Select the blue circle at the center of the drawing and press Enter. A planar surface appears as the PLANESURF command ends.

6. Click the SW corner of the ViewCube to move to a SW isometric viewpoint. The blue planar surface you just created is visible at the top of the dome (see Figure 17.1).

Like dimensions, surfaces can optionally be associated with the profile shapes that define them. Altering the shape of a profile immediately changes the form of its associated surface.

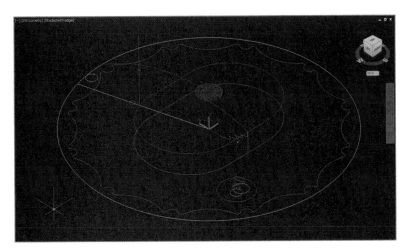

FIGURE 17.1 Creating a planar surface at the top of the dome

Revolving 2D Profile into a 3D Model

Much as you would turn wood on a lathe, you create 3D surfaces by revolving open profiles like lines, arcs, or polylines around an axis. In the following steps, you will revolve a single arc to generate the exterior surface of the dome:

Surface Associativity

1. Select the ribbon's Surface tab, and toggle off the Surface Associativity icon in the Create panel.

2. Select the Revolve tool on the Create panel of the ribbon's Surface tab. Select the blue arc running from the planar surface at the top of the dome down to the white circle at the periphery and press Enter.

3. The command prompt reads:

   ```
   Specify axis start point or define axis by [Object X Y Z]
   <Object>:
   ```

   Type **0,0** and press Enter.

4. The command prompt now says:

   ```
   Specify axis endpoint:
   ```

   Type **0,0,1** and press Enter. Press Enter again to accept the default angle of revolution (360 degrees). The REVOLVE command ends, and the dome surface appears (see Figure 17.2).

The dome is centered on the origin point in the sample file.

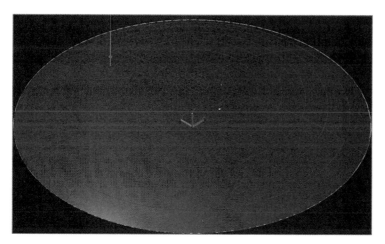

FIGURE 17.2 Revolving an arc to generate the dome surface

5. Type **E** (for Erase), and press Enter. Type **P** (for Previous), and press Enter. Press Enter again to erase the arc that generated the dome surface.

THREE-DIMENSIONAL CARTESIAN COORDINATES

The Z direction extending above and below the ground plane can be specified within Cartesian coordinates simply by adding a second comma followed by the Z value. For example, the coordinates of a point one unit above the origin point are 0,0,1.

6. Type **LA** (for Layer), and press Enter to open the Layer Properties Manager. Double-click the icon representing the Arena layer to set it as current. Click the Dome Membrane layer's lightbulb icon to toggle it off. Click the Auto-hide toggle so that the palette collapses when the cursor isn't over it (see Figure 17.3).

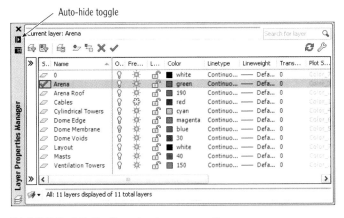

FIGURE 17.3 Changing layer properties

Sweeping Out 3D Geometry

The SWEEP command gives you the ability to create surfaces by pushing an open profile through space following a path. In these steps, you will model the area within the O$_2$ Arena and its internal roof by sweeping open shapes along closed paths:

1. Select the Sweep tool on the Create panel of the ribbon's Surface tab. Select the green arena profile shown in Figure 17.4 and press Enter.

2. The command prompt reads:

        Select sweep path or [Alignment Base point Scale Twist]:

Select the arena sweep path as shown in Figure 17.4. Figure 17.5 shows the resulting 3D arena.

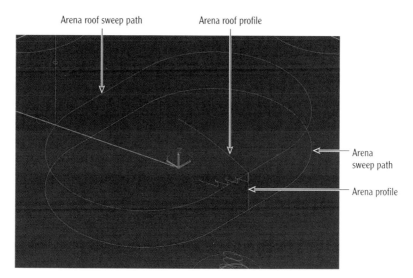

Arena roof sweep path   Arena roof profile

Arena sweep path

Arena profile

FIGURE 17.4 Profiles and sweep paths representing the O2 Arena

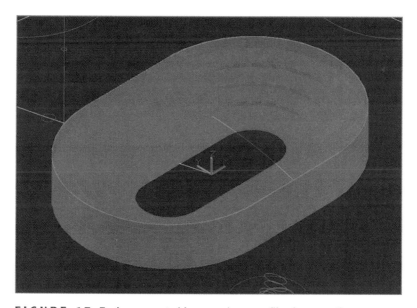

FIGURE 17.5 Arena created by sweeping a profile along a path

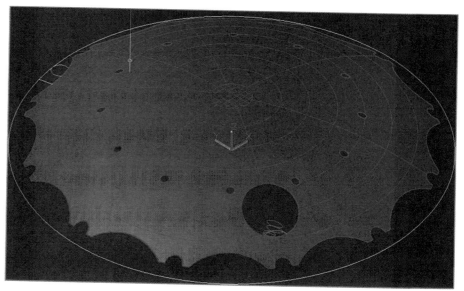

FIGURE 17.15 Trimming holes in the dome to accommodate the masts

Creating Solid Models

The EXTRUDE, REVOLVE, LOFT, and SWEEP commands have Mode options that allow you to select either Solid or Surface.

If surfaces cover a space, solid models enclose a volume. Only with solid objects can you use the MASSPROP command to calculate engineering properties such as volume, centroid, moments of inertia, and so on. Many of the solid modeling tools are the same as the surface modeling tools. If you start these commands with a closed path such as a circle, ellipse, or closed polyline, you will end up with a solid object while open paths generate surfaces. In the following sections, you'll extrude and loft solid objects.

Extruding Solid Objects

The difference between a surface extrusion and a solid extrusion is what's in the middle: nothing in the case of the surface model, and "mass" in the case of the solid. In the next section, you'll see how to affect the solid "mass" with Boolean tools. In the following steps, you'll extrude a circle into a solid and array it around the dome.

1. If the file is not already open, go to the book's web page, browse to Chapter 17, get the file Ch17-C.dwg, and open it. Switch to the 3D Modeling workspace if it's not selected already in the Quick Access toolbar.

2. Select the ribbon's Solid tab, and click the Extrude tool in the Solid panel. Select the cyan circle at the edge of the dome, and press Enter. The command prompt reads:

```
Specify height of extrusion or [Direction Path Taper angle]
<50.000>:
```

Type **30**, and press Enter. The 2D circle becomes a 3D solid cylinder.

3. The O$_2$ Arena features cylindrical towers in pairs. Type **MI** (for Mirror), and press Enter. Type **L** (for Last), and press Enter twice. The command prompt reads:

```
Specify first point of mirror line:
```

Type **0,0** and press Enter.

4. The command prompt now says:

```
Specify second point of mirror line:
```

Type **0,1** to specify a mirror line running vertically along the y-axis, and press Enter. Press Enter once more to accept the default (not to erase the source objects). Figure 17.16 shows the resulting pair of cylinders.

When you are specifying the mirror line, only its direction matters—the distance and units do not.

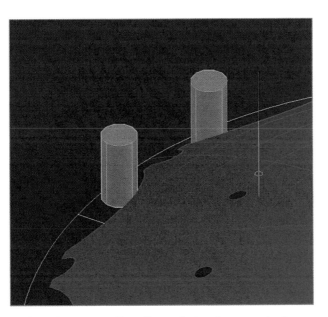

FIGURE 17.16 Extruding and mirroring one pair of solid cylindrical towers

5. You need to place six pairs of cylinders around the dome. Type **AR** (for Array), and press Enter. Select both cylindrical towers, and press Enter. Type **PO** (for Polar), and press Enter. The command prompt reads:

```
Specify center point of array or
[Base point Axis of rotation]:
```

Type **0,0** and press Enter. Type **I** (for Items), and press Enter. Type **6** (for the number of items), and press Enter. Press Enter to accept the default and end the ARRAY command. Figure 17.17 shows the result.

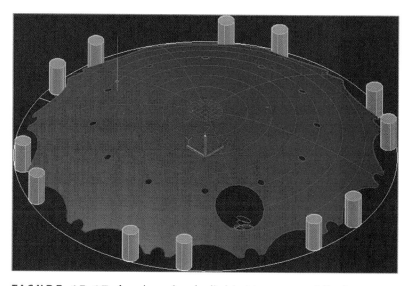

FIGURE 17.17 Arraying pairs of cylindrical towers around the dome

6. Switch to Wireframe using the in-canvas Visual Style Controls menu so that you can see through the dome. Zoom into the yellow vertical line with a hexagon around its midpoint; this represents a structural mast.

7. Hover the cursor over the Layer Properties Manager's title bar to open the palette. Double-click the Masts layer to set it as current.

8. Click the Extrude tool in the Solid panel. Select the hexagon at the midpoint of the vertical line, and press Enter. The command prompt reads:

```
Specify height of extrusion or
[Direction Path Taper angle] <30.000>:
```

Type **T** (for Taper), and press Enter.

9. The command prompt now says:

```
Specify angle of taper for extrusion <15.00>:
```

Type **1**, and press Enter. Verify that Endpoint object snap is running, and click the top endpoint of the vertical line to specify the height of the extrusion. Figure 17.18 shows the result.

Profiles of extruded items are automatically deleted.

FIGURE 17.18 Extruding half of a tapering hexagonal solid mast

10. Select the Extract Edges tool on the Solid Editing panel, select the mast, and press Enter. The Extract Edges tool creates wireframe geometry for solid objects. Hover the cursor over the edges of the mast to see that, with this kind of angular geometry, the wireframe edges are coincident with the original edges of the solid object.

11. Zoom in on the hexagonal bottom of the mast. Type **J** (for Join), and press Enter. Click points A and B shown in Figure 17.19 to create a crossing window that selects the lines, making a hexagon, and press Enter.

12. Select the Extrude tool in the Solid panel, type **L** (for Last), and press Enter twice. Type **T** (for Taper), press Enter, and then press Enter again to select the default one-degree taper angle. Zoom out, and click the lower endpoint of the vertical yellow line to extrude the lower half of the mast down to the ground.

You will union, rotate, and array the masts around the dome in the "Editing Solid Models" section.

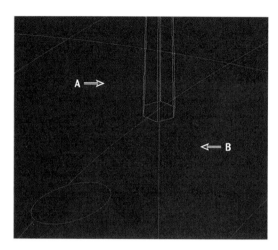

FIGURE 17.19 Joining six edges to form a hexagonal polyline

Lofting Solid Objects

The ventilation tow-ers serve a pair of road tunnels passing under the Thames in London. These tow-ers were *in situ* prior to the construction of the O$_2$ Arena.

Normal means per-pendicular to the surface in question.

Lofting is a modeling technique that lets you create a 3D model from a series of 2D cross sections. In the following steps, you will loft two ventilation towers from a series of circles and ellipses.

1. Hover the cursor over the Layer Properties Manager's title bar to open the palette. Double-click the Ventilation Towers layer to set it as current. Toggle off the Dome Membrane layer.

2. Switch to Shaded With Edges using the in-canvas Visual Style Controls menu.

3. Zoom in on the collection of blue circles and ellipses. Select the Loft tool from the drop-down menu under Sweep, if Sweep is current on the Solid panel, and press Enter. Select profiles A, B, C, and D shown in Figure 17.20, and press Enter. Open the grip menu that appears, and choose Normal To Start And End Sections. Press Enter to end the LOFT command.

4. Press the spacebar to repeat the LOFT command. Select profiles E, F, G, and H, shown in Figure 17.20, and press Enter. Open the grip menu that appears, choose Normal To Start And End Sections, and press Enter. Figure 17.21 shows the result.

5. Save your work as Ch17-D.dwg.

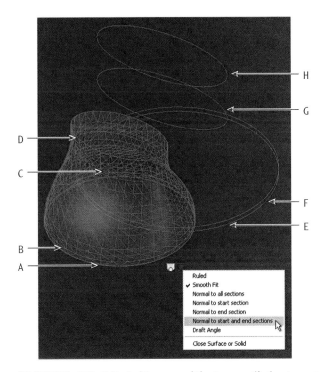

FIGURE 17.20 Lofting one of the two ventilation towers

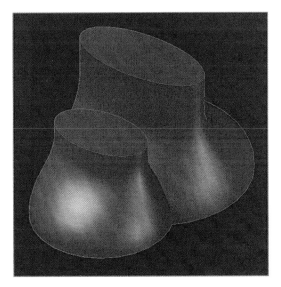

FIGURE 17.21 Lofted ventilation towers

Editing Solid Models

Solid editing tools provide an alternative set of modeling possibilities as compared with surface tools. Boolean tools (named after mathematician George Boole) allow you to union, subtract, and intersect solids (set theory terms) to create new forms. We will explore these tools in the following section and also discuss a variety of specialized solid editing tools.

Performing Boolean Operations

In the following steps, you will unify the top and bottom parts of the mast with the UNION command. You will then rotate and array 12 masts around the dome.

1. If the file is not already open, go to the book's web page, browse to Chapter 17, get the file Ch17-D.dwg, and open it. Switch to the 3D Modeling workspace if it's not selected already in the Quick Access toolbar.

2. Switch to Wireframe using the in-canvas Visual Style Controls menu.

 3. Select the Union tool in the Boolean panel, click the left and right ventilation towers, and press Enter. A curve representing the precise intersection of these two forms' surfaces appears in the wireframe representation (see Figure 17.22).

4. Pan over to the mast objects you extruded in the previous section. Hover the cursor over the Layer Properties Manager's title bar to open the palette. Double-click the Masts layer to set it as current.

FIGURE 17.22 Wireframe representations of two separate lofted ventilation towers (left) and single object (right) created with Boolean union

5. Select the Union tool in the Boolean panel. Drag a crossing window through both mast solids to select them, and press Enter. Although nothing has changed visually, the two solids have been unified as a single object. Zoom into the base of the mast.

6. Select the ribbon's Home tab, and click the 3D Rotate tool in the Modify panel. Select the mast, and press Enter. Click the lower endpoint of the vertical line, which is at the center of the mast, to act as the base point. A 3D rotate gizmo appears (see Figure 17.23).

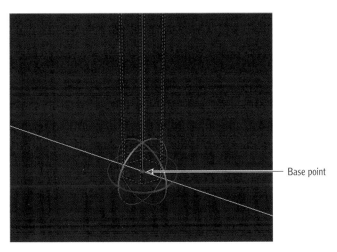

Base point

FIGURE 17.23 3D rotate gizmo displaying three colored rings representing the x-, y-, and z-axes

7. Click the red ring to select the x-axis. The command prompt reads:

   Specify angle start point or type an angle:

   Type **-14**, and press Enter.

8. Press the spacebar to repeat 3DROTATE; then select the mast and press Enter. Click the same base point shown in Figure 17.23, and click the green axis ring to select the y-axis. Type **4**, and press Enter.

9. Zoom out, and select the Erase tool in the Modify panel. Select the edges you extracted from the mast in the previous section and the vertical mast line (see Figure 17.24), and press Enter.

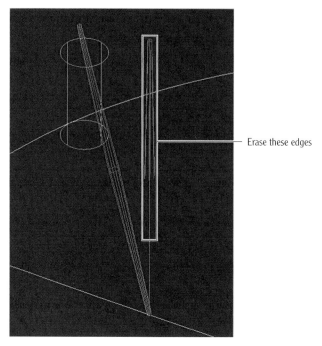

Erase these edges

FIGURE 17.24 Erasing the edges extracted earlier

10. Type **AR** (for Array), and press Enter. Select the solid mast, and press Enter. Type **PO** (for Polar), and press Enter. Type **0,0** (as the center point of the array), and press Enter. Type **I** (for Items), and press Enter. The command prompt reads:

    ```
    Enter number of items or [Angle between Expression] <4>:
    ```

    Type **12**, and press Enter three more times to complete the command.

11. Hover the cursor over the Layer Properties Manager's title bar to reveal the palette. Toggle on the Dome Membrane layer. Switch to Shaded With Edges using the in-canvas Visual Style Controls menu. Zoom out to view the entire model. Figure 17.25 shows the result.

FIGURE 17.25 Arraying rotated masts around the dome

Editing Solids

Rather than having to edit a whole solid object, it is possible to select parts of the object (called *subobjects*) for editing. In the following steps, you will offset a subobject, create an interior shell, and then use AutoCAD's Presspull tool on two faces to perform an automatic Boolean subtraction.

 1. Select the Isolate tool in the Layers panel, select the ventilation towers, and press Enter. Zoom into the ventilation towers.

 2. Select the ribbon's Solid tab, and then select the Offset Edge tool in the Solid Editing panel. Click the top face of the left tower. The command prompt reads:

    Specify through point or [Distance Corner]:

Type **D** (for Distance), and press Enter. Type **1**, and press Enter.

3. The command prompt now says:

    Specify point on side to offset:

Click the center of the top-left face to offset the edge internally. Click the top face of the right tower. Type **D** (for Distance), and press Enter. Type **1**, and press Enter. Click the center of the top-right face, and press Enter to end the OFFSETEDGE command. Figure 17.26 shows the result.

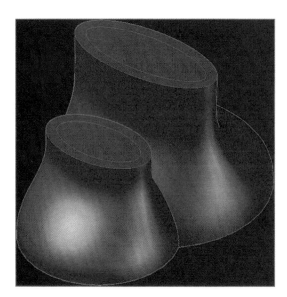

FIGURE 17.26 Offsetting edges on the tops of the ventilation towers

4. Switch to Wireframe using the in-canvas Visual Style Controls menu.

5. Select the Shell tool on the right side of the Solid Editing panel. Select the side of the ventilation towers (not the offset top faces), and press Enter. Type **1** (the same distance you offset in the previous step), and press Enter twice to end the SOLIDEDIT command. A hollow interior shell is generated within each ventilation tower. However, the tops are still solid as the shell is inset 1 unit from all sides (including the top).

6. Select the Presspull tool on the Solid panel. Click point A in Figure 17.27, type **-1**, and press Enter. Click point B, type **-1**, and press Enter twice more.

7. Switch to Shaded With Edges using the in-canvas Visual Style Controls menu. Now you can see the voids you cut in the tops of the ventilation towers in the previous step.

8. Type **LAYUN** (for Layer Unisolate), and press Enter.

9. Select the Thicken tool on the Solid Editing panel. Select the dome membrane, and press Enter. The command prompt reads:

```
Specify thickness <1.000>
```

Type **-0.5**, and press Enter. The dome surface thickens into a solid shell (see Figure 17.28).

10. Save your work as Ch17-E.dwg.

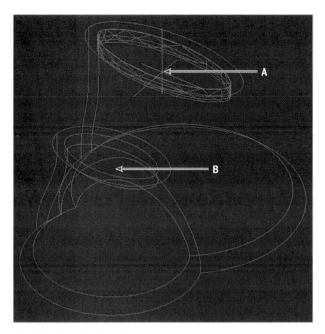

FIGURE 17.27 Using Presspull to remove the tops of the ventilation towers

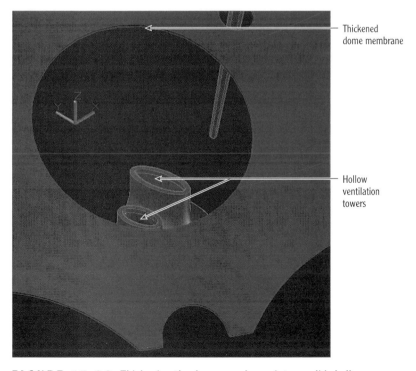

Thickened dome membrane

Hollow ventilation towers

FIGURE 17.28 Thickening the dome membrane into a solid shell

Smoothing Meshes

Mesh objects are represented by discrete polygonal surfaces that can be *smoothed*, meaning their geometrical forms can be rounded out. Mesh objects are ideal for representing organic or sculptural forms. In the following steps, you will convert the ventilation towers into a mesh by smoothing the geometry twice and thereby softening its edges.

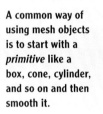

A common way of using mesh objects is to start with a *primitive* **like a box, cone, cylinder, and so on and then smooth it.**

1. If the file is not already open, go to the book's web page, browse to Chapter 17, get the file Ch17-E.dwg, and open it. Switch to the 3D Modeling workspace if it's not selected already in the Quick Access toolbar.

2. Type **LAYISO** (for Layer Isolate), press Enter, select the ventilation towers, and press Enter again. Zoom into the area.

3. Select the ribbon's Mesh tab, and select the Smooth Object tool on the Mesh panel. Select the ventilation tower solid, and press Enter. Click Create Mesh in the warning dialog box that appears (see Figure 17.29). The towers gain a blocky appearance as the curvilinear solid is converted into a polygonal mesh.

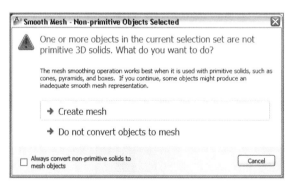

FIGURE 17.29 Mesh warning dialog box

4. Select the Smooth More tool on the Mesh panel, select the ventilation tower mesh, and press Enter. The mesh is subdivided and the result looks smoother (see Figure 17.30).

5. Type **LAYUN** (for Layer Unisolate), and press Enter.

6. Hover the cursor over the Layer Properties Manager's title bar to reveal the palette. Thaw the Cables layer, toggle on the Arena and Arena Roof layers, and toggle off the Layout layer. Figure 17.31 shows the completed project.

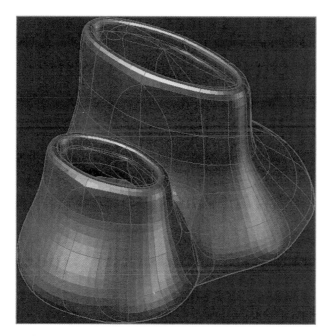

FIGURE 17.30 Smoothing the ventilation towers mesh again

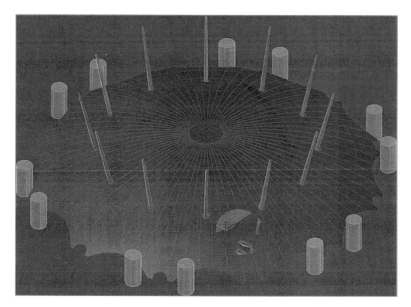

FIGURE 17.31 Completed O2 Arena 3D conceptual model

7. Save your work as Ch17-F.dwg. Your work should now resemble the file of the same name that is provided on the book's web page.

THE ESSENTIALS AND BEYOND

In this chapter, you learned how to use a variety of 3D modeling toolsets, including surfaces, solid, and meshes. You learned how to create planar surfaces and how to revolve, sweep, and extrude surfaces from open profiles. You trimmed a surface with another surface and with edges that you projected onto the surface in question. You also extruded and lofted solid objects, performed Boolean operations, created a shell, and thickened a surface. Finally, you converted a solid into a mesh and smoothed the mesh to soften its edges and give it a sculptural appearance. In short, you now have the skills to model a tremendous variety of 3D objects in AutoCAD.

ADDITIONAL EXERCISE

Experiment shaping surfaces with the NURBS toolset. For example, convert the planar surface at the top of the dome model you made in this chapter into a NURBS object. Then rebuild the surface, giving it five CVs in both U and V directions. Show CVs, and pull up the central CV to deform the surface, making it convex.

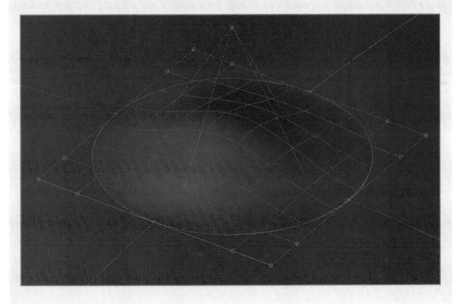

CHAPTER 18

Presenting and Documenting 3D Design

Wireframe, hidden line, and shaded views are helpful means of visualizing models during the design process. However, visual styles leave something to be desired when you are communicating designs to your clients. The general public has come to expect designers to be able to produce the kind of realistic computer-generated imagery regularly seen in movies. This chapter will help you learn to do that by teaching you how to create realistic presentation images using the advanced rendering system in the AutoCAD® program. After you gain client approval, you still need to document your 3D design with relevant 2D plans, elevations, sections, and detail drawings so that your design can be communicated to the building or manufacturing trades. You will learn how to generate these drawings directly from models using AutoCAD 2013's new model documentation features.

▶ **Assigning materials**

▶ **Placing and adjusting lights**

▶ **Creating renderings**

▶ **Documenting models with drawings**

Assigning Materials

Materials describe the way objects interact with light. AutoCAD comes with an extensive library of real-world materials, including numerous types of concrete, metal, glass, brick, paint, leather, carpet, plastic, and so on. In the following steps, you will transfer materials from the Autodesk library to a sample model and then assign them to objects layer by layer:

1. Go to the book's web page at www.sybex.com/go
    /autocad2013essentials, browse to Chapter 18, get the file
    Ch18-A.dwg, and open it. This is a model of the author's house (see
    Figure 18.1).

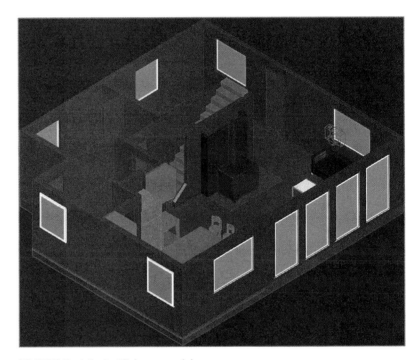

FIGURE 18.1 3D house model

2. Select the 3D Modeling workspace from the drop-down menu on the Quick Access toolbar.

3. Select the ribbon's Render tab, and click the Materials Browser toggle in the Materials panel. In the Materials Browser palette that appears, select the Fabric category in the Autodesk library, scroll down the list of materials in the right pane, and click Velvet – Black to load it into the document (see Figure 18.2).

4. Continue loading materials by single-clicking the materials listed by category in Table 18.1.

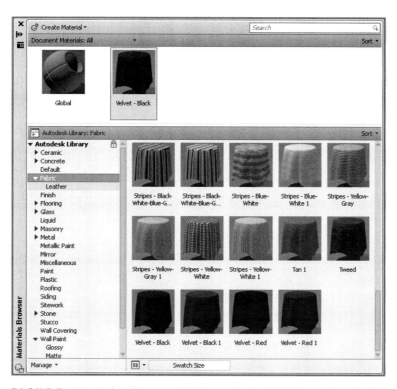

FIGURE 18.2 Loading a material from the Autodesk library into the document

TABLE 18.1: Loading materials from the Autodesk library

Category	Subcategory	Material
Flooring	Stone	Flagstone
Flooring	Stone	Flagstone Light Pink
Flooring	Wood	Natural Maple – Antique
Glass	Glazing	Clear
Masonry	Brick	Uniform Running – Burgundy
Metal	(none)	Chrome Satin 1
Metal	Steel	Stainless – Brushed
Paint	(none)	Black

(Continues)

TABLE 18.1 *(Continued)*

Category	Subcategory	Material
Plastic	(none)	Laminate Light Brown
Wall Paint	Matte	Cool White
Wall Paint	Matte	Flat – Antique White
Wood	(none)	Beech
Wood	(none)	Birch – Solid Stained Dark No Gloss

All drawings have a global material (flat gray) by default.

5. Figure 18.3 shows all the materials loaded into the current drawing. Close the Materials Browser.

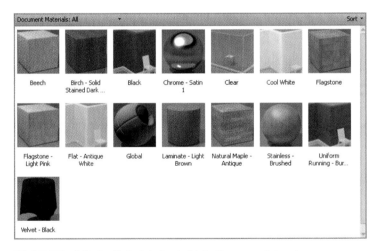

FIGURE 18.3 Materials loaded into the current drawing

6. Expand the Materials panel, and select the Attach By Layer tool. Click the Layer header to sort the list of layers in reverse alphabetical order. Click the Layer header again to sort in alphabetical order. Drag materials from the left side, and drop them on the right side according to Table 18.2 (see Figure 18.4). Click OK to close the Material Attachment Options dialog box.

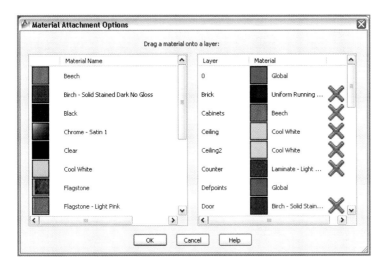

FIGURE 18.4 Assigning materials to layers by dragging from the left pane to the right pane in the Material Attachment Options dialog box

You can also assign materials by dragging them from the Materials Browser onto specific objects in the drawing canvas.

TABLE 18.2: Assigning materials to layers

Layer	Material
0	Global
Brick	Uniform Running – Burgundy
Cabinets	Beech
Ceiling	Cool White
Ceiling2	Cool White
Counter	Laminate Light Brown
Defpoints	Global
Door	Birch – Solid Stained Dark No Gloss
Downlight	Cool White
Equip	Stainless – Brushed

(Continues)

TABLE 18.2 *(Continued)*

Layer	Material
Floor1	Natural Maple – Antique
Floor2	Flagstone
Floor3	Flagstone Light Pink
Seat-Cushion	Velvet – Black
Seat-Frame	Chrome Satin 1
Sink	Stainless – Brushed
Stairs	Birch – Solid Stained Dark No Gloss
Stool	Beech
Stove	Black
Table-Glass	Clear
Table-Legs	Chrome Satin 1
Wall	Flat – Antique White
Wall2	Flat – Antique White
Window-Frame	Cool White
Window-Glazing	Clear
Woodstove	Black

You can also display texture maps in the viewport by clicking Materials/Textures On in the Materials panel.

Texture maps are images used within materials to represent realistic surfaces.

7. Texture maps do not normally appear in the viewport in the Shaded With Edges visual style. Select Realistic using the in-canvas Visual Style Controls menu. Figure 18.5 shows the texture maps in the viewport.

8. Save your work as Ch18-B.dwg.

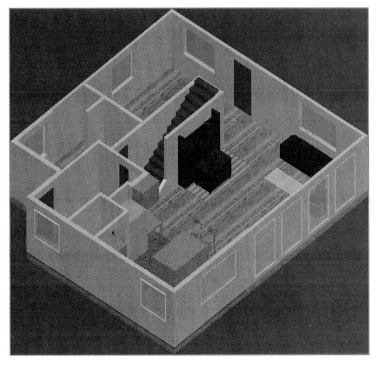

FIGURE 18.5 Using the realistic visual style to display materials' texture maps

Placing and Adjusting Lights

Without light nothing would be visible. AutoCAD uses what is called *default lighting* to illuminate objects in the viewport while you are building 3D models. The default lights are positioned behind the viewer and emit even illumination so that you can always see what is in the viewport. However, default lighting is not realistic and must be turned off as soon as you create artificial or natural light. You will add artificial lights (a series of spotlights mounted in the ceiling) and natural lights simulating the sun and sky light diffused throughout the atmosphere.

Adding Artificial Lights

In the real world, artificial lights are electrical lighting fixtures that are one of the hallmarks of the modern world. In AutoCAD, artificial lights include point, spot, and direct sources. Point sources illuminate in all directions, spot sources illuminate in a cone, and direct lights simulate light coming evenly from a particular direction, illuminating everything like the sun.

AutoCAD has two different lighting methods: standard and photometric. Standard lights were used before AutoCAD 2008, and they are still available so that lights in older DWG files will still be compatible in the current version.

However, I strongly urge you to use photometric lights, which are much more realistic. Photometric lights use real-world lighting intensity values (in American or International lighting units), and light coming from photometric light decays with the inverse square of distance, just as light does in the real world.

In the following steps, you will first change lighting units to turn on the photometric lighting system, and then add a series of artificial lights to illuminate an architectural interior:

The absolute size of the model matters when you are using photometric lights. Natural light can easily overpower artificial light in terms of intensity.

AutoCAD for Mac users can change lighting units in the UNITS command.

1. If the file is not already open, go to the book's web page, browse to Chapter 18, get the file Ch18-B.dwg, and open it. Switch to the 3D Modeling workspace if it's not selected already in the Quick Access toolbar.

2. Select the ribbon's Render tab, and expand the Lights panel. Open the menu that says Generic Lighting Units (used only for the standard lighting method), and select American Lighting Units (or International Lighting Units in metric). Figure 18.6 shows this menu.

FIGURE 18.6 Selecting photometric lighting units in AutoCAD for Windows

3. Click the word Top in the ViewCube to switch to a floor plan view. Choose Zoom Extents in the Navigation bar, and switch to the Wireframe visual style using the in-canvas control.

4. Select the ribbon's Home tab, and expand the Layers panel. Select the Turn All Layers On tool. Light fixtures (down lights) are visible in the viewport (see Figure 18.7).

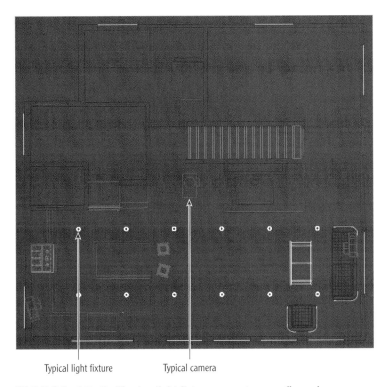

Typical light fixture   Typical camera

FIGURE 18.7 Viewing light fixture geometry on a floor plan

5. Zoom in on the upper-left light by turning the mouse wheel forward. Windows users select the ribbon's Render tab and, on the Lights panel, open the Create Light menu and select Spot. Mac users type **LIGHT**, press Enter, type **S** (for Spot), and press Enter. All users select Turn Off The Default Lighting when the Lighting – Viewport Lighting Mode dialog box appears (see Figure 18.8).

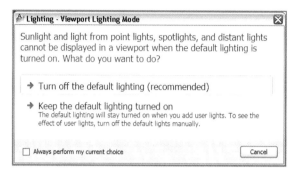

FIGURE 18.8 Turning off default lighting when adding the first artificial light source

6. The command prompt reads:

   Specify source location <0,0,0>:

   Type **.xy**, and press Enter. Click a point visually centered on the light fixture (but do not use center object snap).

7. The command prompt now says (need Z). Type **96** (the ceiling height), and press Enter. The command prompt now reads:

   Specify target location <0,0,-10>:

   Type **.xy**, press Enter, and click the same center point as you did in the previous step. The command prompt now says (need Z). Type **0** (the floor height), and press Enter. Press Enter again to end the SPOTLIGHT command.

8. Press the F8 key if Ortho is not already on. Type **CO** (for Copy), and press Enter. Type **L** (for Last), and press Enter twice. Click a point near the light fixture, zoom out by turning the mouse wheel backward, move the cursor down to the light fixture in the bottom row, and click in the drawing canvas to create the second spotlight. Press Enter to end the COPY command.

9. Press the spacebar to repeat the last command, type **P** (for Previous), and press Enter. Type **L** (for Last) so that you have a selection of two lights, and press Enter twice to end Select Objects mode. Click the start point under the last spotlight and zoom out. The command prompt reads:

   Specify second point or [Array]
   <use first point as displacement>:

Point filters such as .xy, .xz, and .yz allow you to specify the listed coordinate values by clicking in the drawing. Typing the missing coordinate then specifies the 3D coordinates.

Type **A** (for Array), and press Enter. Type **6** (for the number of items), and press Enter. Type **F** (for Fit), and press Enter. Move the cursor under the rightmost light fixture (see Figure 18.9), and click to specify the second point of the array. Press Enter to exit the ARRAY command.

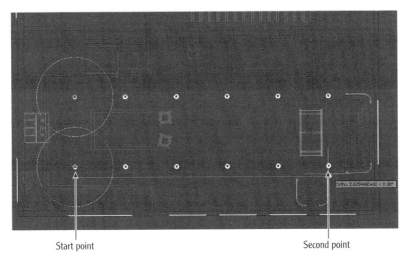

Placing lights within block definitions can help keep source and fixture together.

Start point   Second point

FIGURE 18.9 Copying spotlights in a rectangular array

10. Type **V** (for View), and press Enter. Double-click Camera 1 in the View Manager (see Figure 18.10). Click Apply and OK.

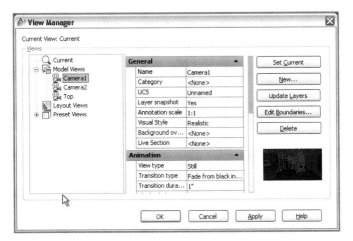

FIGURE 18.10 Selecting a predefined camera view

11. Click the Lights panel menu (a small icon in the lower-right corner of the Lights panel) to open the Lights In Model palette (see Figure 18.11). Select the first spotlight in the list, hold Shift, and select the last spotlight in the list to select them all.

Real-world lamps are typically rated by a color standard and/or color temperature (measured in degrees Kelvin). The Tool palettes have a set of real-world lamps ready for use.

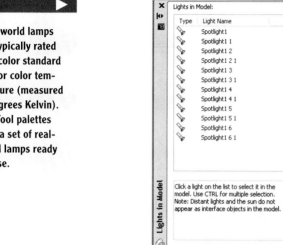

FIGURE 18.11 Selecting lights in the Lights In Model palette

12. Right-click the selected lights in the Light Lister and choose Properties. Select the Lamp Color property, and click the icon to the right of the drop-down menu to open the Lamp Color dialog box. Select the Kelvin Colors radio button, type **5000**, and press Tab. The resulting color changes (see Figure 18.12). Click OK.

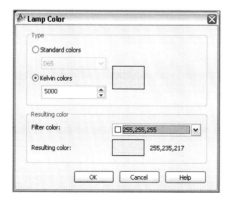

FIGURE 18.12 Specifying lamp color by temperature

13. In the Properties palette, change Lamp Intensity to **15000**, Hotspot Angle to **30**, and Falloff Angle to **60**. Figure 18.13 shows the resulting light glyphs in the drawing canvas. The outer orange cones represent the spotlight's falloff angle and the inner yellow cones represent the area of full light intensity. Close the Properties and Lights In Model palettes. Press Esc to deselect all.

14. Save your work as Ch18-C.dwg.

The viewport shows direct illumination only. Reflected and transmitted light must be rendered.

FIGURE 18.13 Selected spotlights reveal light coverage as seen in the camera view.

Simulating Natural Light

AutoCAD can simulate the light of the sun and/or the light scattered in the sky by the atmosphere for any location on earth and for any time of year and time of day. In the following steps, you will configure the model to use a simulated sun and sky with specific time and space coordinates:

1. If the file is not already open, go to the book's web page, browse to Chapter 18, get the file Ch18-C.dwg, and open it. Switch to the 3D Modeling workspace if it's not selected already in the Quick Access toolbar.

2. Select the ribbon's Render tab if it is not already selected. Click the Sun Status toggle in the Sun & Location panel. The sun is on when the toggle is highlighted in blue.

Mac users control Sun Properties in the Properties inspector.

3. Select the Set Location tool in the Sun & Location panel. In the Geographic Location – Define Geographic Location dialog box that appears, select Enter The Location Values (see Figure 18.14).

You can use Google Earth to specify an exact geographic location if desired.

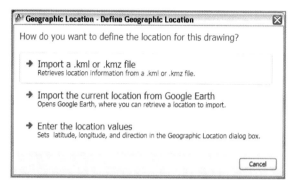

FIGURE 18.14 Using the Geographic Location dialog box to specify latitude and longitude

4. In the Geographic Location dialog box that appears, click the Use Map button. In the Location Picker dialog box, click a point near Vancouver, Canada and the crosshairs will snap there (see Figure 18.15). Click OK.

5. Click Accept Updated Time Zone in the Geographic Location – Time Zone Updated dialog box that appears. Click OK to close the Geographic Location dialog box.

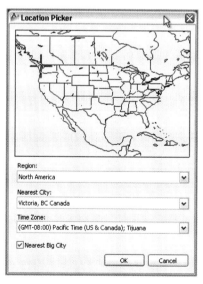

FIGURE 18.15 Selecting a city in the Location Picker dialog box

6. Open the Sky Off menu in the Sun & Location panel, and select Sky Background And Illumination. AutoCAD automatically manages the

color of the sky and degree of sky illumination based on your chosen time and space coordinates.

7. Save your work as Ch18-D.dwg.

Dragging the Date and Time sliders automatically repositions the sun as it would in the real world at the chosen time coordinates.

Creating Renderings

Rendering is the process of converting the geometry, materials, and lighting settings into pixels. Rendering can be a time-consuming process because it typically requires a lot of computation to perform. There are no rendering options in AutoCAD for Mac (just the RENDER command), and the resulting rendering quality isn't as realistic as that available in AutoCAD for Windows, where you have many advanced options. In the following steps, you will use AutoCAD 2013's advanced render settings for Windows to progressively create more realistic renderings:

1. If the file is not already open, go to the book's web page, browse to Chapter 18, get the file Ch18-D.dwg, and open it. Switch to the 3D Modeling workspace if it's not selected already in the Quick Access toolbar.

2. Select the ribbon's Render tab, and expand its Render panel. Select the Adjust Exposure tool. After a few moments, AutoCAD creates a preview that gives you a rough sense of the level of illumination in a rendered thumbnail image. As it appears dark, change the Brightness from **65** to **100** and press Tab. The preview brightens significantly (see Figure 18.16). Click OK to close the Adjust Rendered Exposure dialog box.

F I G U R E   1 8 . 1 6 Adjusting exposure prior to rendering

The "Utah teapot" is the symbol of 3D computer graphics. See `http://en.wikipedia.org/wiki/Utah_teapot` for historical information on this symbol.

3. Open the Render Presets drop-down menu in the Render panel and select Low. Click the teapot icon to initiate the rendering process. Figure 18.17 shows the resulting low-quality rendering that appears after a few moments in the Render dialog box.

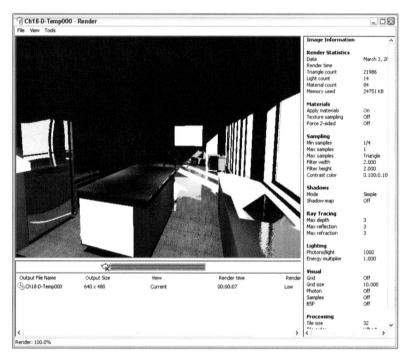

FIGURE 18.17 First test render using Low quality preset

Global illumination is best used in interior spaces to bounce light into areas that are not directly lit.

4. Windows users should click the small icon at the right edge of the Render panel (or type **RPREF** and press Enter) to open the Advanced Render Settings palette. Mac users cannot adjust any advanced render settings. Scroll down in the palette, and toggle on Global Illumination by clicking the lightbulb icon shown in Figure 18.18.

5. Click the Render icon in the Render panel to create another test render. Figure 18.19 shows the result. The global illumination algorithm bounces photons off the floor, and this helps illuminate the ceiling. However, there aren't enough photons for a quality result.

You will be prompted to install the Medium Images Library (700 MB) if it's not already installed when you initiate a render. For the purposes of this book, you do not need to install it.

6. In the Advanced Render Settings palette, change the number of Photons/light to **10000**. More photons will illuminate the dark recess of the architectural interior better. Click the Render icon in the Render panel to create another test render. It is much improved, but photon circles are still visible on various surfaces.

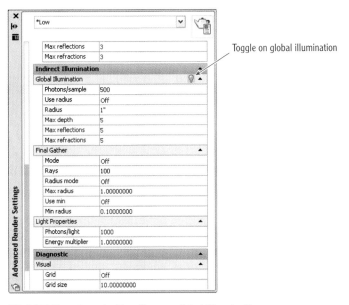

Toggle on global illumination

FIGURE 18.18 Toggling on global illumination

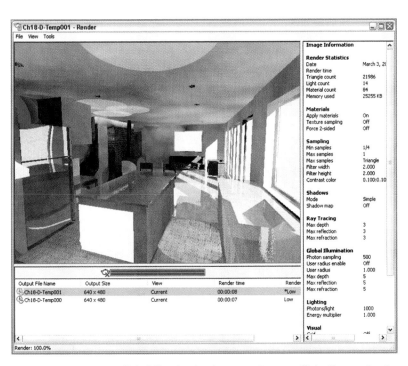

FIGURE 18.19 Global illumination bounces photons off the floor and onto the ceiling.

Final gather can be used with or without global illumination. The final gather algorithm takes a lot of calculation (and thus time), but it produces the highest quality results.

7. Open the shadow menu in the Lights panel, and select Full Shadows.

8. Open the drop-down menu at the top of the Advanced Render Settings palette and select High. Toggle on Global Illumination by clicking the lightbulb icon as you did in step 4. In the High preset, the scene will use *final gather*, which cleans up photon circles. Click the Render button in the top-right corner of the Advanced Render Settings palette to initiate a render. Mac users type **RENDER**, and press Enter. Figure 18.20 shows the final rendering.

F I G U R E 1 8 . 2 0 High-quality rendering using global illumination and final gather

9. Right-click the most recent output file name in the Render dialog box, and select Save in the context menu. In the Render Output File dialog box that appears, open the Files Of Type drop-down menu and select TIF (*.tif). Type **Camera 1** in the File Name text box and click Save. Select the 24 Bits radio button in the TIF Image Options dialog box that appears and click OK.

10. Save your model as Ch18-E.dwg. Your work should now resemble the file of the same name, which is provided on the book's web page.

Documenting Models with Drawings

AutoCAD 2013 introduces a set of model documentation features that allow you to generate 2D plans, elevations, sections, and/or details directly from solid and surface models. In the following steps, you will open a 3D model of a gear and project multiple 2D drawings from it:

1. Open Ch18-F.dwg. This is a 3D solid model of a gear (see Figure 18.21).

FIGURE 18.21 Gear 3D model

Model documentation drawings are created and dimensioned on layouts.

 2. Select the 3D Modeling workspace from the drop down on the Quick Access toolbar. Select the ribbon's Layout tab, which is new in AutoCAD 2013.

 3. Select the Base tool in the Create View panel, and choose From Model Space in the drop-down menu. The command line reads:

    Select objects or [Entire model] <Entire model>:

Select the gear object, and press Enter.

You can also link to Autodesk Inventor base models into AutoCAD in order to generate dimensioned shop drawings.

C

callout symbols, 187
Camera & Target Location grip, 310
CAMERA command, 309
Camera Preview, 310, 310
cameras, 309–311, **309–311**, 355, 355
canceling, 23–24
Cartesian coordinates, 24–25, 43, 320
Cell Styles panel, 294–295
CHAMFER command, 36
Chamfer tool, 36–38
circles
    drawing, 30–34
    hatch boundaries, 150
    planar surfaces, 317
    properties, 101
    smoothness, 34
    squaring, 224
City of Revelation (Michell), 229
Clipboard panel, Match Properties
    tool, 105
closed paths, 330
collinear constraints, 218
color standard, 356
color temperature, 356, 356
color-dependent plot style tables (CTB
    files), 258
columns
    Layer Properties Manager,
        117–118, 118
    rectangular arrays, 67
    table, 286, *287*, 288–291
    text, 192, 194, 195
command line, 11, 18, 73
Command window, 18
commands, 10
    aliases, 13, 22
    AREA, 203
    ARRAY, 329, 332
    ATTDEF, 281
    ATTDIA, 283
    BLEND, 95, 123
    BOUNDARY, 148
    CAMERA, 309
    CHAMFER, 36
    CONVERTCTB, 265
    CONVERTPSTYLES, 265
    COPY, 60–63, *61, 63*, 188, 279
    CVREBUILD, 91
    DCLINEAR, 222
    DDEDIT, 193
    DDPTYPE, 94
    DIMCONSTRAINT, 222
    DIMLINEAR, 208
    DIMRADIUS, 229
    DIMSTYLE, 213
    DIMTEDIT, 214, 215
    DIST, 203
    DISTANCE, 110
    DIVIDE, 70, 87
    EATTEDIT, 296
    editing, 76
    EXPLODE, 137
    EXTEND, 71–72
    EXTRUDE, 330

    FILLET, 36, 37, 45, 74, 122, 165–166
    GCPARALLEL, 219
    GCTANGENT, 226
    GRADIENT, 160
    HATCH, 148, 154
    HATCHEDIT, 154
    HATCHTOBACK, 160
    inquiry, 203, **204**, 206
    INSERT, 283
    JOIN, 84
    LAYERSTATE, 274
    LAYFRZ, 112
    LAYISO, 342
    LAYMCH, 105
    LAYMRG, 100
    LAYOFF, 107, 110
    LAYUN, 342
    LENGTHEN, 72
    LINE, 20, 23, 44, 104, 279
    LOFT, 330, 334
    LTSCALE, 114
    MASSPROP, 330
    MEASURE, 70
    MEASUREGEOM, 203, 206
    MIRROR, **73–74**, *75*, 188
    MOVE, 60–63, 188
    MTEDIT, 192
    MTEXT, **189–192**, 191
    MVIEW, 246
    OFFSET, **73–74**, 111, 123
    OFFSETEDGE, 339
    OPTIONS, 108
    PEDIT, 84
    PLAN, 29
    PLANESURF, 318
    PLOT, 269, 273
    PLOTTERMANAGER, 254
    POLYGON, 34
    PROJECTGEOMETRY, 326, 328
    PURGE, 137
    RECTANGLE, 20, 22
    REGEN, 86, 92, 94, 151
    RENDER, 359, 362
    repeating last, 20, 58, 61
    REVOLVE, 319, 330
    ROTATE, **63–66**, 188
    SCALE, **63–66**, 188
    SELECT, 58
    SELECTSIMILAR, 59
    SETBYLAYER, 138
    SKETCH, 91
    SOLIDEDIT, 340
    SPLINE, 79, 88
    SPLINEDIT, 89–90, 92–94
    STRETCH, 72
    STYLESMANAGER, 258
    SURFTRIM, 324
    SWEEP, 320, 322, 330
    TABLESTYLE, 286, 294
    TEXT, 185–187, 189
    3DFORBIT, 308
    3DORBIT, 308
    3DROTATE, 337
    transparent, 42, 76
    TRIM, **71–72**, 82
    UCS, 28–30

    UCSICON, 28
    UNGROUP, 177
    UNITS, 13, 22, 352
    VIEWBASE, 364
    VIEWDETAIL, 366
    VIEWRES, 34
    VIEWSECTION, 365
    VPORTS, 304
    XPLODE, 137, 143
    ZOOM, 18, 42
Concentric constraint tool, 225
constraint bar, 220
constraint points, 221
constraints, 217
    Auto Constrain tool, 219
    collinear, 218
    concentric, 225
    dimensional, 220–227
    equal, 218
    geometric, **217–220**, 224–227
    hiding, 220
    Infer Constraints mode, 217–218
    linear, 221, 226
    naming, 224
    parallel, 218, 219
    Parameters Manager, 222–223
    parametric changes, 227–229
    perpendicular, 218
    radius, 225, 228
    simultaneous geometry and
        dimension, 224–227
    tangent, 226
content
    globally accessing, 171–174
    storing on tool palettes, 175–177
Content Explorer, 171–174
Content Sources menu, 173
context menu, 22, *22*, 40
continuous linetype, 116, 118
control frame, 88
control vertices (CV), 88–91
Conversion Factor, 291, 293
Convert to Block option, 126, 140
CONVERTCTB command, 265
CONVERTPSTYLES command, 265
Coordinate System menu, 306
coordinate systems
    UCS, 29–30, 62, 305–306, 325
    using, 24–30
    ViewCube, 305–306
    WCS, 30, 305–306
coordinates
    absolute, 25
    Cartesian, 24–25, 43, 320
    cylindrical, 24
    polar, 24, 27–31
    relative, 26–27
    spherical, 24
COPY command, **60–63**, *61, 63*, 188, 279
copying
    arrays, 62, *63*, 332, 338, *339*,
        354–355, 355
    blocks, 130
    lights, 354–355, 355
core, 177, *178*, 180
CPolygon, 57

Create Light menu, 353
Create Mesh, 342
Create View panel, 365, 366
creating solid models, 330–334
    extruding, 330–333
    lofting, 334, 335
creating surface models, 317–323
    extruding 2D geometry into
        3D, 322–323
    planar surfaces, 317–318
    revolving 2D profile into 3D
        model, 319–320
    sweeping out 3D geometry, 320–322
creating text
    to fit, 185–187
    transforming and, 188–189
crossing windows, 55, 55
CTB files. *See* color-dependent plot style
    tables
CV. *See* control vertices
CVREBUILD command, 91
cylindrical coordinates, 24

D

DCLINEAR command, 222
DDEDIT command, 193
DDPTYPE command, 94
decimal units, 12, 14, 236, 293
default lighting, 351
Default Plot Style for Objects, 262
Default Plot Style Table, 262
Defpoints layer, 101
Design Web Format (DWF files), 256, 275
DIMANGULAR, 210
DIMBREAK, 215, 215
DIMCENTER, 208
DIMCONSTRAINT command, 222
DIMCONTINUE, 208
DIMEDIT, 214
Dimension Center Mark, 208
Dimension Continue, 208
dimension objects, **206–208**, **210**, 213
Dimension Style Manager, 198, *199*,
    201–203, 203
dimension styles, 197, 201
    annotative, 235–237
    modifying, 198–201, *200*, *201*, 236
    new, 202, 202
    Standard, 197–199
dimensional constraints, 220–227
Dimensional panel, 225–226
dimensioning, 197
dimensions
    adding, 203–211
    aligned, 209
    angular, 210
    annotative, 235–237
    converting to constraint, 222
    editing, 212–215
    linear, *207*, 208
    paperspace, 248, 249
    radius, *210*, 229
    styling, 197–203
Dimensions panel, 228
DIMLINEAR command, 208

DIMRADIUS command, 229
DIMSTYLE command, 213
DIMTEDIT command, 214, 215
direct distance entry, 28, 43
direct light sources, 351–352
Displacement mode, 61
DIST command, 203
DISTANCE command, 110
DIVIDE command, 70, 87
down lights, 353
Drafting & Annotations workspace, 16
Drafting Settings dialog box, 44
Draw panel, 21–23
drawing
    arcs, 33–34
    circles, 30–34
    ellipses, 85–87
    on layouts, 248–251
    lines, **19–22**, *20*, 27–28
    natural, 91
    polygons, 34–35
    polylines, 79–84
    rectangles, **22–23**, 27, 51
    splines, 88–95
Drawing Recovery Manager, 23
drawing spaces, 6
drawing units
    block definition, 127
    inquiry commands, 204
    setting, 12–14
Drawing View Editor tab, 365
drawings
    base, 364, *365*, 367
    configuring for named plot style
        tables, 262–264
    documenting models with, 363–366,
        365, *366*, 367
    inserting as local block, 166–168
    model documentation, 363–366, *365*,
        366, 367
    navigating, 15–19
    plot style table switching, 265
    referencing external, 177–181
drivers, 254
DWF files, 256, 275
DWFx files, 275, 275
DWT files. *See* AutoCAD Drawing
    Template
dynamic input, 36, 41, 47, 92

E

Earth, 229
EATTEDIT command, 296
edges
    extracting, 333
    offsetting, 339
    projecting onto surfaces,
        325–329, 329
    trimming surfaces with, 328–329
Edit Reference panel, 134
editing
    blocks, 131–138
    commands, 76
    dimensions, 212–215
    grip, 76–77

polylines, 79–84
solid models, 336–340
splines, 88–95
surface models, 324–329
table data, 292–297
table style, 285–286
text, 192–195
ellipses, drawing, 85–87
elliptical arc, 84, 86–87, 87
Endpoint object snap, 333
engineering units, 12
equal constraints, 218
Erase tool, 337
erasing, 23–25, 55, 58–59
Euclidean space, 24
EXPLODE command, 137
Explode tool, 122, 123
exploding blocks, 137–138
exporting to electronic formats, 275
EXTEND command, 71–72
external references. *See* Xrefs
External References palette, 91
Extract Edges tool, 333
EXTRUDE command, 330
Extrude tool, 322, 331, 332, 333
extruding
    solid objects, 330–333
    surface models, 322–323
    taper angle, 332, 333

F

Falloff Angle, 357
Field Category dropdown menu, 290
fields, 277, 289–292
    Conversion Factor, 291, 293
    decimal units, 293
    Imperial units, 291
    names, 290
    text, 291
    units, 291
FILLET command, 36, 37, 45, 74,
    122, 165–166
Fillet option, 23
Fillet tool, 36–38, 122
final gather, 362, 362
Fit Points mode, 88, 92–94
Fit to Paper option, 269
floating modelspace, 273
floating palettes, 4
floating viewports, 241–246
floor plan view, 353
Font Name dropdown, 184, 278, 279
Formatting panel, 192
fractional units, 12
Freeze, 106, 118
French curve, 88
From snap, 49–50
front view, 304
full navigation wheel, 311, 311

G

GCPARALLEL command, 219
GCTANGENT command, 226
general properties, 98

Generic Lighting Units, 352
Geographic Location – Define
  Geographic Location dialog box,
  357–358, 358
Geographic Location – Time Zone dialog
  box, 358, 358
geometric constraints, **217–220**, 224–227
geometric properties, 97–98
geometry
  block definition, 131–132
  extruding into 3D, 322–323
  real-world, 248
  sweeping out 3D, 320–322
  wireframe, 333
global blocks, 126
  accessing, 171–174
  configuring, 167
  redefining local blocks with, 169–170
  working with, 163–170
global illumination, 360, *361*, 362
global material, 348
Google Earth, 358
GRADIENT command, 160
Gradient Tint and Shade button, 160
gradients, hatching with, **159–160**, 161
graphical user interface (GUI), 1–6, 2
GR_CURVED gradient, 160
Grid, 39–42
  spacing, 40, 40
  toggling display, 40, *40*, 41
Grid Display toggle, 40, 41
grips, 24, 58, 59
  Camera & Target Location, 310
  editing, 76–77
  kink, 94
  Lens Length/FOV, 310
  multifunction, 89, 89
Group Edit tool, 143
Group Selection On/Off toggle, 142, 143
groups
  ungrouping, 177
  working with, 141–144
GUI. *See* graphical user interface

H

Hatch Color dropdown, 147–149, 155
HATCH command, 148, 154
Hatch Creation tab, 147, 148
Hatch Editor tab, 150–153
Hatch Layer Override dropdown, 147,
  148, 155, 160
hatch object, 145, 147, **150–151**, 267
hatch patterns
  separating areas, 156–158
  setting origin, 157
  specifying properties, 154–155
HATCHEDIT command, 154
hatching
  associating with boundaries, 151–153
  color, 147–149
  defining, 145
  gradients, **159–160**, 161
  picking points to determine
    boundaries, 145–149

selecting objects to define
  boundaries, 150–151
separating areas, 156–158
specifying areas, 145–151
storing on tool palettes, 175
transparency, 149
HATCHTOBACK command, 160
hidden line visual style, 112, 345
hidden linetype, 114
Hotspot Angle, 357
HP DesignJet 800 plotter, 254, 256–257,
  269, 271

I

images
  raster, 255
  referencing external, 177–181
Imperial units, 236, 271, 291
implied windows, 54–56, *55*, *56*, 133
in-canvas controls, 302, *303*, 304, 306
Infer Constraints mode, 217–218
InfoCenter, 12
In-Place Editor, 191
input, 253
inquiry commands, 203, **204**, 206
INSERT command, 283
Insert Table dialog box, 286–288, 287
inserting blocks, **126–131**, 166–170
  attributed, **282–283**, *283*, 284
  drawing as local, 166–168
Insertion Scale menu, 14, 127
International Lighting Units, 352
Intersection object snap, 35
Island Detection menu, 147
islands, 147
ISO A0 paper sizes, 245
Isolate tool, 326, 339
isolating layers, 109–111, 326, 342
isometric views, 309, *310*, 365

J

JOIN command, 84
Join tool, 123
justifying text, 187, 280

K

Kelvin Colors, 356
keytips, 10, 10
Kink grips, 94

L

Lamp Color dialog box, 356, 356
Lamp Intensity, 357
Layer drop-down menu, 99, 104, *105*, 107
Layer Isolate, 342
Layer Properties Manager
  freezing columns, 118
  freezing layers, 324
  maximizing columns, 117, 118
  new layers, 238
  nonplotting layers, 238, 249

plot style assignment, 265–266
setting current, 329, 332, 336
setting current layer, 320, 322,
  323, 325
thawing layers, 327, 342
toggling layers on/off, 320, 327, 329,
  338, 342
layers, 31, 32
  altering object assignment, 104–106
  attaching materials by, 348–350
  Defpoints, 101
  general property control, 98
  isolating, **109–111**, 326, 342
  locking, 108
  managing properties, **117–118**, 118
  overriding properties, 247
  plot style assignment by, 265–266
  property assignment by, **115–116**,
    118, *119*, 133, 138, 262
  saving states, 111–112
  setting current, **101–104**, 318
  sorting, 348
  states, 106
  Symbol, 282
  Table, 286
  toggling status, 106–108
  visibility, 106–112
  0, 101, 134
  Z-Viewport, 238
Layers panel, 99, 102, 339
  Match tool, 105
LAYERSTATE command, 274
LAYFRZ command, 112
LAYISO command, 342
LAYMCH command, 105
LAYMRG command, 100
LAYOFF command, 107, 110
Layout tab, 363
layout tab, 238
layouts, 231
  base drawing, 364
  creating, 237–241
  drawing on, 248–251
  metric, 271
  overriding layer properties, 247
  paper sizes, 248
  plotting in paperspace, 271–275
  Quick View, 238, 240, 241, 244, 286
  scale, 271
LAYUN command, 342
leader objects, 211
Left view, 306
Length Precision menu, 14
LENGTHEN command, 72
Lens Length/FOV grip, 310
light fixtures, 353
Light Lister, 356
lighting
  adding artificial, 351–357
  arrays, 354–355, 355
  blocks, 355
  copying, 354–355, 355
  default, 351
  methods, 352
  natural, 352, 357–359
  photometric, 352

placing and adjusting, 351–359
properties, *356*, 356–357
standard, 352
types, 351–352
units, 352
viewports, 353
Lighting – Viewport Lighting Mode
     dialog box, 353, 354
Lights In Model palette, *356*, 356–357
Lights panel, 352, 353, 356
LINE command, 20, 24, 45, 104, 279
Linear constraint tool, 221, 226
lines. *See also* splines
     break, 55–56, 72
     drawing, **19–22**, *20*, 27–28
     joining crossed, 37–38
     joining nonparallel, 36–37
     mirror, 331
     orthogonal, 42
     polylines, 56, 79–84, 122, 123, 148,
          152, 317, 319, 330
     properties, 97
     revolving, 319
linetype
     applying, 112–115
     ByLayer, 118, 119
     continuous, 116, 118
     hidden, 114
Linetype drop-down menu, 116
Linetype Manager dialog box, 113
lineweight, 41, *41*, 51, 249
Load or Reload Linetypes dialog box, 113
local block definition
     inserting drawing as, 166–168
     redefining with global
          blocks, 169–170
     writing to file, 163–166
local block references, 126
Lock, 106
Lock Viewport, 246
LOFT command, 330, 334
lofting solid objects, 334, 335
Look tool, 312
LTSCALE command, 114

M

Make Object's Layer Current tool,
     103, 318
Make Viewport, 246
Manage Text Styles, 183
MASSPROP command, 330
Match Properties tool, 105, 157
Match tool, 105
Material Attachment Options dialog
     box, 348
materials
     assigning, 345–350
     attaching by layer, 348–350
     global, 348
     library, 345, 346, *347*, 348
Materials Browser, 346, 348, 349
Materials panel, 346, 348
Maximize Viewport, 250, 304
maximized mode, 250
Maya, 79, 88

MEASURE command, 70
Measure menu, 204
MEASUREGEOM command, 203, 206
Medium Images Library, 360
Merge Cells menu, 292
mesh objects, **342–343**, 343
Mesh panel, 342
Mesh tab, 342
Metric layouts, 271
metric units, 13, 236, 352
Michell, John, 229
Microsoft, 8
Microsoft Excel, 285
Microsoft Internet Explorer, 275
Midpoint marker, 50
Millennium Dome. *See* O2 Arena
Minimize Ribbon button, 9
Minimize Viewport, 251, 297, 304
MIRROR command, **73–74**, *75*, 188
mirror line, 331
mirroring text, 189
MIRRTEXT, 189
model documentation drawings,
     363–366, *365*, *366*, 367
model tab, 238
Model Views, 315
modelspace, 6, 231–233, 238,
     241–245, 242
     annotation scale, 233, 233
     floating, 273
     output, 253
     plotting, 268–271
     real-world geometry, 248
     toggling, 241, 244
Modify Dimension Style, 198–201, *200*,
     201, 236
Modify panel, 58, 61, 71, 73, 74, 337
Modify Table Style, 285–286
Moon, 229
MOVE command, **60–63**, 188
MTEDIT command, 192
MTEXT command, **189–192**, 191
multifunction grips, 89, 89
multileaders, 204, **211**, 212
multiline text, 190, 233
MVIEW command, 246

N

NAME attribute, 281
named plot styles (STB files)
     configuring drawings for, 262–264
     creating, 258–261
named views, 313
natural drawing technique, 91
natural light, 352, 357–359
Navigate 2D panel, 16, *17*, 18
navigating 2D drawings, 15–19
navigating with ViewCube, **305–306**, 307
Navigation bar, 15, *16*, 47, 48, 108
navigation history, 312, 313
Nearest snap, 48
nesting blocks, 135–137
New Dimension Style, 202, *202*
New Page Setup dialog box, 271
node snap, *33*, 34

nonassociative arrays, 329
None object snap, 102
nonuniform rational bases spline
     (NURBS), 79, 88
normal, 334
NURBS. *See* nonuniform rational bases
     spline
NW Isometric view, 306, 314

O

O2 Arena, 300, *300*, 331
object properties
     changing, 97–101
     general, 98
     geometric, 97–98
     layer assignment, 104–106
Object Snap context menu, 31, *31*, 32, 47
object snaps, 31–33
     From, 49–50
     Endpoint, 333
     Intersection, 35
     modes, 47, 47
     move tool, 60
     Nearest, 48
     node, *33*, 34
     None, 102
     running, 46–49, 125
     Tangent, 34
     tracking, 50–52
objects
     annotative, 231–237, 243, 245
     assigning materials to, 345–350
     boundary, 152
     default plot style, 262
     dimension, **206–208**, **210**, 213
     dimensionally constrained, 224–227
     extruding solid, 330–333
     field names, 290
     geometrically constrained, 224–227
     hatch, 145, 147, 267
     hatch boundaries, 150–151
     leader, 211
     lofting solid, **334**, 335
     mesh, **342–343**, 343
     occluded, 299
     parametric changes, 227–229
     plot style assignment by,
          265–266, 267
     property assignment by, 115–116
     region, 148
     selecting for hatch
          boundaries, 150–151
     selecting similar, 59
     solid, 330–334, 335
     subobjects, 339–340
     text, 188–189
occluded objects, 299
OFFSET command, **73–74**, 111, 123
Offset Edge tool, 339
OFFSETEDGE command, 339
On/Off, 106–107
open paths, 330
OPTIONS command, 108
orbiting, 307–209
Ortho mode, 42–44, 51, 58, 64, 72

orthogonal lines, 42
orthogonal views, 306
output, 253
output devices, configuring, 253–257

P

Page Setup Manager, 239–240,
    271–273, 272
page setups
    new, 271
    saved, 271–273
palettes
    Advanced Render Settings, 262, 360
    Authoring Palettes tool, 136
    docking, 4, 5
    External References, 91
    floating, 4
    lamps, 356
    Lights In Model, *356*, 356–357
    storing blocks, 175–177
    storing content, 175–177
    storing hatching, 175
    Tool, 175–177, 356
pan tools, 15
paper sizes
    Arch C, 269, 271
    ARCH E1, 245
    fitting to, 245, 269
    ISO A0, 245
    layouts, 248
    plotting, 269
    title blocks, 248
    viewport scaling, 245
Paper Text Height, 278, 279
paperspace, 6, 231, 238, 243
    dimensions, 248, 249
    output, 253
    plotting layouts, 271–275
    toggling, 241, 244
    viewport frames, 242, 245
parallel constraints, 218, 219
Parameters Manager, 222–223, *223*, 228
parametric changes, 227–229
Parametric tab, 225, 226, 228
PC2 files, 256
PC3 files, 256
PCP files, 256
PDF files, 256, 275
PEDIT command, 84
pen plotters, 184
perpendicular constraints, 218
perspective, 310
photometric lights, 352
Pick Insertion Base Point, 281
PLAN command, 29
planar surfaces, 317–318
PLANESURF command, 318
Plot – Model dialog box, 268, 270
Plot – Plot Scale Confirm, 270
PLOT command, 269, 273
Plot panel, 251
plot preview, 251, 251
plot preview window, 270
Plot Stamp, 269–270, *270*, 273
Plot Style Table dropdown, 239, 241

Plot Style Table Editor, 260–261
Plot Style Table Settings dialog box, 262
plot style tables
    color-dependent, 258
    creating, 258–261
    default, 262
    layer assignment, 265–266
    named, 258–264
    object assignment, **265–266**, 267
    switching, 265
    using, 261–267
plot styles folder, 259
Plot tool, 268
Plotter Configuration Editor, 257
PLOTTERMANAGER command, 254
plotters, 253
    pen, 184
    setting up, **254**, *255*, **256–257**, 257
plotting, 253
    fit to paper, 269
    layouts in paperspace, 271–275
    modelspace, 268–271
    raster images, 255
    scale, 269, 270
    test, 268
point filters, 354
point light sources, 351
Point Style, 32
Polar arrays, **68–70**, *70*, 338
polar coordinates, 24, 27–31
Polar Distance, 44
Polar Tracking mode, 42–44, 64, 72
    MIRROR command, 74
    PolarSnap, 44–45
    running object snaps, 46, 47
PolarSnap, 44–45
polygon, 2, 30
    CPolygon, 57
    drawing, 34–35
    WPolygon, 57, 57
POLYGON command, 34
polylines, 123
    arcs, 79–81, 84
    BOUNDARY command creating, 148
    break lines, 56
    drawing and editing, 79–84
    exploding, 122, 123
    hatch boundaries, 152
    joining, 123
    planar surfaces, 317
    revolving, 319
    solid model creation, 330
Portable Document Format (PDF files),
    256, 275
Presspull tool, 339, 340, 341
Preview tool, 251, 297
preview window, *274*, 274–274
primitives, 342
printers, 254
Project Geometry panel, 325, 326
Project to UCS tool, 325
Project to View tool, 327–328
PROJECTGEOMETRY command, 326, 328
projecting edges onto surfaces,
    325–329, 326
Prompt, 280

properties. *See also* Layer Properties
    Manager; Quick Properties window
    ByBlock, 133, 134
    ByLayer, 115–116, 118, *119*, 133,
        138, 262
    floating, 133–135
    general, 98
    geometric, 97–98
    hatch patterns, 154–155
    layer assignment, 115–116
    lighting, *356*, 356–357
    lines, 97
    managing layer, **117–118**, 118
    matching, 105, 157
    object, **97–101**, 104–106
    object assignment, 115–116
    overriding layer, 247
    saved views, 314
    table cell border, 295, 296
    text, 193
Properties panel, 100–101
PURGE command, 137

Q

Quick Access toolbar, 5, 40
Quick Properties mode, 98–99
Quick Properties window
    block references, 133–134
    current layer in, 102–103
    text, 193
Quick View, 6, 6
Quick View Layouts, 238, 240, 241,
    244, 286

R

Radius constraint tool, 225, 228
radius dimension, *210*, 229
raster images, 255
raycasting, 145, 148, 149
realistic visual style, 350, 351
Rebuild Curve dialog box, 91
Recreate Boundary tool, 152
RECTANGLE command, 20, 22
rectangles, drawing, **22–23**, 27, 51
rectangular arrays, **67–68**, 68
redefining blocks, **138–140**, 169–170
Reference options, 64–65, 66
REGEN command, 86, 92, 94, 151
region object, 148
relative coordinates, 26–27
Remove objects: prompt, 55
RENDER command, 359, 362
Render Output File dialog box, 362
Render panel, 359–360
Render Presets drop-down menu, 360
Render tab, 346, 352, 353, 357, 359
renderings, 299, 359–362
REVOLVE command, 319, 330
Revolve tool, 319
revolving, 2D profile into 3D
    model, 319–320
ribbon, *8*, 8–12, *9*, 10
    minimizing, 9
    View tab, 16

Right-Click Customization, 20–21, 21
Rogers, Richard, 300
roll, 308
ROTATE command, **63–66**, 188
rows, rectangular arrays, 67
rubberband, 20, 41, 64
running object snaps, 46–49, 125

S

saved page setups, 271–273
saving views, 313–315
scale
    annotations, 231–235, *233*, 237,
        243, 244
    layouts, 271
    plotting, 269, 270
    raster image plotting, 255
SCALE command, **63–66**, 188
scale factor, negative, 130
scientific units, 13
SE Isometric view, 304, 306
Select Annotation Scale dialog box,
    233, 233
Select Boundary Objects tool, 150
SELECT command, 58
Select Objects, 281, 354
`Select Objects:` prompt, **53–56**, 58
Select Plot Style dialog box, 265, *265*, 266
Select Template dialog box, 40, 262
selecting similar objects, 59
Selection Cycling, 58, 59
Selection dialog box, 59
selection sets
    creating, 53–59
    `Select Objects:` prompt, 53–56
SELECTSIMILAR command, 59
Separate Hatches option, 156
Set Camera View, 311
Set Location tool, 357
Set To ByLayer tool, 138
SETBYLAYER command, 138
shaded visual styles, 317–318, 345
Shaded With Edges visual style, 302, *302*,
    318, 325, 334, 338, 340, 350
Shaded With Visible Lines visual
    style, 365
Sheet Set Manager, 4
shell, 177, *178*, 180
Show/Hide Lineweight, 41, *41*, 51
SHX fonts, 184
simulating natural light, 357–359
SKETCH command, 91
Sky Background And Illumination, 358
sky illumination, 357–359
Smooth More tool, 342
Smooth Object tool, 342
smoothing meshes, 342–343, 343
smoothness, 34
Snap, 39–42
    object, 31–35, 46–52, 60, 102,
        125, 333
    Polar, 44–45
Solid Editing panel, 333, 339, 340

solid editing tools
    Boolean operations, **336–338**, 339
    subobjects, 339–340
solid modeling tools, 330
solid models
    Boolean operations, 336–338
    creating, **330–334**, 335
    editing, 336–340
    wireframe geometry, 333
Solid panel, 331, 332
Solid tab, 331
SOLIDEDIT command, 340
spherical coordinates, 24
SPLINE command, 79, 88
Spline Fit tool, 92
SPLINEDIT command, 89–90, 92–94
splines
    control vertices, 88–92
    drawing and editing, 88–95
    Fit Points mode, 88, 93–95
    NURBS, 79, 88
    object blending, 95–96
    projecting, 326, 329
    trimming with, 329
spot light sources, 351
squaring the circle, 224
Standard dimension style, 197–198
standard lights, 352
status bar, 40, 51
status toggles, 20
STB files. *See* named plot styles
SteeringWheel, 305, 311–312
STRETCH command, 72
Stretch tool, 143
Stretch Vertex, 218
styles. *See also* dimension styles; plot
    style tables; visual styles
    annotative, 231–237
    cell, 294–295
    plot, 258–261
    point, 32
    table, 285–286
STYLESMANAGER command, 258
subobjects, 339–340
Substitute Block Name, 174
substyles, 197, 198
sun, 357
Sun & Location panel, 357, 358
Surface Associativity, 318, 319
surface modeling tools, 330
surface models
    creating, 317–323
    editing, 324–329
Surface tab, 319, 320, 325, 327, 329
surfaces, 317, 318
    planar, 317–318
    projecting edges, 325–329, 326
    trimming, **324**, 325
    trimming with edges, 328–329
SURFTRIM command, 324
SW isometric view, 309, 318
SWEEP command, 320, 322, 330
sweep path, 320–321, 321
sweeping, 320–322
Symbol layer, 282
system printer, 254, 268, 269

T

tables, 277
    block, 125
    cell border properties, 295, 296
    cell styles, 285, *286*, 294–295
    creating new, 287–289
    editing data, 292–297
    editing styles, 285–286
    fields in cells, 289–292
    inserting and deleting rows and
        columns, 288
    linking to external spreadsheets, 286
    merging cells, 292
    navigating, 288–289
    stretching height, 296
    Text Editor, 291
Table Cell Background Color menu, 295
Table Cell Format dialog box, 293
Table Cell tab, 286
table cells
    merging, 292
    style, 294–295
    Title style, 285, 286
Table layer, 286
table styles, 285–286
Table tool, 286
TABLESTYLE command, 286, 294
Tag, 280
Tangent constraint tool, 226
Tangent object snap, 34
taper, 332, 333
technical pens, 253
Template Options dialog box, 264
templates, 40
Tesla, Nikola, 145
test plot, 268
text
    annotative, **232–235**, 277, 279
    columns, 192, 194, 195
    creating styles, 183–185
    creating to fit, 185–187
    editing, 192–195
    fields, 291
    justifying, **187**, 280
    mirroring, 189
    multiline, 190, 233
    properties, 193
    transforming, 188–189
    transforming and creating, 188–189
    writing and formatting with
        MTEXT, 189–192
    writing lines of, 185–189
TEXT command, 185–187, 189
Text Editor Color Gallery dropdown,
    192, 295
Text Editor context tab, 190, 191, 291, 295
texture maps, 350
Thaw, 106
Thicken tool, 340
3D Basics workspaces, 8
3D geometry
    extruding, 322–323
    sweeping out, 320–322
3D modeling toolsets, 317

3D Modeling workspace, 300, 318, 330, 346
3D Rotate tool, 337
3DFORBIT command, 308
3DORBIT command, 308
3DROTATE command, 337
three-dimensional Cartesian coordinates, 320
tiled viewports, 303–304, 305
TILEMODE variable, 304
Time-Sensitive Right-Click, 21, 21
title blocks, 248, 249
Title cell style, 285, 286
Tool palettes
  lamps, 356
  storing content on, 175–177
toolbars
  docking, 7
  Quick Access, 5, 40
top view, 304, 353
Tour Building wheel, 312
transforming text, 188–189
transparent commands, 42, 76
TRIM command, **71–72**, 82
Trim tool, 82, 329
trimming surfaces, **324**, *325*, 328–329
TrueType, 184
Turn All Layers On tool, 107, 353
Turn Off The Default Lighting, 353
2D profile
  projecting, 325, 326
  revolving into 3D model, 319–320
2D Wireframe visual style, 300

U

UCS. *See* user coordinate system
UCS command, 28–30
UCSICON command, 28
undoing, 23–24
UNGROUP command, 177
Union tool, 336–337
UNITS command, 13, 22, 352
Unlock, 106
user coordinate system (UCS), 29–30, 62, 305–306, 325
user interface
  exploring, 1–12
  graphical, **1–6**, 2
Utah teapot, 360

V

value, 280
value attributes, 280
View Controls menu, 306, 309, 315
View Manager dialog box, 315, *315*, 355, 355
View Object wheel, 312

View tab, 16, 300
VIEWBASE command, 364
ViewCube. 29, 30
  additional controls, 306
  Coordinate System menu, 306
  navigating with, **305–306**, 307
  navigation interface, 305
  rotation limits, 307
  top, 327, 353
VIEWDETAIL command, 366
viewport scale, 231, 242–243
  annotation scale changes, 244
  fitting to paper, 245
  saved page setups, 273
viewports, 6, 231
  floating, 241–246
  frames, 241, 242, 245
  lights, 353
  locking, 246
  making, 246
  maximized, 250, 304
  minimizing, 251, 297, 304
  overriding layer properties, 247
  saving position, 313–315
  tiled, **303–304**, 305
  visual styles, 302
  Z, 238
VIEWRES command, 34
views
  Back, 306
  Bottom, 306
  display properties, 365
  floor plan, 353
  front, 304
  isometric, 309, *310*, 365
  Left, 306
  model, 315
  named, 313
  NW Isometric, 306, 314
  orbiting, 307–309
  orthogonal, 306
  projecting to, 327–328
  saving, 313–315
  SE Isometric, 304, 306
  setting camera, 311
  SW isometric, 309, 318
  top, 304
  X-ray, 315
VIEWSECTION command, 365
virtual cameras, 309–311
Visual Style Controls menu, 304, 332, 336, 340
visual styles, 345
  applying to viewport, 302
  hidden line, 112, 345
  planar surfaces, 317–318
  realistic, 350, 351
  saving, 302
  shaded, 317–318, 345

Shaded With Edges, 302, *302*, 318, 325, 334, 338, 340, 350
Shaded With Visible Lines, 365
2D Wireframe, 300
  using, **299–302**, 303
  wireframe, 301, *301*, 304, 332, 336, 340, 345
  X-ray, 302, 303
Visual Styles drop-down menu, 300, 300
Visual Styles Manager, *301*, 301–302
VPORTS command, 304

W

Walk tool, 312, 313
watched folders, 172, 172
WCS. *See* world coordinate system
Windows Standard Behavior, 20
Windows XP Professional, 1
Wireframe visual style, 301, *301*, 304, 332, 336, 340, 345
word processing, 189–192
workspaces
  3D Basics, 8
  AutoCAD Classic, *7*, 7–8
  Drafting & Annotations, 16
  exploring, *7*, 7–8
  Text Editor, 191
  3D Modeling, 300, 318, 330, 346
world coordinate system (WCS), 30, 305–306
WPolygon, 57, 57
Write Block dialog box, 164

X

XPLODE command, 137, 143
X-ray view, 315
X-ray visual style, 302, 303
Xrefs, 177–181
.xy, 354
.xz, 354

Y

.yz, 354

Z

Z direction, 320
ZOOM command, 18, 42
Zoom Extents, 15, 19, 108, 228
Zoom Previous, 19
Zoom Realtime, 16, *17*, 232
zoom tools, 15, 16, *17*, 47
Zoom Window, 16, 18
Z-Viewport, 238